JOURNAL OF APPLIED LOGICS - IFCOLOG JOURNAL OF LOGICS AND THEIR APPLICATIONS

Volume 6, Number 6

October 2019

Disclaimer

Statements of fact and opinion in the articles in Journal of Applied Logics - IfCoLog Journal of Logics and their Applications (JALs-FLAP) are those of the respective authors and contributors and not of the JALs-FLAP. Neither College Publications nor the JALs-FLAP make any representation, express or implied, in respect of the accuracy of the material in this journal and cannot accept any legal responsibility or liability for any errors or omissions that may be made. The reader should make his/her own evaluation as to the appropriateness or otherwise of any experimental technique described.

ISBN 978-1-84890-316-6
ISSN (E) 2631-9829
ISSN (P) 2631-9810

College Publications
Scientific Director: Dov Gabbay
Managing Director: Jane Spurr

http://www.collegepublications.co.uk

iii

Scope and Submissions

This journal considers submission in all areas of pure and applied logic, including:

pure logical systems
proof theory
constructive logic
categorical logic
modal and temporal logic
model theory
recursion theory
type theory
nominal theory
nonclassical logics
nonmonotonic logic
numerical and uncertainty reasoning
logic and AI
foundations of logic programming
belief change/revision
systems of knowledge and belief
logics and semantics of programming
specification and verification
agent theory
databases

dynamic logic
quantum logic
algebraic logic
logic and cognition
probabilistic logic
logic and networks
neuro-logical systems
complexity
argumentation theory
logic and computation
logic and language
logic engineering
knowledge-based systems
automated reasoning
knowledge representation
logic in hardware and VLSI
natural language
concurrent computation
planning

This journal will also consider papers on the application of logic in other subject areas: philosophy, cognitive science, physics etc. provided they have some formal content.

Submissions should be sent to Jane Spurr (jane.spurr@kcl.ac.uk) as a pdf file, preferably compiled in LaTeX using the IFCoLog class file.

CONTENTS

ARTICLES

Logic and the Concept of God 999
   Stanisław Krajewski and Ricardo Silvestre

Mathematical Models in Theology. A Buber-inspired Model of God and
   its Application to "Shema Israel" 1007
   Stanisław Krajewski

Gödel's God-like Essence 1021
   Talia Leven

A Logical Solution to the Paradox of the Stone 1037
   Héctor Hernández Ortiz and Victor Cantero Flores

No New Solutions to the Logical Problem of the Trinity 1051
   Beau Branson

What Means 'Tri-' in 'Trinity'? An Eastern Patristic Approach to the
   'Quasi-Ordinals' 1093
   Basil Lourié

The Éminence Grise of Christology: Porphyry's Logical Teaching as a
   Cornerstone of Argumentation in Christological Debates of the Fifth
   and Sixth Centruies 1109
   Anna Zhyrkova

The Problem of Universals in Late Patristic Theology 1125
   Dirk Krasmüller

Intuitionist Reasoning in the Tri-unitrian Theology of Nicolas of Cues
   (1401–1464) 1143
   Antonino Drago

Logic and the Concept of God

Stanisław Krajewski
University of Warsaw
stankrajewski@uw.edu.pl

Ricardo Silvestre
Federal University of Campina Grande
ricardoss@ufcg.edu.br

Several important philosophical questions might be posed about God. The most common one, perhaps, is: Does God exist? This is an ontological question. A traditional way to deal with it is through argumentation. Arguments for and against the existence of God have been proposed and subjected to logical analysis in different periods of the history of philosophy. One of the most famous arguments in the history of philosophy, the ontological argument, first proposed by Anselm in his seminal work, the Proslogion, is an argument for the existence of God.[1]

For atheist arguments, the problem of evil occupies a prominent place. Although many times described as an argument against the existence of God, the problem of evil might also be seen as an issue of incompatibility between the propositions that (1) there is an omnipotent, omniscient and wholly good being who created the world and (2) there is evil and suffering in our world.[2] Even though in most cases equivalents, the latter way of presenting the problem illustrates its real point, which is to challenge the rationality of theist belief; a traditional view of rationality is that it prevents inconsistent sets of beliefs.

In fact, arguments for and against the existence of God are a traditional way to conduct the debate on the rationality of theist belief. Besides being attempts to answer the question of the existence of God, these arguments also address the following (epistemological) question: Is the belief in God rational?

---

[1]Other kinds of theist arguments of historical importance are: cosmological arguments, moral arguments, teleological and design arguments and arguments from miracles. We say kinds of arguments because these are actually classes of arguments; what we call ontological argument, for example, is a family of related, but at times quite different, arguments.

[2]If we take the word 'incompatibility" to mean the same as 'inconsistency" we get the logical problem of evil; if we take it to mean evidential incompatibility—in the sense of the existence of evil and suffering standing as evidence against the existence of God—we get the evidential problem of evil. See [12].

In order to properly address the ontological and epistemological questions we must have a minimally clear idea of what "God" means. Unless this is the case, how are we going for example to articulate an argument which ends with the conclusion that God does (not) exist? This is especially relevant when we notice that virtually every religious tradition has its own concept of God. The concept of God of Christianity is different from the one of Judaism, which is different from the one of theist forms of Vedanta, and so on and so forth. Therefore, the conceptual question "What does the concept of God mean?" is prior to the ontological and epistemological questions.

There is however a second, less trivial way in which the conceptual inquiry is prior to the ontological and epistemological ones. And it involves a different conceptual question. From a philosophical viewpoint, the question of what "God" means has been addressed by referring to so-called divine properties. William Rowe [10, p. 335], for example, named as "broad theism" the view according to which God has the following properties: omnipotence, omniscience, omnibenevolence and eternity.[3] From the definition that God is that than whom nothing greater can be thought, Anselm famously arrives not only at the conclusion that God exists (this is his ontological argument), but also at many properties which God supposedly possess. But not only that. He wonders about the individual and conjoint consistency of these properties. In modern terms, he ponders about the following question: Is the concept of God consistent? He writes, for instance, as follows:

> Now, since to be able to perceive and to be omnipotent, merciful, and impassible is better than not to be [any of these], how are You able to perceive if You are not something corporeal, or how are You omnipotent if You cannot do all things, or how are You both merciful and impassible?
> [3, p. 272]

How God can be omnipotent if he cannot do all things? Using a contemporary example, can he create a stone so heavy that he cannot lift? If we say no, then there is something God cannot do, namely to create such a stone; if we say yes, there is also something he cannot do, namely to lift the stone. In either case he is not omnipotent, which is the same as saying that the concept of omnipotence is not consistent. And how can he be both merciful and impassible at the same time? For if he is impassible, he has no compassion. And if he has no compassion, Anselm says, he does not have a heart sorrowful out of compassion for the wretched—which implies that he lacks the attribute of being merciful. Therefore, the concepts of mercifulness and impassibility seem to be inconsistent with one another.

---

[3]Rowe adds to these four properties the extrinsic property that God is the creator of the world [10, p. 335].

Leibniz goes further and ponders about the compossibility of all divine properties. Attempting to fill what he took to be a shortcoming in Descartes' ontological argument, he endeavored to show that all divine properties or perfections can coexist together in a single entity, or that it is possible that there is such a supremely perfect being, or that the concept of God is consistent. Leibniz's so-called ontological argument might therefore be seen as an argument for the consistency of the concept of God.[4]

The same issue arises when we deal with the God of religious traditions. The Christian concept of God, for example, involves the so-called doctrine of Trinity, summarized in the Athanasian Creed as follows: (1) We worship God in Trinity and Trinity in Unity... Neither confounding the persons nor dividing the substance. (2) So, the Father is God, the Son is God, and the Holy Spirit is God. (3) And yet they are not three Gods, but one God. As one might see, it is not hard to derive a contradiction from these three propositions.[5] This is the famous logical problem of Trinity.

The significance of this for the ontological and epistemological questions is obvious: if the concept of God is inconsistent, then it cannot be instantiated. Similar to the concept of squared circle, it would be impossible the existence of an entity which instantiates all properties attributed to God. Therefore, the ontological and epistemological questions would be apprioristically answered in a negative way.

Now, inconsistency is a logical concept. A set Γ is inconsistent if and only if one can derive from Γ (possibly augmented with some analytically or axiomatically true statements) a contradiction of the form "α and not-α", where α is an arbitrary proposition or statement. From a semantic point of view, a set Γ is inconsistent if and only if there is no model which satisfies all members of Γ. Γ is consistent if and only if Γ is not inconsistent. The way one will use this definition to effectively determine whether a set of propositions is consistent or not will depend on her approach to logic. A more technical approach will involve translating the statements into a formal language and viewing concepts such as derivation, model and satisfaction from the perspective a formal logical theory, be it proof-theoretical or semantic or both.

Even though the concepts of inconsistency and consistency are traditionally applied to sets of statements or propositions, they can easily be expanded so as to be applied to concepts. A concept C is consistent or coherent if and only if the set of propositions constructed as follows is consistent: proposition "a is C", a number of propositions of the form "If x is C, then x is ... ", which together define the concept C, and a number of additional definitional propositions dealing with other relevant

---

[4]For a brief historical introduction to the ontological argument (and its formalization) which contemplates Anselm's, Descartes' and Leibniz's contributions, see [11].

[5]See [9], for instance.

concepts. A concept is inconsistent if and only if it is not consistent. The concept of squared circle is inconsistent because the set {"a is a squared circle", "If x is a squared circle, then x (as a square) has four sides", "If x is a squared circle, then x (as a circle) has no sides", "If x has no sides, then it is false that x has four sides"} is inconsistent.

Our second conceptual question is therefore, perhaps beyond anything else, a logical question. Thus, logic is a crucial element for the analysis of the concept of God. This, of course, is only one way according to which logic might be seen as relevant to the philosophical analysis of the concept God. For other approaches to the concept of God, in particular more metaphorical ones in which God is not an object at all [5], logic will be pertinent in a quite a different way.

The concept of God, or of gods, constitutes the central theme of theology, or rather theologies. This is a vast subject that cannot be introduced briefly in its entirety. In the present issue of the *Journal of Applied Logics* we focus on a specific topic, namely logical aspects of the concept of God, where 'God' is understood principally according to the Biblical traditions. This collection does not present, however, a comprehensive survey of logical problems arising in relation to possible or realized conceptualizations of the divine. Only a few themes are explored, each an important one. As many as five papers deal with logical problems implied by the Christian concept of Trinity. The remaining three papers hardly have a common denominator with those dealing with Trinity, and with each other (except, of course, that they all deal with the logical analysis of the concept of God): one analyzes the traditional paradox of omnipotence mentioned above (the paradox of the stone), another one the concept of the divine developed by the eminent logician Gödel, and the third, one that opens this collection, deals with a mathematical model of God and the issue of mathematical models of the divine in general. Its initial and concluding parts can be seen as an introduction to the general problem of the value of mathematical models for theology.

This issue has been put together in the wake of the Second World Congress on Logic and Religion that took place at the University of Warsaw in June 2017. It is not the only publication following the congress; there is an already published special issue on formal approaches to the ontological argument [13] and another one is being prepared.

Logic is understood rather broadly in this collection. The authors refer to various logical systems, also non-classical ones and, in the second paper, to the Cantorian set theory, and in addition, in the first paper, to the models of mathematical systems in other mathematical theories, which constitutes a major topic in mathematical logic. Mathematics is not the same as logic—despite the arguments to the contrary by Frege and Russell—but they are related, and moreover, mathematics can be seen as a domain where logic reigns supreme as nowhere else. That is why mathematical considerations having theological significance belong here. The first paper, "Mathematical Models in Theology. A Buber-inspired Model of God and its Application to Shema Israel" by Stanisław Krajewski [5], one of the editors of this issue of the Journal of Applied Logics, deals with the problem of mathematical models in theology, a topic that nowadays seems rather neglected. Mathematical models representing religious issues can be seen as far-reaching logical examples of theological metaphors. They can be as misleading as every other metaphor. How useful are they? The problem is studied in reference to the example of a new theological model based on projective geometry and inspired by the thought of Martin Buber. In addition, this model can be used as a tool assisting meditation during the Jewish prayer involving the well-known verse Shema Israel "Hear, oh Israel, ... "

In the second paper, "Gödel's God-like Essence" by Talia Leven [7], another mathematical metaphor is proposed for "Godlikeness", or, more specifically, for Gödel's central monad modelled after a Leibnizian idea. She argues that it is the cumulative hierarchy of sets—arising in the transfinite process of repeatedly taking "the set of" previously obtained sets—forming the universe accepted by mathematical logicians that can play the role of the God-like essence.

The third paper, "A Logical Solution to the Paradox of the Stone" by Héctor Hernández-Ortiz and Victor Cantero-Flores [4], contains a discussion of the paradox of omnipotence, e.g., whether an omnipotent being can create a stone which he cannot lift. The authors argue for the solution based on the recognition of the limitations that must be present in the concept of omnipotence, namely that a coherent notion of omnipotence implies many impossibilities, in particular logical ones. One can, however, ask whether logical paradoxes genuinely follow from theological concepts. Don't they rather follow from the logically extremal interpretation of the concept of omnipotence? In the Biblical language, omnipotence can be perceived as indication of a gigantic power, incomparable with anything we know from human experience, rather than an absolutely maximum power. On the other hand, the fact is that logically interesting issues result from these extremal interpretations.

The block of papers dealing with various logical issues referring to the Trinity begins with the fourth paper of the collection, "No New Solutions to the Logical Problem of the Trinity" by Beau Branson [1]. It contains a presentation of the logical problem of the Trinity. A solution is given by a logical formalism in which all the relevant propositions are accepted but no inconsistency follows. The author argues that all solutions—and many have been proposed—belong to one of a finite number of categories, defined in a way that makes them controversial, heretical, or inconsistent.

The fifth paper, "What Means 'Tri-' in 'Trinity'?" by Basil Lourié [8], combines the insight perceived in the writings of the Eastern Church Byzantine Fathers with modern logical notions. When they said that Trinity is Oneness and Oneness is Trinity they meant, it is argued in the paper, neither cardinal numbers nor natural numbers; rather, they meant a paraconsistent order breaking the axiom of extensionality and the law of identity. What emerges can be called 'quasi-ordinal' numbers governed by some kind of 'super-reflexive logic': the elements are identical not only to themselves but to all others.

The sixth paper, "The Éminence Grise of Christology: Porphyry's Logical Teaching as a Cornerstone of Argumentation in Christological Debates of the Fifth and Sixth Centuries" by Anna Zhyrkova [14], assumes a strictly historical approach. It is argued that Neoplatonic logic, in particular Porphyry's logical account of substance, were useful for the explanation of the double—human and divine—nature of Christ, as well as in Trinitological considerations.

In the seventh paper, "The Problem of Universals in Late Patristic Theology" by Dirk Krausmüller [6], the historical approach referring to the first Millennium of the Christian era is continued. The contemporary reactions are studied to the claim of the sixth century Alexandrian philosopher-theologian John Philoponus who contended that the human nature in one individual was not the same as the human nature in another individual. The specific problem of Christian theology implied by the concept of Trinity is transferred to the realm of general ontology.

The eight and last paper, "Intuitionist Reasoning in the Tri-Unitarian Theology of Nicholas of Cues (1401–1464)" by Antonino Drago [2], contains an interpretation of the writings of Cusanus on the name of God. It is argued that to understand them it is best to assume that in the 15th century there was an awareness of intuitionistic logic, in particular of the failure of the double negation law. Cusanus applied the insight to the problem of Trinity. Furthermore, the paper contains the thesis that Christian revelation can be seen as an introduction of intuitionist logic into the history of mankind.

Even from this summary it should be clear that interesting explorations are possible when theology and logic are simultaneously taken into account. The papers of this collection constitute only a sample. We hope that more research will follow.

References

[1] B. Branson. No New Solutions to the Logical Problem of the Trinity. *Journal of Applied Logics* 6(6), 1051–1092, 2019.

[2] A. Drago. A. Intuitionist Reasoning in the Tri-Unitarian Theology of Nicholas of Cues (1401-1464). *Journal of Applied Logics* 6(6), 1143–1186, 2019.

[3] B. Folz, (ed.) *Medieval Philosophy: A Multicultural Reader*. New York: Bloomsbury Academic, 2019.

[4] H. Hernández-Ortiz and V. Cantero-Flores. A Logical Solution to the Paradox of the Stone. *Journal of Applied Logics*, 6(6), 1037–1050, 2019

[5] S. Krajewski. Mathematical Models in Theology. A Buber-inspired Model of God and its Application to Shema Israel. *Journal of Applied Logics*, 6(6), 1007–1020, 2019.

[6] D. Krasmüller. The Problem of Universals in Late Patristic Theology. *Journal of Applied Logics*, 6(6), 1125–1142, 2019.

[7] T. Leven. Gödel's God-like Essence. *Journal of Applied Logics*, 6(6), 1021–1036, 2019.

[8] B. Lourié. What Means 'Tri-' in 'Trinity'? *Journal of Applied Logics*, 6(6), 1093–1108, 2019.

[9] D. Molto. The Logical Problem of the Trinity and the Strong Theory of Relative Identity. *Sophia: International Journal of Philosophy and Traditions*, 56: 227-245, 2017.

[10] W. Rowe. The Problem of Evil and Some Varieties of Atheism. *American Philosophical Quarterly*, 16: 335-41, 1979.

[11] R. Silvestre. A Brief Critical Introduction to the Ontological Argument and its Formalization: Anselm, Gaunilo, Descartes, Leibniz and Kant. *Journal of Applied Logics*, 5: 1441-1474, 2018.

[12] R. Silvestre. On the Concept of Theodicy. *Sophia: International Journal of Philosophy and Traditions*, 56: 207-226, 2017.

[13] R. Silvestre and J.-Y. Beziau, (eds.). Special Issue on Formal Approaches to the Ontological Argument, *Journal of Applied Logics*, Vol. 5, issue 6, 2018.

[14] A. Zhyrkova. A. The Éminence Grise of Christology: Porphyry's Logical Teaching as a Cornerstone of Argumentation in Christological Debates of the Fifth and Sixth Centuries. *Journal of Applied Logics*, 6(6), 1109–1124, 2019.

 Received July 2019

Mathematical Models in Theology. A Buber-inspired Model of God and its Application to "Shema Israel"

Stanisław Krajewski
University of Warsaw
stankrajewski@uw.edu.pl

Abstract

Mathematical models representing religious issues can be seen as far-reaching logical examples of theological metaphors. They have been used since at least Nicholas of Cusa. Although rarely appreciated today, they are sometimes invoked by modern theologians.

A novel model is presented here, based on projective geometry and inspired by an idea stated by Martin Buber. It models God and transcendence, especially in the framework of one central Jewish prayer. Actually, it models our relation to God rather than God as such, which is more in keeping with the approach of Judaism as well as negative theology in general.

Models can help us understand some theological concepts and aspects of the traditional vision of the relationship of the world and its creator. The model presented here can also be used for the purpose of visualization in prayer: it can be used as a tool assisting meditation during the Jewish prayer involving the well-known verse *Shema Israel* "Hear, oh Israel, ..." (Deut. 6:4), often designated as the Jewish credo.

Yet, mathematical models can be as misleading as every other metaphor. Is the model presented here a model of the Biblical God, the God of Judaism, or just of the "Buberian God"? Do the shortcomings of mathematical models annul their usefulness?

Keywords: Model, mathematical model, metaphor, theology, projective geometry, projective hemisphere, Martin Buber, Eternal Thou, Jewish prayer, *Shema Israel*, meditation.

Mathematical models in theology can be seen as a result of the use of logic for constructing elaborate metaphors. Metaphors are indispensable in our thinking. Our language depends on them, as emphasized by Lakoff and his followers. (See [24].) In theology they are particularly important because we refer to intangible

Vol. 6 No. 6 2019
Journal of Applied Logics — IfCoLog Journal of Logics and their Applications

realities. Can metaphors be "logical" in some sense? In every metaphor a situation at hand is compared to another one, presumably better known. The situation to which we compare the less known reality usually have some structure, and we can try to find a "logic" behind it. What seems even more relevant, metaphors can refer to rigid, well determined structures that can be abstract. Their description can be logical in the sense of being a full description of all possibilities as regards the aspects taken into account. This inevitably brings us close to mathematics. The best source of such abstract structures is to be found in the existing mathematics. Mathematical models representing religious issues can be seen as extreme examples of theological metaphors of a logical variety.

Such models have been used since at least Nicholas of Cusa. In *De docta ignorantia* (II.5) he wrote that "since the pathway for approaching divine matters is opened to us only through symbols, we make quite suitable use of mathematical signs because of their incorruptible certainty." (Cf. [27, p. 100]) He was fond of infinite figures, or rather indefinitely growing finite figures, metaphorically representing the infinity of God. Thus a sequence of mutually tangent circles coinciding in one point and growing in an unlimited way was to be identified with an infinite line, namely its common asymptote. Such a circle in infinity, Cusanus argued, is indistinguishable from a similarly arising triangle in infinity. (*De docta ignorantia* I,13.) In *Idiota de mente* he wrote that "we give our name 'number' to number from the Divine Mind." (Cf. [27, p. 101].) Thus mathematics can reflect God's mind. Nicholas of Cusa claimed that the divine unity is symbolized by the number 1. This theological approach to number 1 was also maintained by Leibniz. He developed the binary system of notation and was delighted that 0 and 1 suffice to represent every number. He referred to the Biblical description of Creation, "It is true that as the empty voids and the dismal wilderness belong to zero, so the spirit of God and His light belong to the all-powerful One." In addition, because for Leibniz, who continued the Pythagorean tradition, the essence of everything is number, in every created thing there is 0 and 1, or both nothingness due to us and perfection coming from God. (Cf. [4, p. 491] in [17].)

Speculations similar to those of Cusanus or Leibniz now strike us as rather naïve. Nowadays, mathematical models are so rare that in the monumental volume Models of God ([8]), presenting dozens of models of divinity, they do not appear at all. Nor are mathematical models mentioned in Bradley's 2011 survey of the connections between mathematics and theology [3]. However, mathematical models are sometimes invoked by modern theologians. In Section 1 some examples are given. In Section 2 an original model is presented (first mentioned in [19] and [20]) using a mathematical model used to show the consistency of plane projective geometry. In addition, use of the model (the application that is not mentioned in the previous papers) as a possible support for meditation during the (Jewish) prayer "Shema Israel" is indicated in Section 3. Along the way, and then in a more focused manner in Section 4, an assessment of mathematical models in theology is attempted. Whatever their merits, they are a far cry from scientific models: it seems that they cannot be creative. Yet, whereas their shortcomings are serious, they can still be useful as illustrations of ideas. The present paper is similar to a Polish article ([22]), and complements another one ([18] in [23]), where theological background of mathematical concepts is studied.

1 Examples of contemporary mathematical metaphors in theology

An extremely simple but instructive example of an interesting mathematical metaphor applied to theology was proposed by the late Józef Życiński. Answering a natural, if naïve, criticism of the Christian concept of Trinity as an absurdity because it would mean that $1 + 1 + 1 = 1$, he indicated that for infinite cardinal numbers the equality does hold. As is well known, $\aleph_0 + \aleph_0 + \aleph_0 = \aleph_0$. The retort is clever, but a moment's reflection discloses its limitations. After all, also $\aleph_0 + \aleph_0 + \aleph_0 + \aleph_0 = \aleph_0$, which means that the concept of a "Quadrity" would be equally well justified. Moreover, it is doubtful that it makes sense to refer to mathematical addition of numbers, finite or infinite, as corresponding to the "addition" of the persons of the Trinity. Perhaps it would be better to refer to the operation of the Boolean union? In Boolean algebras adding the (Boolean) unity to itself results in the same unity. In addition, it is the only element (of the algebra) that is greater than each of the remaining ones. It has, therefore, a "divine" quality, and since it is unique, it can be seen as modeling monotheism. Yet, obviously, this model is no better than the previous one. It forms a speculation that is as shallow as it is arbitrary. Życiński's retort is good as a riposte, and it was meant as such, but not as a genuine mathematical model.

Another well-known example is provided by the modal logic version of the ontological argument. The contemporary version, developed by Gödel following Leibniz, has been extensively studied and explored. It deals with an object having all maximal positive properties within a formal system of modal logic. A critic would say that it is extremely doubtful that such an object has anything to do with the God of religious traditions, especially in view of the often present realization that God is no "object". Yet one can also say, "Even if one concludes that even this form of an ontological argument is no sufficient proof of God, it is a help for clarifying the notion of a property as used in the context of properties of God." (After [10,

p. 320].)

Another modern example seems to be even more widely known. The metaphor provided by the concept of absolute infinity in Cantor's vision of the universe of sets has been invoked by theologians. (See, e.g., [6], [32].) The class of all sets, that of all ordinal numbers or that of all cardinal numbers — all such "proper" classes are not only infinite, but beyond reach of our necessarily limited constructions. This alone, independently of Cantor's theological arguments in favor of his theory of sets, can serve as a mathematical analogue of transcendence. While there is hardly anything directly theological in the class of all sets, it naturally suggests talking about hugeness, inaccessibility, indescribability, ineffability — the terms that set theorists have used to define some purely formal properties of the universe of sets. (See, e.g., [15].)

These examples provide illustrations, but do they offer models? To me it is rather doubtful, even though I admit that there is hardly a hard and fast border between metaphoric illustrations and genuine models. Yet there exist attempts to construct genuine mathematical models for theology. For example, James B. Miller in 1998 ([26], the paper is currently not available, which is a proof that it is not true that nothing is ever lost in the internet) presented a rather advanced one, based on the normal (Gaussian) distribution, in order to explain the supposedly paradoxical belief that submission to God's will provides more freedom than does disobedience. While this is difficult to explain in everyday language, it becomes understandable when the Gaussian curve is considered in the "option space", that is, in the space of all possible options in a given moment of one's life. On the y-axis the number of options is indicated, and on the x-axis their quality — from animal ones, on the left, to the opposite ones, resulting from the human hubris, on the right hand side. Under the curve the available options are indicated. Miller assumes that the most agreeable to God are the options belonging to the "middle way", somewhere between the pole of the "animal" and that of human "hubris". The acceptable options are not much different from those in the middle, distant no more than one standard deviation. As a result, we model free will, as there are many possible options to choose from. At the same time, since the columns near the middle position are relatively larger, the way that pleases God offers more opportunities. Submission provides more freedom! Furthermore, sin can be illustrated as a deformation and dislocation of the Gaussian curve: then what the sinner takes to be the middle way is in reality distant from the genuine "divine" middle way.

It should be apparent that several assumptions, the described model rests on, must be made to use it, such as the meaningfulness of the parameter indicated on the x-axis, the adequacy of the (arbitrarily invoked) curve, the identification of God's will with the options belonging to the golden middle. The value of the model for theology is debatable. It is commendable if it helps someone to grasp some theological ideas. However, Miller himself is careful to refer to the model as a (mere) mathematical metaphor. It can help us understand a theological concept that "is not easily describable in traditional or everyday language."

Another proposal has been made, related to the idea that is current in — to use the term advocated by Ruben Hersh in [14] — "the kitchen of mathematics," according to which the set of all true sentences is included in the "divine" knowledge. (Cf. [18] in [23].) Making use of logical and set-theoretical notions one can try to express "divinity" as nothing more, and nothing less, than the set of all true sentences. John Post does this in the spirit of Quine's naturalism and minimalism in order to express the foundations of theism, avoiding "metaphorical, analogical, symbolic, mythical" talk about God. ([28, p. 736–7].) He tries to paraphrase, as suggested by Quine in [29], the statements about God in a possibly restricted language so that one can get sentences that are "literally true." ([28, p. 738].) Thus "Godhead" is defined as the smallest set G such that its transitive closure (that is, the totality of its elements, elements's elements, etc.) includes the set of all true sentences about sets, the set of true sentences about justice, virtues, religious experience (whatever this may mean for us), etc. The set G is mysterious, "combines transcendence with immanence," contains complete knowledge, and the "mythic" personal God is its "intended object." ([28, p. 740].) Even this short summary suggests that this construction can be easily criticized as contributing nothing to theology. The model can be easily undermined by asking, e.g., whether devout people really pray to a set. Even disregarding this, many critics would see this sophisticated reduction of theology to the vocabulary of logic as singularly futile.

Another proposal has been recently made by Ilya Dvorkin (still unpublished) who has used category theory to indicate a model of God as present in the system of Franz Rosenzweig. God is, or rather corresponds to, a (special) category. It is a metaphor that perhaps illustrates well the theologico-philosophical system of Rosenzweig with its fundamentally dynamic character. This is possible because category theory can illustrate movement, while set theory is static. I am sure that there have been other attempts by theologians to model God in mathematics. The above-mentioned ones use relatively serious mathematics and I take them as representative. My guess is that such models are usually vague metaphors or imprecise suggestions rather than genuine mathematical models. When they use precise mathematics, their relevance is questionable. Before discussing the problem of how good those models are I present another way in which religious ideas can be illuminated thanks to mathematical knowledge and mathematical structures.

2 A new model

I vividly remember the moment, long ago, when I was learning Martin Buber's vision of God presented as a consequence (or background or implication) of interhuman relations. In 1923, in the book *I and Thou*, he wrote, "The extended lines of relations meet in the eternal Thou." ([5, p. 75].) To anyone acquainted with projective geometry this picture seems familiar. In this system of plane geometry the direction of each straight line constitutes a point of a new type, and this point at infinity is common to all parallel lines. Thus, every pair of straight lines (in the plane) intersects in exactly one point, with no exceptions. For parallel lines this point of intersection is in infinity, but in projective geometry these infinitely far located points have the same status as do the usual points of the plane. What is more, the totality of the points at infinity constitutes one "straight line in infinity." This line ca be see to correspond to God in Buber's vision. For him, similar to the situation in projective geometry, the line of relation between two arbitrary individuals always reaches the same God.

The emerging picture is very attractive. It is even more adequate than it seems at first sight. The mathematical model can suggest interesting claims of philosophical or theological nature. For example, in the projective geometry the same point in infinity is reached on both "ends" of the straight line. This would mean that from whichever of the two sides the interhuman relation is considered, it leads to the same point "in God", which is exactly what was depicted by Buber, who stressed symmetry of the relation. Furthermore, one point does not determine a line; in order to reach the line in infinity two (arbitrary) points are needed. This is also in accordance to Buber's conception, according to which a single human being cannot enter into the relation with God, that is, "to address the eternal *Thou*," since it is possible only through the relation with another being: "the inborn Thou is realized in each relation and consummated in none. It is consummated only in the direct relation with the *Thou* that by its nature cannot become an *It*." ([5, p. 75].) Each finite point in the projective plane belongs to this world of ours, and that is why it can function also as an "it". The points at infinity are not directly tangible. They are transcendent. The line in infinity becomes the area of transcendence. It is an interesting mathematical model of the transcendent, or the realm beyond this world of ours, but in close connection to us.

The parallel between the projective geometry and Buber's vision can be extended even further. And here a genuine mathematical model is invoked. (See, e.g. [9, p. 544–546].) Namely, one of the best known models of the projective plane in Euclidean (three-dimensional) geometry is given by a hemisphere. Let us imagine the Northern hemisphere together with the equator. All the points above the equator constitute the proper (finite) points of our model, and the points on the equator constitute the points at infinity. Straight lines are the semicircles with the centers coinciding with the center of the sphere (the Earth). These "great circles" deserve to be called straight lines because they form the shortest way between two points. (To see the connection of the model to the plane let us imagine a bulb in the center of the globe and a horizontal plane touching the sphere only at the Northern Pole; the projection of the hemisphere fills up the plane and the equatorial points are projected to an "infinity".) One more move needs to be made to get a model of the projective plane geometry. In order to have only one point corresponding to the direction of a line, the opposite points of the equator must be identified. They must be treated as one entity, one point "at infinity." The resulting objects cannot be easily imagined, but it is also possible to assume that the whole line segment joining two opposite points of the equator constitutes, *ex definitione*, one "improper point." The totality of these improper points forms a plane figure, or a disc determined by the equator. In our model this figure is the basis of the hemisphere. Thus God is here the foundation of the world, unattainable directly, but appearing, in some way, everywhere: being the direction of every line joining two points, it is indirectly present in every relation between the beings of this world.

This model of the projective plane models God and transcendence. Actually, it models our relation to God, or a configuration involving an allusion to God, rather than God as such, which is more in keeping with the approach of Judaism and the tradition of negative theology in general, stressing unknowability of God.

This projective plane model is more successful than previous attempts made to use mathematical metaphors to illustrate Buber's concepts. For example, Will Herberg in his introduction to a selection of Buber's writings quotes the phrase about the extended lines of relations, and adds, "God is the center of the circle of existence, the apex of the triangle of life." ([13, p. 16].) I think that this reference to elementary geometrical figures gives no useful explanation, and harms rather than helps understanding of Buber's vision. It is worth mentioning that Buber himself used the image of a circle in another context (and perhaps that was the source of Herberg's remark). He applied his concept of God to social theory. He indicated an external center, which moreover is of a "divine" character, as a pillar of a true community (in addition to the existence of I-Thou relations between its members). "The real origin of community is undoubtedly only to be understood by the fact that its members have a common relationship to the center, superior to all other relations: The circle is drawn from the radii, not from the points of the periphery. And undoubtedly, the primal reality of the center cannot be known if it is not known as transparent into the divine."[1]

Buber's model of the situation is simple: it is a circle. Its center is the divine Center and the circumference is composed of the members of the community. All the points are at the same distance from the center. The radii, which connect to the center, stabilize the circle. In this way the idea that each of the community members is in the same relation to God is nicely expressed. Nothing else, however, is expressed by this model. My model, the hemisphere with opposite points of the equator pairwise identified, does the same job as the circle: here of course the Center is the center of the ball, and each point on the hemisphere is in the same relation to the Center. Yet my model achieves more. It includes the concept of God as the meeting points of the prolonged lines of the I-Thou relations. In addition, the center identified with the line at infinity is sufficiently unusual and "otherworldly" to represent the transcendent God. Thus all the principal aspects of Buber's concept of God are included in the model presented in this paper.

3 An application of the model to one prayer

The model introduced in Section 2 can be applied in another religious context. Namely, it can be seen as a tool suitable for interpreting one important prayer, namely, the well-known verse *Shema Israel* "Hear, O Israel, ... " (Deuteronomy 6:4), often designated as the Jewish credo. The verse has many interpretations within Judaism, but I want to propose a particular way of approaching it, namely as a meditative phrase. Meditation as such is not new within Judaism (cf. [16]), but the point here is to use the projective geometry model as a means to visualize the meaning of the Biblical verse. So the model can be used as a tool assisting meditation performed during the Jewish prayer involving the *Shema*.

The verse Deut. 6:4, presented in the standard Jewish way (with the Tetragrammaton replaced by the word "Hashem," or "the Name"), reads: "*Shema Israel Hashem Eloheinu Hashem echad.*" Its translation: "Hear, O Israel: Hashem, our God, Hashem (is) one." Other translations are possible, but this is not relevant here because it is assumed that the meditation refers to the Hebrew original. (On the other hand, using a translation seems also doable.)

Now when I — and this can apply to everyone — say "*Shema Israel*" I imagine the hemisphere; its (proper) points are human beings (which is a universalizing reading of "Israel", possible according to some thinkers, for example Levinas ([25]), who explains the ultimate meaning of Israel as being fully human and with unlimited

---

[1]From 1931 article "On Community", quoted after [2, p. 244]; almost exactly the same is repeated in "Paths in Utopia"; see, e.g., [13, p. 129].

responsibility), and I am seeing myself as one of those points. Furthermore, I am in relation to another point, another human being. The fundamental I-Thou relation is symbolized by the shortest arc between the two points. Fortunately, between any two proper points there exists such an arc that forms a fragment of a great circle; this circle meets the equator in two exactly opposite points.

Next, when I hear *"Hashem"*, uttered within prayer as *"A-d-o-n-a-i,"* or "my Lord," I realize an undefined realm of transcendence which is difficult to imagine because it is beyond our world. It is, however, immediately specified à la Buber: I imagine the point at infinity beyond my partner in the relation; at the same time, I feel the point at infinity behind my back and I know it is exactly the same point I perceive behind the partner. I know it is the same because this is how it is in our model, the hemisphere made into a projective plane.

After that I say *"Eloheinu,"* or "our God." This term with the suffix *"nu,"* meaning "our,"[2] makes me realize that there are plenty of various relations between us, human beings, and in particular between me and other Jews who refer to God understood in the same way and, moreover, pray using the same verse. Israel becomes a network of relationships. As does humanity. Then I say *"Hashem"* again and I realize that all "the extended lines of relations" refer to the Name. They do it whether the individuals who are in relation see the ultimate background in this way or don't. All the indicated points at infinity have one reference. And here comes, appropriately enough, the word *"echad,"* or "one."

"One" means that the two points appearing at the two sides of my relation with someone as well as all the other points at infinity that arise from all possible relations of that kind are one. They are to be identified with each other. All the lines of relations "meet in the eternal Thou." And it is One. The sheer saying "one" is, however, not enough for the appropriate visualization. What is needed is the image of all the equatorial points becoming one point. This last move is hard to imagine, and it is not part of the standard mathematical construction or the accepted use of the hemisphere model. We go beyond projective geometry here. What happens is that the whole line at infinity, representing transcendence, becomes just *one* point. The equator shrinks to one point, or the whole disk that is the basis of the world becomes one point. Of course this is in no way an Euclidean point.

The fact that this last transformation is so hard to imagine as a geometrical action is not a problem for this modelling; it is actually valuable because it makes us realize that transcendence is paradoxical. We must not imagine it as a realm very distant but otherwise similar to the world around us, a kind of outer space. It is of

---

[2]Actually, the very term „Elohim" to which the suffix is added, is also in plural. It is not clear why. My philosophical explanation is given in [21].

different nature, which is what theologians and religious leaders always say.

While creating such a model is relatively easy, the question of its value and usefulness is less simple.

4 How useful can a mathematical model be for theology?

The model presented in Section 2 has a lot of charm. It helps to explain Buber's theological idea; it provides assistance in one prayer; it models paradox using mathematical concepts. It seems, at least to me, extremely natural: I guess it is possible that Buber had heard about projective geometry before he described his vision. The hemisphere model was already known, and I wouldn't exclude the possibility that the philosopher was inspired by this impressive piece of mathematics. Also, as we have seen, the model illustrates nicely the Buberian social-theological understanding of community. Despite all the advantages, the value of the model can be questioned in at least two ways.

First, one can say that even though mathematics used in the model is more advanced than that used by Nicolaus of Cusa, the achievement is not more significant than it was 500 years ago: it illustrates matters that have nothing to do with mathematics. And perhaps in 500 years the mathematical points will be as obvious as pictures invoked by Cusanus are to us now — and will be felt to be similarly naïve. The answer to this criticism is that for the moment the model does not seem trivial and, in addition, its use for meditation can be helpful for some individuals, which is a proof of its value.

The second criticism is more fundamental. It can be expressed in the form of two questions. One, does the geometrical model enable us to achieve a significant progress in our quest to understand theology? Two, does it make possible an unexpected conclusion in the field of theology? A positive answer to any of the questions would constitute a proof of a genuine value of the model. I must admit that I am not sure whether positive answers can be properly justified.

Buber's vision was forcefully presented by its author without mathematical pictures. The model presented in this paper illustrates the issue but does not advance it. Unclear or controversial issues pertaining to it are not made easier by projective geometry; they are beyond the model. For example, the model will not help to answer the question whether the relation that opens the dimension of the transcendent may hold also between a human being and an animal or an object such as a tree (as Buber himself was claiming). There are also limitations to the analogy. Mathematical research related to the projective plane include many more issues and deep theorems than the features mentioned above. For example, the non-orientability of the projective plane or the fact that a straight line does not divide the plane into two regions.[3] Such properties and facts seem to have no theological parallels. And I am sure that if someone zealously insisted on finding such a parallel, it would almost certainly lead him astray.

There is a certain incongruence between the mathematical picture and theological vision. If our geometrical model is seen as an adequate description of the philosophico-theological idea, philosophy and theology look meager compared to mathematics. If, on the other hand, one believes that it is primarily philosophy and theology that deal with important problems of humankind and the world, then the mathematical models becomes no more than an illustration — perhaps suggestive, but insufficient and fundamentally irrelevant.

Mathematical models, as much as every other metaphor, can be as misleading as they can be illuminating. An analysis of their adequacy is always needed. Regarding the model presented here, is it a model of God *tout court*, the Biblical God, the God of Judaism or merely the "Buberian God"? We can imagine arguments in favor of each of these options. However, every answer would be highly subjective. In other cases the same limitation is again unavoidable: models can help us to grasp the ideas of theologians, but can they help us understand the reality to which religious discourse refers?

On a more general level, my guess is that theologians — and also philosophers —always have a metaphorical model in mind when describing divine matters. If we can recover it we will know better the vision of the author. In this sense all models, mathematical as well, are important and useful. Yet, to go from an understanding of the mind of theologians to the claim that we can get knowledge of God is very risky. It is similarly difficult to know if we can achieve an understanding of a seemingly easier matter than ungraspable God Himself, namely the relationship between the Creator and the world.

The objections to the value of the mathematical models mentioned in Section 1 and also to the merits of model from Section 2 illustrate a universal problem: even in science, all mathematical models are merely models, that is, they reflect only some aspects of reality. This is a shortcoming, but let us realize that in physics or cosmology models reflect the most essential aspects, or at least so we believe. Moreover, and most importantly, such models can be creative, revealing unexpected properties of the modelled world. For example, Michael Heller reminds us that "all properties of quarks have been deduced from mathematical models, in which,

---

[3]See, e.g., [9, p. 547], or [30, pp. 164nn]. I am grateful to the anonymous referee for the mention of Richeson's book as well as for some other remarks. I have decided, however, not to follow the suggestion to give a fuller mathematical presentation of projective plane geometry.

nota bene, quarks initially had been absent." ([11, p.111–112], also included in [12].) Therefore, for us mathematics is "to some extent," says Heller, a Leibnizian "divine language": in the God-given name — here, in mathematical description — all properties of the denoted object are contained. Thus, the question is whether non-scientific uses of models can be similarly creative.

Adequate and fruitful application of mathematical models in the humanities are rare, if at all present. The best example I can think of is the catastrophe theory developed by René Thom ([31]). Similarly ambitious but incomparably less convincing is the set-theoretical modelling of being and events by Alain Badiou ([1]) who identifies ontology with set theory. I do not know if a truly successful model has ever been proposed in theology.

The projective geometry model of Section 2 is nice but it is unclear if it captures all essential aspects of the situation described by Buber. It is, of course, even less clear whether it reflects the "true" properties of God as conceived in Judaism, other Biblical traditions, other religions, let alone God *tout court*. This model is certainly fine as a metaphor, a general suggestive picture, and as a helpful visualization in certain prayer/meditation. Similarly to the other models, it lacks, however, the creativity present in genuine scientific models. This is a most essential point. What new property of the theological reality can be revealed through the model? Does it even make sense to expect that? What is more, it seems unreasonable to expect from it any predictive power. Scientific models can help us predict events or outcomes of experiments. It seems to me that not only in theology but in the humanities in general this is not possible. This would mean that mathematical models, for all their usefulness, function there in a different way than in science. Their role is less deep. They do not reveal the inner structure in a similarly adequate manner. They are illustrations rather than models in the strict sense. To be sure, some reservations are needed here: for example, statistical analysis certainly provides new facts in sociology and other endeavors. I doubt, however, if such uses can be applied in theology, although they can in the science of religion, when comparisons of various religions or religious objects or texts can be assisted by statistical analysis.

To sum up, mathematical models in theology can be valuable but their value is limited. Illustration via mathematical metaphor is not the same as a genuine mathematical model in the sense known from science. Perhaps for „genuine" applications of models in theology and other branches of humanities another mathematics is needed? Interestingly, this suggestion was made by mathematician Keith Devlin. In his 1997 book *Goodbye Descartes* ([7]) he describes difficulties in applying current mathematics and logic to descriptions of human communication and suggests that "soft mathematics" is needed. That novel mathematics would avoid reductionism: so far, mathematics achieves incomparable precision by reducing live situations to rigid abstract structures; in addition, let me add, it does not sufficiently take into account context and time. If "soft math" emerges may be it will also be applicable to theology? In the realm of logic, perhaps "softer" logical systems can be proposed, and be more suitable for theology?[4]

References

[1] Alain Badiou. *Being and Event.* Continuum, New York, 2005. French orig.1988.

[2] Asher D. Biemann, editor. *The Martin Buber Reader.* Palgrave Macmillan, New York, 2002.

[3] James Bradley. Theology and Mathematics — Key Themes and Central Historical Figures. In J. Bradley, editor, *Theology and Science*, volume 9, pages 5–26. 2011.

[4] Herbert Breger. God and Mathematics in Leibniz's Thought. In Koetsier, Teun and Luc Bergmans, editor, *Mathematics and the Divine: A Historical Study*, pages 485–498. Elsevier, 2005.

[5] Martin Buber. *I and Thou.* T. and T. Clark, Edinburgh, 1937. German orig. 1923.

[6] Joseph W. Dauben. *Georg Cantor, His Mathematics and Philosophy of the Infinite.* Harvard University Press, Cambridge, Mass., 1979.

[7] Keith Devlin. *Goodbye, Descartes: The End of Logic and the Search for a New Cosmology of the Mind.* John Wiley & Sons, New York, 1997.

[8] Jeanine Diller and Asa Kasher, editors. *Models of God and Alternative Ultimate Realities.* Springer, Dodrecht, 2013.

[9] Marvin Jay Greenberg. *Euclidean and Non-Euclidean Geometries. Development and History, fourth edition.* W. H. Freeman and Co., New York, 2008.

[10] Petr Hajek. Gödel's Ontological Proof and Its Variants. In Matthias Baaz, Christos H. Papadimitriou, Hilary W. Putnam, Dana S. Scott, and Jr. Charles L. Harper, editors, *Kurt Gödel and the Foundations of Mathematics*, pages 307–321. Cambridge Univ. Press, 2011.

[11] Michał Heller. *Czy fizyka jest nauką humanistyczną? [Polish].* Biblos, Tarnów, 2000.

[12] Michał Heller and Stanisław Krajewski. *Czy fizyka i matematyka to nauki humanistyczne? [Polish].* Copernicus Center Press, Kraków, 2014.

[13] Will Herberg, editor. *The Writings of Martin Buber.* Meridian Books, Cleveland and New York, 1956.

[14] Reuben Hersh. Mathematics has a front and a back. *Synthèse*, 88:127–133, 1991.

[15] Akihiro Kanamori. *The Higher Infinite : Large Cardinals in Set Theory from Their Beginnings (2nd ed.).* Springer, 2003.

[16] Aryeh Kaplan. *Jewish Meditation. A Practical Guide.* Schocken Books, New York, 2003.

---

[4]A noteworthy attempt is due to the investigations of Talmudic logic, conducted by Dov Gabbay and others.

[17] Teun Koetsier and Luc Bergmans, editors. *Mathematics and the Divine: A Historical Study*. Elsevier, 2005.

[18] Stanisław Krajewski. Theological Metaphors in Mathematics. In *Volume „Theology in Mathematics?", Studies in Logic, Grammar and Rhetoric 44 (57)*.

[19] Stanisław Krajewski. *Czy matematyka jest nauką humanistyczną? [Polish]*. Copernicus Center Press, Cracow, 2011.

[20] Stanisław Krajewski. Matematyka w teologii, teologia w matematyce [Polish]. *Zagadnienia filozoficzne w nauce*, 60:99–117, 2016.

[21] Stanisław Krajewski. An Explanation of the Plural Form of God's Name. *Eidos*, 2(4):115–121, 2018.

[22] Stanisław Krajewski. O pewnym matematycznym modelu Boga i jego zastosowaniu [Polish]. *Roczniki filozoficzne*, LXVII(1):5–18, 2019.

[23] Stanisław Krajewski and Kazimierz Trzęsicki. *Volume „Theology in Mathematics?", Studies in Logic, Grammar and Rhetoric 44 (57)*. 2016.

[24] George Lakoff and Mark Johnson. *Metaphors We Live By*. University of Chicago Press, Chicago, 2008. Updated; first ed. 1980.

[25] Emmanuel Levinas. Judaisme et kénose. In *A l'heure des nations*. Editions de Minuit, Paris, 1989.

[26] James B. Miller. From the Garden to Gauss: Mathematics as Theological Metaphor. `www.aaas.org/spp/dser/03_Areas/beyond/perspectives/Miller_James_Paper_gauss/Miller_James_Paper_gauss.shtml`; `http://www.aaas.org/spp/dser/RESOURCE/miller/GAUSS4.htm`, 1998. Paper presented at the 7th European Conference on Science and Theology, March 31-April 4, 1998, Durham, England); it was available at AAAS Dialogue on Science, Ethics, and Religion, but is not there anymore.

[27] Roman Murawski. Between Theology and Mathematics. Nicholas of Cusa's Philosophy of Mathematics. In *Volume "Theology in Mathematics?", Studies in Logic, Grammar and Rhetoric 44 (57)*, pages 97–110. 2016.

[28] J. F. Post. New Foundations for Philosophical Theology, Quine with God. *The Journal of Philosophy*, 7:736–748, 1974.

[29] Willard Van Orman Quine. *Word and Object*. MIT Press, Boston, 1960.

[30] David S. Richeson. *Euler's Gem. The Polyhedron Formula and the Birth of Topology*. Princeton University Press, Princeton and Oxford, 2008.

[31] René Thom. *Structural Stability and Morphogenesis: An Outline of a General Theory of Models*. Addison-Wesley, Reading, MA, 1989.

[32] Aaron R. Thomas-Bolduc. Cantor, God, and Inconsistent Multiplicities. In *Volume "Theology in Mathematics?", Studies in Logic, Grammar and Rhetoric 44 (57)*, pages 133–146. 2016.

Received 27 May 2019

Gödel's God-like Essence

Talia Leven

Department of Computer Science, The Open University of Israel, Levinsky College of Education

taliale@openu.ac.il

Abstract

In the 1970s, the great logician Kurt Gödel proposed an argument for the existence of what he called "Godlikeness". At the time, Gödel wished to rescue David Hilbert's program, which he knew was impossible because of his own incompleteness theorems. Gödel named his new program "Gödel's Program". In this paper I argue that the cumulative hierarchy of sets V could play the role of Godlikeness, meaning that V could play the role of Gödel's central monad. Thus, proving the existence of Godlikeness actually means proving the existence of the cumulative hierarchy of sets V. According to Gödel there is a connection between epistemology, ontology and formal systems. If something exists, we will someday have the ability to recognize it. Therefore, it is reasonable to conclude that the ability to know the complete set of axioms of the cumulative hierarchy of sets V, which I attempt to show is the God-like essence, is an argument in favor of the success of Gödel's Program.

Keywords: God-like, Gödel's Program, Essence, Positive Property, Primitive Property, Complete Set of Axioms.

1 Introduction

In the 1970s, the great logician Kurt Gödel wished to rescue David Hilbert's program, which calls for the formalization of all mathematics and their reduction to a finite and consistent set of axioms. The method of proof according to Hilbert's Program must also be finite. Gödel knew that Hilbert's plan could not be implemented because of his own incompleteness theorems. Consequently, Gödel defined a new program, named "Gödel's Program", which relinquished the notion of finiteness. Gödel believed that the axioms of set theory describe mathematical reality and that the world of sets, which is the hierarchy of sets V, is a well-determined reality [13, p. 181]. At the same time, Gödel proposed an argument for the existence of what he

called "Godlikeness", which bears striking similarities to Gottfried Leibniz's ontological arguments. Gödel described his general philosophical theory to Hao Wang as
a "monadology with a central monad like the monadology of Leibniz in its general
structure" [38, p. 8].

In this paper, I attempt to argue that the cumulative hierarchy of sets V could
play the role of Godlikeness, which means that V could play the role of Gödel's
central monad. Accordingly, proving the existing of Godlikeness means claiming the
existence of the cumulative hierarchy of sets V. Since according to Gödel there is a
connection between knowing and existing, we have the ability to know this world of
sets. Therefore it is reasonable to conclude that the ontological argument indicates
an optimistic view of the success of Gödel's Program.

It is important to emphasize that I do not wish to find flaws in the ontological
argument or defend it. Rather, I intend to show why it is reasonable to claim that
the cumulative hierarchy of sets V could fill the role of Godlikeness.[1]

2   Gödel's Program

Gödel's Program grew out of the remains of Hilbert's Program, with the aim of
searching for new axioms to add to those of set theory ZF in order to complete
our understanding of the world of sets V. Gödel believed that the way to improve
Hilbert's Program is by searching for new axioms of set theory to add to the standard
axioms of set theory ZFC in order to attain a complete set of axioms.[2]

From 1963, Gödel started looking for new axioms that would resolve the continuum hypothesis. The need to add more axioms developed as a result of Gödel's
proof of the failure of Hilbert's Program, namely, the confirmation of any theorem
concerning natural numbers in a finite number of steps. It is known that the theorem concerning natural numbers can be proved using real numbers and transfinite
induction (which is not a finite technique) tools, which were rejected by Hilbert.[3]
Therefore it was natural for Gödel to think that in order to describe the entire world
of sets, he needed to understand the higher infinite cardinals. At some point, Gödel's
belief in the existence of such cardinals was based on arguments appealing to the
uniformity of the universe of sets:

The universe of sets does not change its character substantially as one

---

[1]For example, Anderson H. [28] and [23] pointed out different flaws in the ontological argument.

[2]Gödel anticipated that the independence of the continuum hypothesis would eventually be
proved. In his 1947 paper 'What is Cantor's Continuum Problem', he provides examples which
demonstrate the inability to prove the continuum hypothesis from the axioms of set theory.

[3]Gentzen proved the consistency of PA using real numbers in 1936.

goes from smaller to larger sets or cardinals; that is, the same or analogous state of affairs appears again and again [10, pp. 45–53].

Gödel envisaged an axiom which would state a certain maximum property of the system of all sets. I am arguing that the proof of the existence of Godlikeness informs us that this program is possible, since it is possible to perceive the primitive concept of the world well enough that the complete set of axioms will be spread before us. This idea was incompatible with Gödel's incompleteness theorem, according to which no single finite formal system for set theory can be complete. Thus, it is certain that according to Gödel's Program there is a single, complete, infinite formal system for set theory. Gödel was a Platonist who believed in the existence of one world of math, meaning the existence of one world of sets. Only a complete set of axioms is capable of describing this one world of mathematics.

3 Gödel's ontological argument

Gödel's ontological argument is a formal argument for a being which Gödel referred to as âĂŸGodlikeness'. This Godlikeness is defined as having the maximum "positive properties". Gödel's argument is that a being with maximum positive properties is possible, and that if this being is possible, then it is necessarily possible and therefore exists.

Oskar Morgenstern recorded in his diary entry for 29 August, 1970, that Gödel would not publish his ontological proof because he was afraid that others might think "that he actually believes in God, whereas he is only engaged in a logical investigation (that is, in showing that such a proof with classical assumptions—completeness, etc., and the corresponding axiomatization—is possible)" [19, p. 388].The ontological proof must be grounded in the concept of value (if p is positive then ¬p is negative and vice versa, if ¬p is positive than p is negative). The proof itself is written in logical notation [7, pp. 403, 430]. I reproduce Gödel's notes here with less technical notation, to indicate his line of thought. This version of the proof appears in the Stanford Encyclopedia of Philosophy based on [27], [39, p. 7].

Definition 1: x is God-like if and only if x has as essential properties those and only those properties which are positive. Definition 2: A is an essence of x if and only if for every property B, x has B necessarily if and only if A entails B. Definition 3: x necessarily exists if and only if every essence of x is necessarily exemplified. Axiom 1: If a property is positive, then its negation is not positive. Axiom 2: Any property entailed by—i.e., strictly implied by—a positive property is positive. Axiom 3: The property of being God-like is positive. Axiom 4: If a property is positive, then it is necessarily positive. Axiom 5: Necessary existence is positive. Axiom 6: For any property P, if P is positive, then being necessarily P is positive. Theorem 1: If a property is positive, then it is consistent, i.e., possibly exemplified. Corollary 1: The property of being God-like is consistent. Theorem 2: If something is God-like, then the property of being God-like is an essence of that thing. Theorem 3: Necessarily, the property of being God-like is exemplified.

For Gödel, something is God-like if and only if it has all the positive properties , and only positive properties[4]. Oppy's comment is of importance here: "No definition of the notion of 'positive property' is supplied with the proof. At most, the various axioms which involve this concept can be taken to provide a partial, implicit definition. If we suppose that the 'positive property' form a set, then the axioms provide us with the following information about this set: (1) If a property belongs to the set, then its negation does not belong to the set; (2) The set is closed under entailment; (3) The property of having as essential properties just those properties which are in the set is itself a member of the set; (4) The set has exactly the same members in all possible worlds; (5) The property of necessary existence is in the set; (6) If a property is in the set, then the property of having that property necessarily is also in the set. According to Gödel's theoretical assumptions, we can show that any set which conforms to (1)—(6) is such that the property of having as essential properties just those properties which are in that set is exemplified. Gödel wants us to conclude that there is just one intuitive, theologically interesting set of properties which are such that the property of having as essential properties just the properties in that set is exemplified. But, on the one hand, what reason do we have to think that there is any theologically interesting set of properties which conforms to the Gödelian specification? And, on the other hand, what reason do we have to deny that?" [27, p. 9].

According to Gödel, all the terms occurring in mathematical propositions either have a fixed definition or are primitive terms such as 'set'. Positive properties are taken as primitive. "Positive means positive in the moral aesthetic sense, independently of the accidental structure of the world" [38, p. 113]. Positive in this sense means that positive properties are independent from the "actual structure of the world". According to Gödel, it is possible to interpret positiveness as perfective. A property is perfective if and only if it implies no negation of the perfective.

A property is positive if and only if its negation is not positive. Gödel argued that the result of a conjunction of properties which are positive is a new property that is also a positive property. Gödel's claim is that if a property is positive, it is necessarily so, and if it is not positive, then likewise necessarily so. Being a positive

---

[4]Much has been written about the Gödelian notion "positive property", about its meaning and the question concerning the consistency of the union of all positive properties; see, for example, [23, 2, 35], and many others.

property is hence necessary. Gödel then argues, in theorem 1, that each positive property is "possibly exemplified", meaning applies at least to some object in the world. Positivity in this sense means "independent of the 'accidental structure of the world"'. In addition, according to Gödel, it is possible to indicate for every property whether it is a positive property or not [7, p. 404].

The notion of a positive property is taken as primitive, meaning that all other properties are constructed out of the primitive property by an operation of disjunction. Van Atten and Kennedy discuss and provide examples concerning Gödel's primitive concept [34, p. 432–3]. They write that "the main difficulty in carrying out the project of philosophy as an exact theory may have been specifying the primitive terms." Examples of primitive properties which appear in their paper include object, relation, good and will. For Gödel, monads are primitive concepts, but Wang informs us that he does not know what sorts of things the primitive concepts of metaphysics would be for Gödel. Nonetheless, Gödel gave us a hint which does not tell us very much: "Force should be a primitive term in philosophy" [38, p. 297]. According to Gödel, "the notion of existence is one of the primitive concepts with which we must begin as given. It is the clearest concept we have" [38, p. 150].

Gödel suggests two readings—"positive in the moral-aesthetic sense" and positive as involving only "pure attribution". The only further comment in the notes on the first interpretation is to the effect that 'positive' in this sense is independent of the "accidental structure of the world." The second notion is said to be "opposed to privation properties", which are essential to the world. A "positive property" is something that is inherent to the nature of the universe, and separate from the details of the world. "Necessary positive" is something without which the world cannot exist. Is there any relationship between positivity as a moral-aesthetic concept and positivity as pure attribution? I would like to think that the answer is yes. That which is moral or aesthetic typically enhances or deepens being.

Godlikeness is entirely determined by its essence. If essence exists at all, it is unique to its individuals. According to axiom 3, the property of being God-like is positive. In theorem 3 Gödel concludes that Godlikeness is exemplified. From theorem 2, definition 3 and using axiom 5 and theorem 3 it can be concluded that Godlikeness exists.[5] "Exists" is a primitive property and hence a positive property, since every primitive property is a positive property as well [7, pp. 404, 435].

> Existence: we know all about it, there is nothing concealed. The concept of existence helps us to form a good picture of reality. Wang [38, p. 150]

The first theorem of Gödel's proof tells us that the essential property of God-

---

[5] [2] explains the ontology proof in a most detailed way, including Subol's objection.

likeness is being God-like [7, pp. 404, 104]. "If a property is an essential property, then any one which has this property necessarily has all the other properties which are entailed by it" [38, p. 114]. The question that then remains open is, therefore, What is a God-like essence? I will address this question later and suggest a definable answer for it. Gottfried Leibnitz was Gödel's point of reference concerning the proof of the existence of Godlikeness, which is entirely determined by its essence [7, p. 403]. An individual essence involves each of its properties, and insofar as this is the case, it is correct to say that "Gödel's essence is like Leibniz's complete individual concepts" [28, p. 259].

Godlikeness is complete and unique. It is complete because it has all the positive properties. According to Gödel's argument, it is possible for a being to possess all the positive properties, since from the conjunction of all positive properties we attain a property which is positive. Since existence is a positive property, we can say that a property is necessary if it is necessary that everything has the property. From the above we understand that a being necessarily exists. A property is consistent if it is possibly exemplified, meaning, there is a being that possesses this property. This being is Gödel's Godlikeness and Godlikeness necessarily exists. Gödel defined necessary existence in terms of essences: Something necessarily exists only if its essence necessarily exists. As was noted above, for Gödel, necessary existence is a positive property.

Informally, if something is God-like then there necessarily exists something that is God-like, and if there is a God-like thing which exists, then necessarily there is something that is God-like. Meaning, the system of all positive properties is fit to exemplify Godlikeness, as concluded by Gödel's final axiom [7, p. 403].

$$x = x \text{ is positive} \quad x \neq x \text{ is negative.}$$

Gödel's was a Platonist who believed in the existence of one world of mathematics, meaning the existence of a unique world of sets. Only a complete set of axioms is capable of describing this one world of mathematic. It should be clear that because the essence of a God-like being entails all the positive properties, Godlikeness is unique[6]. Gödel never gives a reason why positive properties cannot be inconsistent. The move from "a necessary being is possible" to "a necessary being exists" is problematic. My claim is that this being with maximum positive properties is V, i.e., the world of sets.

---

[6]Brandon claims that Gödel does not address the uniqueness of Godlikeness directly [3, p. 515], and I think that it is clear why: Gödel did not need to. According to my claim that Gödel's Godlikeness is the V world of sets, its essence is a complete set of ZFC axioms. Consequently, there is a unique world of sets and there is only one Godlikeness.

4 Sets, Monads and Godlikeness

Leibnitz was Gödel's hero regarding everything related to the proof of the existence of God. Although Leibniz's basic units are monads while Gödel's basic units are sets, it is not difficult to see the similarities between monadology and set theory. Thus, in both cases we have a universe of objects where the objects resemble, in some sense, the whole, and the actual universe is, in some sense, the best out of a collection of possible universes. In the monadology, God chooses a universe or world to actualize from a collection of possible worlds, according to certain criteria for which one is the best. For Leibniz, the best universe means a world that is "the simplest in hypotheses and the richest in phenomena" [24, A VI iv 1538/AG 39]. For Gödel, the best universe of sets is the actual world of sets, and this actual world has the simplest set of axioms, namely a minimum and complete set of axioms and maximum consistent existing sets [?, p. 144]. Gödel also believed that Cantorial set theory is a true theory which describes a well-determined reality. Gödel asserted to Paul Benacerraf that "the monads have unambiguous access to the full set-theoretic hierarchy" [13, p. 181].

In his paper "What is Cantor's continuum problem?" [17, p. 272], Gödel compares mathematical and physical objects and notes that the question of the objective existence of the objects of mathematical intuition is an exact replica of the question of the objective existence of the outer world. He then proceeds to the issue of mathematical intuition. Objects exists and therefore sets exist, and some concepts exist as well. According to Gödel, it appears that there is a direct correlation between the understanding of a mathematical concept and the knowledge of its existence[7] [38, p. 210].

Robert Adams pointed out that Leibniz's thesis that mathematical objects have their existence in God's mind-might well be acceptable to a mathematical Platonist, given the necessary existence of God, the independence of God's thought from, in particular, human thought, and given the independence, in particular, and eternal truths of God's will [1, p. 751]. It is therefore not surprising to see Gödel's Platonist remark in a notebook from 1944, a time when he was studying Leibniz intensely (1943–1946), asserting that "the ideas and eternal truths are somehow parts of God's substance", that "one cannot say that 'they are created by God', and that they rather 'make up God's essence'." Gödel also writes that when mapping from

---

[7]According to Gödel, sets exist, and this is the main objective fact about mathematics. Set-like monads are units which are a multitude. Being a multitude is the opposite of a unity. Gödel pointed out that it is surprising that the fact that multitudes are also units leads to no contradictions [38, p. 254]. Gödel also believed that sets are objects, but that concepts are not objects. According to Gödel, we perceive objects and understand concepts.

propositions to states of affairs, the correct one is the one which is realized in God's mind [35, p. 6].

This can be further understood through a discussion of **the Reflection Principle**, according to which for any property of the universe of all sets, we can find a set with the same property. If clearly conceived, this specific set is said to reflect the universe with that property. Therefore, any true statement of the universe V already holds some initial segment of V.

Gödel's analogy between the universe of monads and the universe of sets is based on mirroring Leibniz's "principle of harmony" using the reflection principle. Here is a typical example of Leibniz's formulation of his principle of harmony: "Each simple substance has relations that express all the others and is in consequence a perpetual living mirror of the universe" [25, sec. 56].

The analogy is based on the idea that the reflection principle is true in set theory for exactly the same reason that a certain monadological proposition is true in the universe of monads.[8] Both principles are based on a reflection of the universe or some of its properties in its segment. Gödel never published the argument but he did present it to Wang [38, p. 284]. The justification of the reflection principle can be also treated independently of the justification of monadology. According to Gödel, the justification for the reflection principle is a fundamental form of justification, meaning that it cannot be explained by more primitive concepts, as would be the case, for example, if one introduced in the study of Euclidean the concepts of space, point and line. Therefore, the reflection principle has to be, and remains, informal. The strength of the principle increases with every application of it because the resulting stronger system gives rise, in turn, to the formulation of stronger properties to reflect. Gödel's analogy is important here because of its theological implications:

> There is also a theological approach, according to which V corresponds to the whole physical world, and the closeness aspect to what lies within the monad and in between the monads. According to the principle of rationality, sufficient reason, and pre-established harmony, the property P(V,x) of a monad x is equivalent to some intrinsic property of x, in which the world does not occur. In other words, when we move from monads to sets, there is some set y to which x bears intrinsically the same relation as it does to V. Here there is a property Q(x), not involving V, which is equivalent to P(V,x). According to medieval ideas, properties containing V or the world would not be in the essence of any set or monad [38, p. 284].

---

[8]The question whether Gödel's analogy is convincing or not is discussed by [35].

The approach is "theological" because in the monadological setting, only the monad that is God perceives the whole universe perfectly. It follows that the perceptions of all monads, except the central monad which is God, are necessarily limited. No part of the universe expresses the whole universe perfectly. Gödel then proposes that we move from monads to sets and obtain from this, by analogy, the reflection principle for sets[9]. In the move from monads to sets, the immediate analogy shifts from Leibniz's God to Gödel's God-like V, a God that contains all sets. There is also an analogy drawn from a part of the universe of monads, a collection of monads, to a part of the universe of sets, hence a collection of sets. But according to Gödel's set of axioms for set theory, any collection that is properly contained in V and that cannot be mapped one-to-one is not a proper class but a set, since only a proper class is not a member of another entity. Thus, the immediate analogy of a collection of monads that does not perfectly express the universe of monads is a collection of sets that does not perfectly express V. Gödel adds the explanation that according to medieval ideas, properties containing V, or the world, "would not be in the essence of any set or monad" [38, p. 284].

Gödel believed that there is only one world of sets, named 'V', which one day will be accessible to us. The paradoxes that appear in set theory are further proof that mathematical objects exist independently of our minds, and that we will eventually overcome all obstacles and paradoxes in order to understand them as they are. This rationale is no more nor less real than the expectations of a physicist that his theory is true even though his conclusions were reached by sensory perceptions which he knows very well are misleading. There is no reason to trust intuition derived from the senses any more than the intuition of reason [17, p. 268].

A proper class is a class that is not an element of another class. Such classes are called by Gödel 'set-like'. Set-like indicates that it is not a set; set-like sets are over and above the many sets. For example, V is set-like. Therefore, Godlikeness would be over and above the many polytheistic gods, who do not possess every positive property.

In summary, both Leibniz and Gödel have a universe of objects which resemble, in some sense, the whole, actual universe. God chooses the best universe according to some criteria. Leibniz's God chose the world of monads, which is the simplest in hypotheses and the richest in phenomena. Gödel's Godlikeness presents the best world, which is the world that has a complete, minimum set of axioms and maximum existing sets. Sets are objects in Godlikeness, in V. Only Godlikeness contains all the objects of the world of sets. All objects except V are limited, since each set

---

[9]Van Atten and Kennedy argue [35] that the analogy is ineffective. This is not the place to argue with this. Rather, the focus should be on the purpose of Gödel's analogy and what light it sheds on Gödel's 'divine essence'.

contains some sets but not every set. Only V contains all the objects in the world of sets.

5   Formalism and Essence

Since the world of sets itself is not a set, but set-like, understanding the concept of a set is not good enough. For Gödel it was clear that the standard, iterative concept of set has the property of reflection. Some properties possessed by the totality of ordinals is possessed by some ordinals. Indeed, as Wang reports, "the central principle is the reflection principle, which presumably will be understood better as our experience increases" [38, pp. 283, 285]. According to Gödel's incompleteness theorem, no single, finite, formal system for set theory can be complete, and the reflection principle that Gödel discusses is precisely meant to be the fundamental way to arrive at additional axioms to extend any given system.

Gödel's Program provides interesting ties between the ontology and epistemology of mathematics, for it seems that any solution to an unsolvable question in math must be accompanied by a better understanding of the concepts concerning this problem. In other words, we need to increase our interpretational power in order to form a complete picture of "the world of sets", which in turn necessitates deep connections between mathematical ontology and epistemology. The inability to "separate epistemology, ontology and theology" in Gödel's work guarantees that it is possible to bring realistic elements to Gödel's ideal objects. The existence of Godlikeness guarantees that human epistemology can capture the abstract mathematical world and explain in detail the connections between the objective existence of the mathematical world, on the one hand, and the ability to express this objective mathematical world formally, on the other.

From Gödel's point of view, this new program was inevitable, since he believed that the axioms of ZFC describe a "well-determined reality" and that this program could mathematically decide interesting questions independent of ZFC, using well-justified extensions of ZFC. The program explains that the only way to resolve the continuum hypothesis would be by investigating the very high infinite (as described above) and to add new axioms to ZFC, which would be helpful in understanding the concept of "the world of sets" as a whole. In the 1970s, Gödel wrote three documents concerning the higher infinite, and also worked on his proof of the existence of Godlikeness. Gödel claimed that the question relating to the continuum hypothesis has meaning only if there is one world of sets that is connected to the iterative concept of sets. Gödel was optimistic regarding the capability of understanding the world of sets despite its remoteness from the physical world [17, p. 286]. His proof of the existence of Godlikeness is evidence of his optimism and of his belief that his program could be carried out.

6 The God-like Essence

Gödel believed that "in the world of the future, man will have philosophy in place of religion" [38, p. 112]. Wang writes that Gödel often identified theology with metaphysics. Gödel also linked the definition of a concept to the axioms that concern it. The clear perception of a concept is connected to its set of axioms and it is not connected to any model since it is the set of axioms that defines it. Therefore, as I understand Gödel, the clearer a concept becomes to us, the more complete its system of axioms becomes. We shall overcome the gap between ontology and epistemology by the true analysis of a concept, which means linking the definition of a concept to the axioms that concern it [38, p. 233].

It is therefore logical to conclude that the proof of Godlikeness shows that it is possible to perceive the primitive properties of set theory clearly enough to set up its complete set of axioms. With the help of the reflection principle, we can attain a complete set of axioms for set theory. This complete set of axioms isa God-like essence, since the complete set of axioms of set theory shows that a single world of sets exists, and that every true statement about this world of sets-and therefore about its primitive concept-can be inferred from it. I would like to argue that viewing the complete set of axioms of set theory as the essence of Godlikeness is defensable. Such a defense is based on the claim that the property of "being God-like" is compatible with the complete set of axioms of set theory as fulfilling the task of being the essence of Godlikeness.[10]

There is a connection between thought and existence. According to Gödel, the clearer a concept is to us, the stronger the certainty of its existence

---

[10]Kurt Gödel began to study Husserl's work in 1959. In his paper "The Modern Development of the Foundation of Mathematics" [16], Gödel wrote that his own main aim in philosophy was to develop metaphysics-specifically, something like the monadology of Leibniz transformed into exact theory-with the help of phenomenology. It is in this light that I argue that Gödel's theological claims can be supported on the basis of Edmond Husserl's methodology and his views on evidence and intuition. Gödel turned to the phenomenology of Husserl in order to extend the explanation of the cognitive process and to find out what really appears [38, pp. 158, 372]. This process is (or in any case should be) a procedure or technique that produces in us a new state of consciousness in which we describe in detail the basic concepts we use in our thought, or grasp other basic concepts hitherto unknown to us. The more a concept becomes clear to us, the more the certainty of our knowledge strengthens. This process ends with formalization. Namely, having a complete set of axioms of a property permits its existence. Husserl's phenomenology gives us tools with which we are capable of perceiving the primitive concepts of metaphysics clearly enough to set up the axioms.

becomes, as he put it: "We can say that a mathematical concept objectively exists only when it becomes so clear to us that its complete set of axioms spreads out in front of us" [15], [4, p. 262].The evidence of the existence of abstract mathematical elements is no less strong than the evidence regarding the existence of physical objects.

> But, despite their remoteness from sense experience, we do have something like a perception also of the objects of set theory, as is seen from the fact that the axioms force themselves upon us as true. I don't see any reason why we should have less confidence in this kind of perception, i.e., in mathematical intuition, than in sense perception, which induces us to build up physical theories and to expect that future sense perception will agree with them [15], [4, p. 271].

Thus, it appears that the clearer the understanding of a mathematical concept becomes, the more certain becomes the knowledge of that concept [38, p. 210], [16]. The higher the degree of abstraction or idealization, the lower the degree of clarity. As the degree of clarity of an entity weakens, the certainty of the recognition of that entity also declines. according to Gödel[11]. The increasing degree of uncertainty found in the gap between classical mathematics and set theory. As mathematics is developed ever further, the overall degree of certainty rises, yet the relative degree remains the same [38, p. 217]. Despite the fact that our intuition regarding the arithmetic of higher infinite cardinals and their logic is very weak, most mathematicians would agree that these concepts are clear (even though this is not a basic or a primitive concept). The fact that we can differentiate between different cardinals is proof that the concept 'cardinal' is clear to us at some level [17, p. 372]. According to Gödel, the full concept of class is not used in mathematics, and the iterative concept, which is sufficient for mathematics, may or may not be the full concept of class.

From the proof of the existence of Godlikeness we learn that if x is an object in a certain world, then a property ϕ is said to be an essence of x if $\phi(x)$ is true in

---

[11]Despite the significant differences that exist between physical and abstract elements, there are more similarities than differences in the way we perceive them. Abstract elements have objective aspects and subjective aspects, just like physical objects. Objective aspects of abstract elements are expressed by the ability to perceive them immediately, although not by sense perception. On the other hand, as in the case of physical elements, mathematical elements are perceived based on the structure of the mind,and in this respect, abstract elements are subjective. Gödel, like Kant before him, believed that mathematical intuition also applies to abstract and infinite objects as well. The knowledge of the existence of abstract objects is (as already stated) immediate, just like the knowledge of physical elements.

that world and if ϕ necessarily entails all other properties that x has in that world. We also infer from the proof that any two essences of x are necessarily equivalent. Since Godlikeness has all and only positive properties, its essence of "being God-like" must also entail all and only positive properties and therefore Godlikeness is unique. Since each positive property is possibly exemplified, existence is a positive property and Godlikeness must exist.

7 Summary

The proof of Godlikeness demonstrates that it is possible to perceive primitive properties and therefore positive concepts. The complete set of axioms of Godlikeness is the God-like essence, and this God-like essence can be found and therefore exists. Since the cumulative hierarchy of sets V can fill the role of Godlikeness, it is possible to perceive the primitive properties of set theory (the elements that constitute the world) well enough that with the help of the reflection principle, the complete set of axioms for set theory will be spread before us and every true statement about the world of sets will be inferred from them. Godlikeness is unique, and as a Platonist, Gödel believed that only one world of sets exists as well.

Therefore, we can attain the complete set of axioms which determine V uniquely and completely. V, Godlikeness, is determined by its essence, which is its complete set of axioms. The likelihood of finding a complete set of axioms for set theory exists, which would allow Gödel's Program to be successful. Therefore, the existence of Godlikeness gives hope for Gödel's Program. Gödel was optimistic and believed that if something exists it will be possible someday to recognize it. Therefore, I claim that it is reasonable to conclude that the proof of the existence of the God-like essence bodes well for the success of Gödel's Program.

> Leibniz had defined the ideal by giving a preliminary formulation of monadology. Husserl had supplied the method for attaining this ideal. Plato had proposed in his rudimentary objectivism in mathematics an approach that could serve as foundation for Husserl's method and at the same time, make plausible for Gödel the crucial belief that we are indeed capable of perceiving the primitive concepts of metaphysics clearly enough to set up the axioms [38].

References

[1] Adams, R.M. 1983. 'Divine Necessity', *Journal of Philosophy* 80, 741-751.

[2] Anderson, A. 1990. 'Some Emendation of Gödel ontological proof', *Faith and Philosophy* **7(3)**, 291-302.

[3] Brandon, C. L. 2006 'Some Remarks on the Ontological Arguments of Gödel and Leibniz' in Einheit in der Vielheit: Akten des VIII. Internationalen Leibniz Kongresses, edited by H. Breger et al. Hanover: Hartmann, 510-517.

[4] Benacerraf, P. and Putnam, H., ed. 1964. *Philosophy of Mathematics* New Jersey: Prentice Hall.

[5] Dawson, J. W. 1997. *Logical Dilemmas*, Massachusetts, Wellesley, A. K. Peters.

[6] Feferman, S. et al eds. 1990. *Kurt Gödel Collection Works, Vol. 2*, New York: Oxford University Press.

[7] Feferman, S. et al eds. 1995. *Kurt Gödel Collection Works, Vol. 3*, New York: Oxford University Press.

[8] Forgie, J. W. 1974. "Existence Assertion and the Ontological Argument" in *Mind 73*, 260-62.

[9] Friedman, J. 1975 "On some relations between Leibniz monadology and transfinite set theory." In K. Muller, H. Schepers, and W. Toke, ed. International Leibniz-Kongresses. Hannover Juli 1972 19-22 V. XIV.

[10] Gödel, K. 1933. 'The present situation in the Foundation of Mathematics' lecture at the meeting of the American Association in S. Feferman et al eds. *Kurt Gödel Collection Works*, Vol. 2, 45-53, New York: Oxford University Press.

[11] Gödel, K. 1938. The Consistency of the Axiom of Choice and of the Generalized Continuum-Hypothesis, Proceedings of the National Academy of Sciences of the United States of America (National Academy of Sciences) **24(12)**.

[12] Gödel, K. 1939. 'Lecture at Gottingen' in S. Feferman et al eds., *Kurt Gödel Collection Works*, Vol. 3, 127-155, New York: Oxford University Press.

[13] Gödel, K. 1940. 'Lecture on the Consistency of the Continuum Hypothesis' in S. Feferman et al, *Kurt Gödel Collection Works*, Vol. 3, 175-185, New York: Oxford University Press.

[14] Gödel, K. 1944. 'Russell's Mathematical Logic' in P. Benacerraf and H. Putnam eds., *Philosophy of Mathematics*, 211-232, New Jersey: Prentice Hall.

[15] Gödel, K. 1947. 'What is Cantor's Continuum Problem' In P. Benacerraf and H. Putnam eds., *Philosophy of Mathematics*, 258-273, New Jersey: Prentice Hall.

[16] Gödel, K. 1961. 'The Modern Development of the Foundations of Mathematics in the Light of Philosophy' in S. Feferman et al eds., *Kurt Gödel Collection Works*, Vol. 3, 374-387, New York: Oxford University Press.

[17] Gödel, K. 1964. 'What is Cantor's Continuum Problem' in Feferman. S. et al eds. 1990. *Kurt Gödel Collection Works*, Vol. 2, 254-270, New Jersey: Prentice Hall.

[18] Gödel, K. 1972. 'On an Extension of Finitary Mathematics Which Has Not

Yet Been Used' in S. Feferman et al eds., *Kurt Gödel Collection Works*, Vol. 2, 271-280, New York: Oxford University Press.

[19] Gödel, K. 1995. 'Some basic theorems on the foundations of mathematics and their implications' in S. Feferman et al eds., *Kurt Gödel Collection Works*, Vol. 3, 304-323, New York: Oxford University Press.

[20] Hauser, K. 2006. 'Gödel's program revisited' Part 1: The Turn to Phenomenology, *Bulletin of Symbolic Logic*, **12**, 529-590.

[21] Husserl, E. 1927-1928. Phenomenology (drafts of the Encyclopedia Britannica Article). In: Psychological and transcendental phenomenology and the confrontation with Heidegger (1927-1931). Kluwer, Dordrecht, 83-194, 1997

[22] Husserl, E. 1931. *Cartesian meditations*, English translation1960: (Trans: Cairns D), Springer, Kluwer Academic Publication.

[23] Koons, Robert C. 2005. "Sobel on Gödel's Ontological Proof" (linked to `http://www.scar.utoronto.ca/%7Esobel/OnL_T`).

[24] Leibniz, G. 1686(1989). *Discourse on Metaphysics*, Springer, Kluwer Academic Publication

[25] Leibniz, G. 1714 (1991). *Monadology* University of Pittsburg Press.

[26] Oppy, G. 1995. *Ontological Arguments and Belief in God*, New York: Cambridge University Press.

[27] Oppy, G. 1996. 'Gödelian Ontological Argument', *Analysis* **56(4)**, 226-230.

[28] Sobel, J.H. 1987. 'Gödel Ontological Proof', *On Being and Saying. Essays for Richard Cartwight* 241-161. MIT Press.

[29] Steel, J. 2012. 'Gödel's program' in J. Kennedy, *Interpreting Gödel, Critical Essay*, 153-179, Cambridge: Cambridge University Press.

[30] Tiezen, R. 2002. 'Godel and the intuition of concepts', *Synthese* **133(3)**, 363-391.

[31] Tieszen, R. 2011. After Gödel, Oxford: Oxford University Press.

[32] Tieszen, R. 2011a. 'Monad and mathematics', *Axiomath* 22,31-52 Springer

[33] Tiezen, R. 2015. 'Arithmetic, Mathematical Intuition, and Evidence', *Inquiry*, **58(1)**, 26-58.

[34] Van Atten, M. and Kennedy, J. 2003. 'On the Philosophical Development of Kurt Gödel', *Bulletin of Symbolic Logic*, **9(4)**, 425-476.

[35] Van Atten, M. 2009. 'Monads and Sets on Gödel Leibniz and the Reflection Principle. Judgment and Knowledge', *Papers in Honor of B.J. Sundholm*. London: College Publication.

[36] Van Heijenoort, J. 1967. *From Frege to Gödel, A Source Book in Mathematical Logic 1879-1931*, Harvard: Harvard University Press.

[37] Wang, H. 1987. *Reflection on Kurt Gödel*, London: London MIT Press.

[38] Wang, H. 1996. *A Logical Journey*, Cambridge: Cambridge MIT Press. Stanford Encyclopedia of Philosophy

[39] Stanford Encyclopedia of Philosophy
https://plato.stanford.edu/entries/ontological-arguments/
#GodOntArg

 Received 27 May 2019

A Logical Solution to the Paradox of the Stone

Héctor Hernández Ortiz and Victor Cantero Flores
Universidad del Caribe, Cancún, México
hhernandez@ucaribe.edu.mx, vcantero@ucaribe.edu.mx

Abstract

In this paper, we discuss the paradox of the stone (the question whether an omnipotent being can create a stone which he cannot lift) and propose a promising solution, not only to this particular paradox, but also to any other puzzle of the same type. First, we discuss some virtues and difficulties of two classical solutions to the paradox (one due to George I. Mavrodes, the other to C. Wade Savage). Later, we present and defend our own proposal. We argue that, even using an unrestricted quantifier, a coherent notion of omnipotence and of power imply many impossibilities (all things incompatible with them, including the existence of the stone in question) and hence it is false that if a being is omnipotent, then he must be able to do absolutely everything.

1 Introduction

It has been argued that a series of puzzles, including the well-known paradox of the stone, show that the notion of omnipotence leads to contradiction and so an omnipotent being cannot exist. The basic argument is usually presented as a dilemma. Can an all-powerful being create a stone he cannot lift? Two answers are available. Either such a being can do it, but then he is not omnipotent, for there is something he cannot do, namely, to lift such a stone; or he cannot do it, but then he is not omnipotent either, for there is something he cannot do, namely, to create such a peculiar stone. In either case, the supposedly omnipotent being would not be omnipotent. So, the existence of an omnipotent being is not possible.

Several authors have proposed some ways to solve this paradox, but these are not completely satisfactory. In this paper we discuss the paradox of the stone, and propose a promising solution, not only to this particular paradox, but also to any other puzzle of the same type.

The structure of the paper is as follows. First, we address two classical solutions to the paradox. One is due to George I. Mavrodes [11] and the other to C. Wade Savage [15]. Some virtues and difficulties of both proposals are considered. In the second part, we present and defend our own proposal. We address the problem by means of distinguishing three types of tasks (or the corresponding possibility to perform them[1]): 1) tasks which are logically impossible in themselves, 2) tasks logically possible, but incompatible with omnipotence, and 3) tasks that are logically possible and compatible with omnipotence.

The fact that some being cannot do something logically impossible does not undermine his omnipotence. We argue that omnipotence should be restricted to what is logically possible. That is, not being able to do logically impossible things does not represent a limitation to the power of an omnipotent being. On the other hand, a coherent notion of omnipotence has to imply many impossibilities, namely, everything that is incompatible with it. In particular, the existence of a stone an omnipotent being cannot lift is incompatible with the existence of an omnipotent being. This and other impossibilities (such as being able to be defeated by an enemy, being able to fail in solving a problem, being able to get tired, etc.) derived from the very nature of omnipotence do not constitute a limitation to the powers of an omnipotent being. On the contrary, these possibilities (to be defeated, to fail at something, to die, to lose some powers, etc.) put at risk the omnipotence itself. Finally, among the logical possibilities compatible with omnipotence, we rule out those that are useless, for they do not contribute to the powers of an omnipotent being. For this reason, these possibilities can be excluded without affecting the omnipotence of an omnipotent being. Therefore, the following proposition is false:

If a being is omnipotent, then he must be able to be or do absolutely everything.

Our solution avoids the problems Mavrodes' and Savage's proposals have. In the last section, we confront our proposal with a potential difficulty raised by Earl Conee [2]: he argues that the notion of omnipotence must be interpreted as absolutely unrestricted. We argue that this interpretation renders the notion of omnipotence incoherent by definition, so if it leads to a contradiction, this does not imply any decisive conclusion in favor of or against the possibility of omnipotence. All things considered, our proposal offers a neat solution to all those paradoxes similar to the stone paradox.

---

[1]However, not every possibility to perform some task constitutes a power. Possibilities which do not represent an advantage are not powers. For example, the possibility to lose powers is not a power because not only it does not represent an advantage, but it represents a disadvantage.

2 Mavrodes' solution

Mavrodes [11] argues that, on the assumption that God is omnipotent, the statement "a stone too heavy for God to lift" is self-contradictory; hence something logically impossible is presupposed to be possible in this paradox. Normally, the statement "some being x can make a stone that is too heavy for x to lift" is not self-contradictory. However, it becomes self-contradictory — logically impossible — when x stands for an omnipotent being, for it becomes "a stone which cannot be lifted by him whose power is sufficient for lifting anything". The "thing" described by a self-contradictory phrase is absolutely impossible and so "a stone an omnipotent being can't lift" is an impossible object. It describes nothing, and "its failure to exist cannot possibly be due to some lack in the power of God." [11, p. 222].

On the other hand, if an objector insists that the description "a stone too heavy for an omnipotent God to lift" is self-coherent and therefore describes an absolutely possible object, then "such a stone is compatible with the omnipotence of God. Therefore, from the possibility of God's creating such a stone it cannot be concluded that God is not omnipotent." [11, p. 222].

3 Problems with Mavrodes' solution

Savage has identified at least four problems in Mavrodes' solution.

> First, the paradoxical argument need not be represented as a *reductio*; in A it is a dilemma.[2] Mavrodes' reasoning implies that the paradoxical argument must either assume that God is omnipotent or assume that He is not omnipotent. This is simply false: neither assumption need be made, and neither is made in A. Second, "a stone which God cannot lift" is self-contradictory — on the assumption that God is omnipotent — only if "God is omnipotent" is necessarily true. "Russell can lift any stone" is a contingent statement. Consequently, if we assume that

---

[2] A is the following formulation of the argument, which Savage presents as a dilemma:

1. Either God can create a stone which He cannot lift, or He cannot create a stone which He cannot lift.

2. If God can create a stone which He cannot lift, then He is not omnipotent (since He cannot lift the stone in question).

3. If God cannot create a stone which He cannot lift, then He is not omnipotent (since He cannot create the stone in question).

4. Therefore, God is not omnipotent. [15, p. 74].

Russell can lift any stone we are thereby committed only to saying that creating a stone which Russell cannot lift is a task which in fact cannot be performed by Russell or anyone else. Third, if "God is omnipotent" is necessarily true — as Mavrodes must claim for his solution to work — then his assumption that God exists begs the question of the paradoxical argument. For what the argument really tries to establish is that the existence of an omnipotent being is logically impossible. Fourth, the claim that inability to perform a self-contradictory task is no limitation on the agent is not entirely uncontroversial. [15, pp. 74–75].

We agree with Savage's criticisms and now we present his solution.[3]

4   Savage's solution

Savage states the paradox in a much clearer form that avoids the unjustified assumption made by Mavrodes, namely, that God is omnipotent. His proposal is the following.

Where x is any being:
B

1. Either x can create a stone which x cannot lift, or x cannot create a stone which x cannot lift.

2. If x can create a stone which x cannot lift, then, necessarily, there is at least one task which x cannot perform (namely, lift the stone in question).

3. If x cannot create a stone which x cannot lift, then, necessarily, there is at least one task which x cannot perform (namely, create the stone in question).

4. Hence, there is at least one task which x cannot perform.

5. If x is an omnipotent being, then x can perform any task.

6. Therefore, x is not omnipotent. [15, p. 76].

He argues that the fallacy in the supposed paradox lies in the falsity of the premise 3, for "x cannot create a stone which x cannot lift" *does not* logically imply "There is a task which x cannot perform."

---

[3]Another objection is in [6].

The phrase "cannot create a stone" *seems to imply* that there is a task which x cannot perform and, consequently, seems to imply that x is limited in power. But this illusion vanishes on analysis: "x cannot create a stone which x cannot lift" can only mean "If x can create a stone, then x can lift it." It is obvious that the latter statement does not entail that x is limited in power. [15, p. 77].

To defend this conclusion Savage offers the following representation, C, of the paradox:

C

$(1)(\exists y)(Sy \cdot Cxy \cdot \neg Lxy) \vee \neg(\exists y)(Sy \cdot Cxy \cdot \neg Lxy)$

$(2)(\exists y)(Sy \cdot Cxy \cdot \neg Lxy) \supset (\exists y)(Sy \cdot \neg Lxy)$

$(3)\neg(\exists y)(Sy \cdot Cxy \cdot \neg Lxy) \supset (\exists y)(Sy \cdot \neg Cxy)$

Where S = stone, C = can create, and L = can lift; x is any being; and the universe of discourse is *conceivable entities*. According to Savage, "$(\exists y)(Sy \cdot Cxy \cdot \neg Lxy)$" logically implies "$(\exists y)(Sy \cdot \neg Lxy)$", but "$\neg(\exists y)(Sy \cdot Cxy \cdot \neg Lxy)$" does not logically imply "$(\exists y)(Sy \cdot \neg Cxy)$". Therefore, $C3$ is false.

In sum, "x cannot create a stone which x cannot lift" does not entail that there is a task which x cannot perform and, consequently, does not entail that x is not omnipotent. [15, p. 77].

5   Problems with Savage's solution

A difficulty in Savage's approach is that his solution depends on the falsity of $C3$, which in turn depends on his formulation of $C3$. His solution requires that the implication used in $C3$ must be a logical one, but in the structure of the paradox, that is not necessarily so. The paradox emerges even using a simple indicative conditional. But even using only entailments, other formulations can be given in which the consequent is logically implied by the antecedent. For example $C3^*$:

$$\neg(\exists y)((Sy \cdot Cxy) \cdot \neg Lxy) \supset (((\exists y)(Sy \cdot \neg Lxy)) \supset ((\exists y)(\neg Cxy)))^4$$

Therefore, $C3$ can be true or false, depending on how it is presented. That is why those who reject omnipotence could argue that the way Savage formalizes the original argument can be misleading and biased in favor of his position. In its place, we propose the following way, D, to formalize it, which is more faithful to Savage's

---

[4]This formula is just an instance of a more general principle, which asserts that if nothing satisfies three properties then, if something satisfies two of them, then it does not satisfy the third property.

own form B (where we add $Ox =$ "x is omnipotent", $Tx=$ "x is a task" and $Pxy=$"x can perform y"):

D

1)$\exists y(Sy \cdot Cxy \cdot \neg Lxy) \vee \neg \exists y(Sy \cdot Cxy \cdot \neg Lxy)$

2)$\exists y(Sy \cdot Cxy \cdot \neg Lxy) \supset \exists z(Tz \cdot \neg Pxz)$

3)$\neg \exists y(Sy \cdot Cxy \cdot \neg Lxy) \supset \exists z(Tz \cdot \neg Pxz)$

4) $\therefore \exists z(Tz \cdot \neg Pxz)$

5)$Ox \supset \forall z(Tz \supset Pxz)$

6) $\therefore \neg Ox$

It can be objected that creating that sort of stone is not a genuine task, for that possibility is not open to an omnipotent being or someone whose power to lift stones is unlimited. But that does not mean that it is not a task. At most, it would show that it is an impossible task or one that cannot be done by an omnipotent being. It is reasonable to accept that this kind of stone only can be made by someone who is limited in his power to lift stones. So, if an omnipotent being exists, it would not have to be able to create such a peculiar stone. We admit with Savage that "x cannot create a stone which x cannot lift" does not necessarily imply "x is limited in power", but clearly implies that there is a task which x cannot do, namely, to create the stone in question. For Savage that *is not a task*, but that position is very hard to maintain because many of us are perfectly capable of performing that task. Besides, Savage himself admits the existence of self-contradictory tasks and the existence of tasks which, in fact, cannot be performed by anyone. He says: "Consequently, the correct solution side-steps the question of whether an agent's inability to perform *a self-contradictory task* is a limitation on his power." [15, pp. 76–77]. He also says:

> "Russell can lift any stone" is a contingent statement. Consequently, if we assume that Russell can lift any stone we are thereby committed only to saying that creating a stone which Russell cannot lift *is a task which in fact cannot be performed by Russell or anyone else.* [15, p. 75] (The italics are ours).

Savage finds the premise $D4$ false because of the falsity of $D3$, but $D3$ is false only if we accept that creating a stone which x cannot lift is not a task. Ultimately, Savage's solution depends on the definition of "task", and allows for each side in the debate to choose the more convenient to their position. In this sense, it is not a satisfactory answer to the paradox.

6 Our solution

For Savage the premise $D3$ is false. In contrast, we think that $D5$ is the one that is false.

$$Ox \supset \forall z(Tz \supset Pxz)$$

We differ from Savage in the assertion: "In general, 'x cannot create a stone which x cannot lift' *does not logically imply* 'There is a task which x cannot perform'." [15, p. 77]. We can accept that there is such an entailment, but that does not logically imply "x is limited in power". It depends rather on the type of task we are considering. Some tasks are compatible with the omnipotence of x and some of them are incompatible with it. In the case of a task that is incompatible with omnipotence, it is reasonable that an omnipotent being cannot perform it, just for having omnipotence. This and other impossibilities (such as being able to be defeated by an enemy, being able to fail in solving a problem, being able to get tired, etc.), derived from the very nature of omnipotence, do not constitute a limitation at all to the powers of an omnipotent being. This is not a restriction *ad hoc*, for there are many mutually exclusive predicates and most of the predicates or concepts used in ordinary life exclude others (for example to be completely red excludes to be completely green). Even an opponent of omnipotence, J. L. Cowan, admits the following simple fact:

> There are perfectly respectable, non-self-contradictory predicates, predicates meaningfully and even truly predicable even of such lowly beings as you and me, predicates which, however, are such that the capacity to have them truly predicated of one logically excludes the capacity to have other similarly non-self-contradictory predicates truly predicated of one. [4, p. 104].

As Cowan observes, "it is important to note, moreover, that the existence of such mutually exclusive predicates is a matter of logic." [4, p. 104]. So, it should not be surprising that a coherent notion of omnipotence has to imply many impossibilities, namely, everything that is incompatible with it. Therefore, the following proposition is false: if a being is omnipotent, then he must be able to be or do absolutely everything. At least, every logically impossible task and the tasks that are incompatible with omnipotence must be excluded. These include the task of creating a stone which x cannot lift because, as Savage observes:

> [...] God's inability [or the inability of any omnipotent being x] to create a stone which He cannot lift is nothing more nor less than a

1043

necessary consequence of two facets of His omnipotence. For if God is omnipotent, then He can create stones of any poundage and lift stones of any poundage. And "God can create stones of any poundage, and God can lift stones of any poundage" entails "God cannot create a stone which He cannot lift." [15, pp. 78–79].

In this way, we can accept the premises $D1$ to $D4$ in the formalization D, but block the paradox in $D5$ ("$Ox \supset \forall z(Tz \supset Pxz)$") because it is false.

The fact that some being x cannot do some tasks does not undermine his omnipotence if he is omnipotent. On the contrary, the very existence of some possibilities (to be defeated, to fail, to die, to lose some powers, etc.) puts at risk the omnipotence itself. That means that if we use a coherent concept of omnipotence, many propositions of the form "$(Tz \cdot \neg Pxz)$" will be true. Hence, $D4$ is true, but it does not imply that x is limited in power, for such impossible tasks emerge from the very fact that x is omnipotent. So, this imposes an inevitable restriction to any coherent notion of omnipotent being:

A being x is omnipotent if and only if x can do any logically possible task which is compatible with his omnipotence.[5]

In this way, if omnipotence is to be coherent, it must be understood in a restricted sense: it excludes all that is incompatible with it, and an example would be the existence of a stone that an omnipotent being cannot lift.[6] Mavrodes himself says: "And, interestingly, it is the very omnipotence of God which makes the existence of such a stone absolutely impossible" [11, p. 222]. That means that if a task is incompatible with the omnipotence of x, then x could do it only if x is not omnipotent. So, the fact that x cannot do it is not a limitation of his powers. If this is correct, Savage's $B5$ (or our $D5$) is false, and the paradox does not arise.

---

[5]A proposed counterexample to this definition is the following. Given that we and you are perfectly capable to sit in a chair at a time when God is not sitting there, and given that God does not seem to be capable to do so, one can think that this is a case of a logically possible task (because you and we can do it), which God cannot do [3, p. 200]. However, as Alvin Plantinga points out in a slightly different example [13, p. 236], this is just a confusion with respect to the scope of the modal expressions used. On one interpretation of the example, we have a logical impossibility, for God cannot be seated and not be seated at the same time. On the other interpretation, we have a logical possibility: God is not now sitting in this chair, but God could have been seated in this chair. In either case, there is no conflict with our notion of omnipotence.

[6]This is a better conception of omnipotence than those discussed by Peter Geach [7, p. 9]. Our proposal is not open to the objections he poses against those other four conceptions. Most of his objections attack the fact that the omnipotent being in question is meant to be God (for example, He must be omnibenevolent). We are not assuming anything in that respect. In this sense, our proposal can be generalized to other forms of the paradox and to other omniconcepts such as omniscience.

7 Unrestricted omnipotence

As it should be clear in our solution, we agree with Mavrodes' view that omnipotence must be restricted. But Mavrodes limits his proposal only to the self-contradictory, whereas our restriction excludes also logical possibilities incompatible with omnipotence.[7] However, this may be disputed. Earl Conee [2] argues that omnipotence as absolutely unlimited power is philosophically fruitful and consistent.

> The intuitive view of omnipotence requires an omnipotent being to be able to bring about all sorts of impossibilities. There are propositions that assert all sorts of impossibilities, e.g., the physical impossibility that something travels seven trillion miles in seven seconds, the metaphysical impossibility that Richard Nixon is a photon, and the logical impossibility that something is nothing. An omnipotent being would be able to have any of these propositions be true [2, pp. 449–450].

Conee supports this view on two reasons: 1) intuitions about the universality of the "all" in the paraphrase of "omnipotent" as "all-powerful", and 2) the following argument with two premises:

P1 If a being is omnipotent, then the being is able to will any proposition to be true and able to will any proposition to be false.

P2 If an omnipotent being is able to will a given proposition to be true, and able to will the proposition to be false, then the being is able to have the proposition be true and able to have the proposition be false.

C If a being is omnipotent, then the being is able to have any proposition be true and able to have any proposition false. [2, pp. 450–451].

Regarding his first reason, intuitions may go in the opposite direction. We have seen some cases in which it is very natural to think that there are some predicates that an omnipotent being should not be able to have them be true of himself. "Being able to get tired", "being able to be defeated by a weaker enemy", etc. are some

---

[7]Furthermore, our solution also differs from Mavrodes' solution at least in the following points:
1) He considers the argument as a *reductio*.
2) Mavrodes needs to assume that God exists and that God is omnipotent or not.
3) The statement "God is omnipotent" has to be necessarily true in Mavrodes' answer.
4) Mavrodes conflates "to be logically possible but incompatible with the omnipotence" with "to be logically impossible or self-contradictory".
5) Mavrodes does not refer to the meaning of "power" in his proposal.

of these predicates that go directly against his omnipotence. Moreover, millions of Christians around the world do not have any problem with calling God "All-powerful" and, at the same time, admitting that He cannot lie, He cannot die, and He cannot get tired and loss his powers, etc. This points to a very compelling intuition that omnipotence, by its very nature, should be restricted.

With respect to his second reason, we can say the following. By $P1$, the proposition A: "An omnipotent being O is able to will to do something that is not a deed" is true, and, by $P2$, the proposition B: "An omnipotent being O is able to do something that is not a deed" is true. But Conee himself would reject this conclusion, as he argues that it is part of the semantics of "do anything" that an omnipotent being can only do deeds: "But not even an omnipotent being would be able to 'do' e.g. a physical object. Only deeds can be done by any being, even an omnipotent being." [2, p. 448]. Even so, "[t]his is not a limit on any being's powers. It is a limit on meaningful expressions." [2, p. 448].

Conee could reply that A is not a proposition, but then C: "An omnipotent being O is able to will that A be a proposition" is a proposition. In that case, C is a proposition which O is not able to have true if Conee is right about the semantic restriction mentioned before.

Some other examples are not difficult to come by. There is the perfectly intelligible proposition that an omnipotent being O can lose most of his powers irreversibly. If this is a legitimate proposition, then, by premise $P1$, O is capable of willing this proposition to be true. By premise $P2$, O is capable to have it true. So, it follows that if O is omnipotent, then he can lose most of his powers irreversibly. However, this is an odd result.[8] If O loses most of his powers, he would stop being omnipotent. That possibility clearly goes against the omnipotence of O, for it is expected that a truly omnipotent being should not be able to lose his powers.

So, absolutely unrestricted omnipotence seems to have odd results. In contrast,

---

[8] An omnipotent being O can receive his powers from an external source. O may lose some of his powers temporarily without affecting his nature. In contrast, if O has his powers intrinsically, then he cannot lose them without changing his nature. Whether his omnipotence is intrinsic or extrinsic is a matter of great discussion. Both cases, however, are consistent with our proposal. Whether omnipotence is intrinsic or extrinsic, it is still true that omnipotence, by its very nature, is incompatible with some other things (tasks, predicates, properties, propositions). This is all we need for our proposal to work. However, Sarah Adams [1] seems to think that here are the makings of a new paradox for omnipotence. She argues that omnipotence implies a contradiction, namely, that it must be intrinsic and extrinsic at the same time. On reflection, what she shows is only that there is a series of arguments in favor of each view, but she does not show that we are reasonably forced to accept both series of arguments and, in consequence, we are forced to accept a contradiction. At most, she shows two things: (1) there is an open debate as to whether omnipotence is intrinsic or extrinsic, and (2) there are arguments in favor of each position, which may lead to certain impasse (but no contradiction). No case shows that omnipotence falls prey of a new paradox.

we think that, so understood, the notion is either incoherent or trivial. In either case, this unrestricted notion is of little or no use to settle the debate between the friend and the opponent of the possibility of omnipotence.[9] For if O is omnipotent in an unrestricted sense, then O is able to do any logically impossible thing, for instance, being omnipotent and not being omnipotent at the same time. So, O could be a being that cannot lift a certain stone and, at the same time, omnipotent. This conclusion would be rejected by the friends of omnipotence as well as its opponents.[10] No gain is obtained from this way of understanding omnipotence. In fact, an unrestricted notion of omnipotence would make invalid any attempt of a *reductio*. For suppose we have an unrestricted notion of omnipotence; then there is a logically impossible thing which an omnipotent being can do. In holding this, then we are assuming that it is possible to have a contradiction be true. If we derived (unsurprisingly) from it another contradiction, we cannot reject the original hypothesis because we are assuming that any consequence (even a contradiction) deduced from an unrestricted notion of omnipotence can be true.

All we have said before, at first, seems to point to the unrestricted reading of the universal quantifier 'all' in 'an omnipotent being can do all deeds' as the source of the paradox. In discussions different from the intelligibility of the notion of omnipotence, absolutely unrestricted quantification is a source of great concern. So, it would not be a surprise that this notion might bring in trouble in our present context. Expressions such as "all the beer cans are empty", "she always gets to everywhere late", "they are talking about the coach's resignation everywhere", etc. are most of the time read in a restricted way. To read them in an unrestricted way brings trouble.[11] If this is what is happening in the debate around the intelligibility of omnipotence, it may be a further reason to adopt a restricted notion. However,

---

[9]The problem with unrestricted omnipotence does not have to do only with impossible deeds, but also with necessary deeds. As such, a necessary deed or state of affairs is one that would have happened no matter what. It does not matter whether there is a being capable of doing it. So, it is controversial whether an omnipotent being can do necessary deeds — and presumably he should not be able to undo them. They are just there. Our focus here is on impossibilities, but it is worth keeping in mind that necessary facts may also be an important source of concern for an unrestricted notion of omnipotence. See the entry "Omnipotence" in the *Stanford Encyclopedia of Philosophy* by Joshua Hoffman and Gary Rosenkrantz [9], for arguments against the possibility that an omnipotent being can do necessary things. In contrast, Brian Leftow [10, pp. 391–415] discusses several ways the theist can accommodate omnipotence and necessary facts.

[10]Another possibility is that both opponents believe that an unrestricted notion of omnipotence speaks in favor of their own position without thinking that the adversary thinks the same (compare, for example, Cowan [4] with Frankfurt [6]).

[11]Florio [5] offers an overview of the main arguments in favor and against the possibility of quantifying over a domain comprising absolutely everything as well as the problems and further implications that unrestricted quantification brings in.

the quantifier is not the culprit in this case because, even using an unrestricted quantifier, this runs over all and only the powers. But if a mere possibility is not a power, an omnipotent being is not forced to actualize it.

Our proposal is not restricted to the particular case of the stone. There are some other similar supposed paradoxes that may be solved in a similar fashion. Some tasks clearly represent a logical impossibility, for example, drawing a square triangle. These do not represent a problem, for they are not genuine possibilities. That an omnipotent being is not capable of performing something that is not possible does not count against his omnipotence.[12] Other groups of tasks are logically possible, but incompatible with omnipotence. For instance, creating something that is not a creation of an omnipotent being.[13] For the reasons we have given, these do not represent a problem either.

There is a third group of tasks or capacities that are logically possible and compatible with omnipotence. These should not represent any problem. However, some people have thought that, among the tasks of this last group, there are some that may cause trouble to omnipotence. For instance, if an omnipotent being O is benevolent, he cannot lie or be cruel.[14] However, these do not represent any problem to our present view. The reason why O cannot lie is not that he is lacking in power. He is perfectly capable of doing it, otherwise he would not have any moral merit in avoiding it. He may have moral reasons to never lie, and so "He cannot lie" means that He will never lie even when He has the capacities to do it.

There are still other possibilities which seem to be useless (Plantinga's example of a man that is capable only of scratching his ear [12, p. 170]) or even disadvantageous (for example, O can believe 2+2=5 [8, p. 98]), in the case that these are compatible

---

[12]Can an omnipotent being change the past? If this is logically possible, then we can say that an omnipotent being can do it. However, if it is an impossible task, we can say that an omnipotent being is not forced to do it to count as omnipotent. However, whether it is possible or not, our proposal can accommodate the result.

[13]A more sophisticated example is the existence of another omnipotent being. A compelling argument that shows that existence of more than one omnipotent being is impossible is in Adams [1, pp. 776–778]. The core of this argument fits well with our proposal because it does not require assuming either other attributes such moral perfection or determining whether omnipotence is intrinsic or extrinsic, as Adams seems to do.

[14]We will not deal with this case because it will take us far from the issue at hand. See [16] and [17] for a detailed discussion. However, we can at least mention Plantinga's view on this [14, p. 190]. He also imposes restrictions on omnipotence. In particular, he argues that God cannot create just any possible world, but only those that are compatible with two factors: his omnibenevolent nature and his wish to create beings that are free with respect to their actions. Our proposal does not require presupposing any of these additional restrictions and so we do not have the problem of accepting the existence of necessarily unexercised powers. This is the problem that Hill attributes to several authors that distinguish between powers and possibilities [8, pp. 105–108].

with omnipotence. But note that this task and other similar tasks are not really powers. Being capable of doing them does not necessarily represent an advantage over someone that cannot do them. The powers an omnipotent being has are not mere possibilities, but capacities, skills or abilities to do something in a positive way. In some other examples, where supposedly you and we, simple mortals, can do things that God cannot, these tasks more than powers, they are weaknesses. It would be rather strange to argue that we have the power of getting older and weaker, and that in being capable of doing that where God cannot, we are more powerful than God. Now we can complete our previous concept of omnipotent being by adding an additional restriction:

A being x is omnipotent if and only if x can do any logically possible task which is compatible with his omnipotence and constitutes a power.

8 Final Comments

All things considered, we have arrived at the same conclusion as Mavrodes' (a restricted notion of omnipotence), but by using Savage's method (analyzing the meaning of two key words: "omnipotence" and "power"). In other words, the main problem in the paradox of the stone does not necessarily have to do with the unrestricted quantifier as traditionally has been considered. Rather, everything points to the very notion of power as the source of the problem. Even accepting an unrestricted quantification over all powers, there is room for a restriction: all and only powers are admitted. This was the key strategy in Savage's solution, but he focused on the notion of "task" instead of the notion of "power". And many of the tasks that the opponent offers do not seem to count as either genuine possibilities or genuine powers, such as to make false a necessary proposition, to propose a math problem which its maker cannot solve, to get old, to do something that makes you sick, etc. These are not genuine powers, even if they are genuine tasks or possibilities. There may be some ambiguity in the expression "all mighty", especially in the "might", for it may suggest that an omnipotent being can actualize every possibility. However, it is just a confusion. Powers are not mere possibilities, but skills. In conclusion, there are three types of tasks that, even if an omnipotent being cannot do, they do not undermine his omnipotence: logical impossibilities, logical possibilities incompatible with omnipotence and logical possibilities compatible with omnipotence, but that are not powers.

References

[1] Adams, S. (2015). A new paradox of omnipotence. *Philosophia*, 43(3): 759-785.

[2] Conee, E. (1991). The possibility of power beyond possibility. *Philosophical Perspectives*, 5: 447-473.

[3] Cornman, J. W.; Lehrer, K. & Pappas, G. S. (1987). *Philosophical problems and arguments: An introduction*. Cambridge: Hackett Publishing Company.

[4] Cowan, J. L. (1965). The paradox of omnipotence. *Analysis*, 25(Suppl-3): 102-108.

[5] Florio, S. (2014). Unrestricted quantification. *Philosophy Compass*, 9(7): 441-454.

[6] Frankfurt, H. G. (1964). The logic of omnipotence. *The Philosophical Review*, 73(2): 262-263.

[7] Geach, P. T. (1973). Omnipotence. *Philosophy*, 48(183): 7-20.

[8] Hill, S. (2014). Giving up omnipotence. *Canadian Journal of Philosophy*, 44(1): 97–117.

[9] Hoffman, J. & Rosenkrantz, G. (2017). Omnipotence. *The Stanford Encyclopedia of Philosophy* (Winter 2017 Edition), Edward N. Zalta (ed.), URL = <https://plato.stanford.edu/archives/win2017/entries/omnipotence/>.

[10] Leftow, B. (2012). *God and necessity*. Oxford: Oxford University Press.

[11] Mavrodes, G. I. (1963). Some puzzles concerning omnipotence. *The Philosophical Review*, 72(2): 221-223.

[12] Plantinga, A. (1967). *God and other minds. A study of the rational justification of the belief in God*. Ithaca: Cornell University Press.

[13] Plantinga, A. (1969). De re et de dicto. *Nôus*, 3(3): 235-258.

[14] Plantinga, A. (1974). *The nature of necessity*. Oxford: Clarendon Press.

[15] Savage, C. W. (1967). The paradox of the stone. *The Philosophical Review*, 76(1): 74-79.

[16] Steinberg, J. R. (2007). Concerning the preservation of God's omnipotence. *Sophia*, 46(1): 1-5.

[17] Wielenberg, E. J. (2000). Omnipotence again. *Faith and Philosophy*, 17(1): 26-47.

Received 27 May 2019

No New Solutions to the Logical Problem of the Trinity

Beau Branson
Bresica University, Owensboro, Kentucky
Beau.branson@gmail.com

Abstract

Analytic theologians have proposed numerous "solutions" to the Logical Problem of the Trinity (LPT), mostly versions of Social Trinitarianism (ST) and Relative Identity Trinitarianism (RI). Both types of solution are controversial, but many hold out hope that further "Trinitarian theorizing" may yield some as yet unimagined, and somehow importantly different, solution to the LPT. I first give a precise definition of the LPT and of what would count as a solution to it. I then show how, though there are infinitely many possible solutions, all solutions can be grouped together into a finite, exhaustive taxonomy, based precisely on those features which make them either controversial, heretical, or inconsistent. The taxonomy reveals why ST and RI have been the major proposed solutions, and also proves that there can be no *importantly* different, new solutions to the LPT.

1 What is the Logical Problem of the Trinity?

1.1 Introduction

Consider the following set S of natural language sentences:

(S1) The Father is God

(S2) The Son is God

(S3) The Holy Spirit is God

(S4) The Father is not the Son

(S5) The Father is not the Holy Spirit

(S6) The Son is not the Holy Spirit

(S7) There is exactly one God[1]

Call the set of propositions that the sentences of S express P, and call each of the propositions each S-n expresses P-n.

Of course, P is not the entirety of the doctrine of the Trinity.[2] But it is an important subset of it, or is at least logically entailed by it. Intuitively, what is called "the logical problem of the Trinity" (LPT) is just the question how, or whether, P is consistent.

On the one hand, at a certain level the anti-Trinitarian only wants to prove that the doctrine of the Trinity is *false*. And the anti-Trinitarian wins on that point if the doctrine of the Trinity simply includes or entails false metaphysical or theological claims. Thus, theological and metaphysical arguments are by no means irrelevant here. But, on the other hand, in the context of the LPT, the anti-Trinitarian typically portrays his argument as a "knock-down" – a matter of logic – not just another of the many uncertain arguments found in metaphysics, in philosophy generally, or in biblical hermeneutics. Thus, it would be a major embarrassment to the anti-Trinitarian if the purely formal argument against the doctrine of the Trinity were to fail. In that case, it would not, after all, be a "knock-down." It would be less like a refutation of the claim "it's both raining and not raining" – as the anti-Trinitarian wants to portray it – and more like a debate between, say, endurantists and perdurantists in the metaphysics of time.

And of course, it would be more than an embarrassment to the Trinitarian if the doctrine really could be shown to be formally inconsistent.

1.2 Outline

Perhaps because of a bad analogy to Plantinga's "defense" against the Logical Problem of Evil,[3] there has been an attitude to the effect that, even if all of the major

---

[1] [8] seems to be the first to have formulated it this way in the current debate, and most follow him.

[2] For example, the proposition that "the Father begets the Son" is plausibly an essential part of the doctrine of the Trinity. But of course, adding additional propositions can only yield an inconsistent set from a consistent one, not vice-versa. So adding additional propositions could only help the anti-Trinitarian, not the Trinitarian, so the Trinitarian has no reason to complain about focusing on just this set. On the other hand, anti-Trinitarians have not relied on additional propositions in their formulations of the LPT, and if they really *needed* more propositions to be added to make the set inconsistent, then it is unclear that the resulting problem would deserve the name "the Logical Problem of the Trinity." Thus, most in this debate would likely agree that if P could be shown to be consistent, we could say the LPT had been solved, even if there might be other possible arguments to raise against the doctrine.

[3] I discuss this bad analogy in [3].

proposed defenses fail for various reasons, there are infinitely many possibilities out there for a "defense" of the doctrine of the Trinity. In the words of one analytic theologian, the "business of trinitarian theorizing" is merely "unfinished."[4] At the same time, many authors will speak of Social Trinitarianism (ST) and Relative Identity Trinitarianism (RI) as "the major" or "most common" proposed solutions to the LPT. This comes close to acknowledging that these are really the only two viable solutions, but without quite committing to whether there couldn't be others.

In the interests both of making sharper the distinction between the arguments about the plausibility of Trinitarian *metaphysics*, and the (allegedly) purely *formal* inconsistency of the doctrine (the LPT), of clarifying what exactly the options for both sides of the debate are, and of hopefully pushing the discussion forward in light of both of those projects, in what follows I will do the following in turn. First, in section 2, I give a more precise definition both of what the problem is and of what exactly would constitute a "solution" to it. In section 3, I explain how various proposed solutions to the LPT implicitly attribute different logical forms to P. And finally in section 4, I show how, despite the fact that there are infinitely many logical forms one could attribute to P, we can create an exhaustive taxonomy of all possible logical forms attributable to P based precisely on the logical features of the proposed answers to the LPT that cause them to be either inconsistent, heretical or controversial. Although the result does not map onto the usual dichotomy between ST and RI precisely, the taxonomy allows one to see why these two approaches might appear to be the only viable ones, as well as the ways in which a possible solution might subtly differ from proposals given so far.

For anti-Trinitarians, the taxonomy will show that, if just a handful of objections could all be pressed simultaneously, the doctrine of the Trinity would be decisively defeated. For the Trinitarian, the taxonomy will reveal where one really ought to focus one's efforts if one wants to defend the doctrine.

2 What Is the Problem? What Would Be a "Solution"?

2.1 A Precise Statement of the Problem

If the LPT is supposed to be a "knock-down," if it is supposed to show the doctrine of the Trinity, or at least P, to be formally inconsistent, the question is, how would one show, using the tools of modern logic, whether or not a set of *propositions* is formally consistent or inconsistent? The modern logician's methods of determining

---

[4] [26, p. 165]. At least, this was his claim before finally giving up on the doctrine of the Trinity altogether.

consistency and inconsistency only apply to *sentences* or *formulae* within the artificial languages they construct. So in order to make any use of the tools developed by the logician, a set of propositions Π must be given some regimentation Φ in some formal language L such that the logical forms of the formulae in Φ accurately represent the logical forms of the propositions in Π. Within this artificial language, questions of consistency can be determined (if at all) with mathematical precision. Thus, if a regimentation, Φ in L, of Π can be found such that all parties to the debate can agree that:

1. the formal language L is suitably expressive that there are possible formulae of L that could capture the logical forms (or at least all of the relevant aspects of the logical forms) of the propositions in Π (for short "L is a formally adequate language for Π"), and

2. the logical forms of the formulae of Φ in L do reflect the logical forms (or at least the relevant aspects of the logical forms) of the propositions in Π (for short "Φ is a formally adequate regimentation of Π")

then the question of the formal consistency of the propositions in Π can be decided on the basis of the formal consistency of the formulae Φ in L.

So, in any debate over the formal consistency of a set of propositions Π, the real work, and matter for debate, lies not in proving the formal consistency or inconsistency of any set of formulae, but in finding a suitable artificial language L and a suitable regimentation Φ, such that it can be shown that:

1. L is a formally adequate language for Π, and

2. Φ in L is a formally adequate regimentation for Π.

With one important exception, most philosophers in this debate agree that standard versions of predicate logic with (Leibnizian, classical, absolute, non-relative) identity ("PLI" for short) would be formally adequate for P. What will be called "pure" Relative Identity Trinitarianism (Pure RI) seems to be the only camp in the debate that demands the use of an importantly different formal language in which to address the issue.[5] Since rejecting PLI is controversial in itself, we will adopt a certain mild "prejudice" toward PLI. Specifically, as long as a view *can* be given a

---

[5]Strictly speaking, it may be going too far even to say that Pure RI requires a different formal language. Peter van Inwagen has pointed out to me that every formula that is valid in standard PLI remains valid in his Relative Identity Logic. It is simply that a proponent of Pure RI refuses to *make use of* the standard identity predicate as a way of correctly formalizing any natural language statements. However, I will ignore this complication in what follows as I don't think it affects my

formally adequate regimentation in PLI, we will regiment it in PLI. In other words, if it is *possible* to represent a certain logical form *via* formulae of PLI, we will use formulae of PLI as the means by which we will represent that logical form.[6]

There are two senses in which we might say that a set of formulae Φ in a formal language L is inconsistent. It may be that, given the rules of inference that are valid in L, Φ entails a contradiction, entails its own negation, or for whatever reason, the inference rules for that language say that the conjunction of the members of Φ must be false. If this is so, Φ is *"syntactically inconsistent* in L." If there is no such valid proof in L, Φ is *"syntactically consistent"* in L. This is the strict meaning of "consistency," and pertains, obviously, to syntax.

On the other hand, it may be that there is no interpretation I of the non-logical constants of L such that all of the members of Φ are true in L on I (i.e. there is no "model" for Φ in L). If this is so, Φ is not *"satisfiable"* with respect to the class of possible interpretations of the non-logical constants of L. If there *is* such an interpretation (a model) for Φ in L, Φ *is* satisfiable in L. This is not strictly consistency. It pertains not to syntax but to semantics. But it is just as important a consideration, and in a formal language with the features of *soundness* and *completeness*, the syntactic feature of consistency and the semantic feature of satisfiability go hand in hand.

Since our concerns encompass both syntax and semantics, it would seem that our ordinary use of the word "inconsistent" should cover both strict, syntactic inconsistency, and the semantic notion of unsatisfiability. Thus, I will say that a set Φ of formulae of L is "inconsistent in L" if and only if it is *either* syntactically inconsistent in L *or* merely unsatisfiable in L. Likewise, I will say that Φ is "consistent" in L if and only if it is *both* syntactically consistent in L *and* satisfiable in L.

Now in any formal language L worth studying, any language with the property of *"soundness,"* if Φ is syntactically inconsistent in L, then it will be unsatisfiable in L as well. So, although these are not the only ways to do so, a usually good strategy for showing the inconsistency of Φ is to *give a proof* of the negation of the conjunction of the members of Φ (because the syntactic feature of inconsistency will show the semantic feature of unsatisfiability as well), and a usually good strategy for

---

ultimate conclusion. Ultimately, I will conclude that one way to solve the LPT is to adopt an analysis of counting statements that does not work by way of classical identity, and that conclusion remains, even in the face of this complication. It may be that van Inwagen's proposal could be placed into the category of "Impure" RI, rather than "Pure" RI. But the general taxonomy I will construct can proceed at an abstract level, regardless of how precisely to classify van Inwagen himself, or his proposal.

[6]It's important to emphasize here that nothing in our proof hangs on this "prejudice," since, even if there are other languages that are formally adequate for P, as long as PLI is *one* formally adequate language, then we *may* choose to work entirely within that language if we so choose.

showing "formal consistency" is to *give a model* for all of the members of Φ (because the semantic feature of satisfiability will show the syntactic feature of consistency as well).

So, why does the anti-Trinitarian think that P is inconsistent?

Suppose we take "Father," "Son," and "Holy Spirit" univocally as names for individuals wherever they appear in S. Suppose we also take "God" in S1 through S3 univocally as the name of an individual. Suppose we take "is" univocally as the "is" of (classical) identity in S1 through S6. And suppose we analyze the counting statement expressed by S7 in a standard way, and understand "is God" as it occurs there in the same way we did in our interpretation of S1 through S3. The logical form of the claims expressed by S on this interpretation of it can be represented in PLI as:

$\Phi_{\text{LPT-1}}$:
($1_{\text{LPT-1}}$)   f=g
($2_{\text{LPT-1}}$)   s=g
($3_{\text{LPT-1}}$)   h=g
($4_{\text{LPT-1}}$)   f≠s
($5_{\text{LPT-1}}$)   f≠h
($6_{\text{LPT-1}}$)   s≠h
($7_{\text{LPT-1}}$) $(\exists x)(\forall y)(x=g \ \& \ (y=g \rightarrow y=x))$

$\Phi_{\text{LPT-1}}$ is inconsistent in PLI.[7] (($7_{\text{LPT-1}}$) is not strictly necessary to derive a contradiction here; I include it only for completeness' sake.)

On the other hand, suppose we instead take "is God" in S1 through S3 univocally but take "God" to be a predicate nominative ("a god") and "is" to be the "is" of predication. Suppose we again analyze the counting statement expressed by S7 in the standard way, and understand "is God" as it occurs there in the same way we did in our interpretation of S1 through S3. And suppose we otherwise leave our regimentation unchanged. The logical form of the claims expressed by S on this interpretation of it can be represented in PLI as:

$\Phi_{\text{LPT-2}}$:
($1_{\text{LPT-2}}$)   Gf
($2_{\text{LPT-2}}$)   Gs
($3_{\text{LPT-2}}$)   Gh
($4_{\text{LPT-2}}$)   f≠s
($5_{\text{LPT-2}}$)   f≠h

---

[7] Proof is trivial.

($6_{\text{LPT-2}}$) s≠h

($7_{\text{LPT-2}}$) $(\exists x)(\forall y)(Gx\ \&\ (Gy \to y=x))$

$\Phi_{\text{LPT-2}}$ is also inconsistent in PLI.[8]

Since both of the logical forms we have in mind here *can* be represented in PLI, we will use PLI. So, a more precise way to put the anti-Trinitarian argument would be as follows:

1. PLI is a formally adequate language for P, and

2. at least one of $\Phi_{\text{LPT-1}}$ in PLI or $\Phi_{\text{LPT-2}}$ in PLI is a formally adequate regimentation of P, and

3. both $\Phi_{\text{LPT-1}}$ and $\Phi_{\text{LPT-2}}$ are (syntactically) inconsistent in PLI.

4. So, by definition of "formally adequate language" and "formally adequate regimentation," P is formally inconsistent.

But, if this is the "problem"... what exactly would count as a *solution*?

2.2   What Would Be a Solution?

If the anti-Trinitarian argument above is right, then P is formally inconsistent, and that is the "answer" to the LPT. There is no solution, but rather there is, as we might say, a "non-solution." So the Trinitarian must maintain that *neither* regimentation, in PLI, is formally adequate for P (or else that PLI itself is not formally adequate for P).

Let us define a "*proposed* answer" to the LPT as a set that includes:

1. Exactly one formal language L in which to regiment P, and

2. Exactly one set Φ of formulae of L with which to regiment P,[9] and

3. A purported proof of the formal consistency or inconsistency of Φ in L.

Let us say that a "*formally adequate* answer" to the LPT is a proposed answer to the logical problem of the Trinity such that:

---

[8]Proof is trivial.

[9]We will relax this requirement in an obvious and non-problematic way in the case of a couple of dilemmas, where two different possible regimentations are offered, and the claim made is only that at least one of them is formally adequate. Specifically, the anti-Trinitarian regimentations LPT_1 and LPT_2, and the Naïve Modalist regimentations NM_1 and NM_2.

1. L is a formally adequate language for P, and

2. Φ in L is a formally adequate regimentation of P

3. (and the proof of formal consistency or inconsistency of Φ in L is correct.)

A "proposed *solution*" to the LPT is a proposed answer to the logical problem of the Trinity that purportedly proves that Φ is formally consistent in L.

A "proposed *non-solution*" to the LPT is a proposed answer to the logical problem of the Trinity that purportedly proves that Φ is formally inconsistent in L.

A "formally adequate *solution*" to the LPT is a formally adequate answer that is a proposed solution (i.e., a formally adequate answer to the LPT that proves that Φ is formally consistent in L).

A "formally adequate *non-solution*" to the LPT is a formally adequate answer that is a proposed non-solution (i.e., a formally adequate answer to the LPT that proves that Φ is formally inconsistent in L).

Thus, the anti-Trinitarian argument above can be seen as a constructive dilemma. One of two proposed non-solutions to the LPT (call those LPT$_1$ and LPT$_2$) is formally adequate. Thus, there is some formally adequate non-solution to the LPT.[10] So, by definition of "formally adequate language" and "formally adequate regimentation," P is formally inconsistent.

Thus, to defend P, the Trinitarian must argue at least that it might (for all we know) be the case that neither LPT$_1$ nor LPT$_2$ is a formally adequate answer to the LPT, or even that PLI itself is not a formally adequate language for P, that is, either:

1. PLI is not a formally adequate language for P, or

2. Neither Φ$_{LPT-1}$ in PLI nor Φ$_{LPT-2}$ in PLI is a formally adequate regimentation of P.

   (Or both.)

In principle, this very weak response ("for all we know," either the language is inadequate or the regimentations are) would be a sufficient defence of P. But most philosophers in the literature have wanted to do more. They have wanted to argue that it can be *shown* that P really is consistent (not just that it's not unreasonable

---

[10]It should be obvious that if there is one formally adequate solution, all formally adequate answers are solutions, and that if there is one formally adequate non-solution, all formally adequate answers are non-solutions, since a set of propositions is either consistent or not.

for us to *believe* that it is).[11] But it might seem hard to see how one would argue that PLI is not formally adequate for P, except by arguing that some other language L *is* formally adequate for P, and that L is importantly different from PLI in some relevant way. Likewise, assuming that PLI is formally adequate for P, it might seem hard to see how one would argue that neither Φ_{LPT-1} in PLI nor Φ_{LPT-2} in PLI is a formally adequate regimentation for P, except by arguing that some other regimentation Φ in PLI *is* a formally adequate regimentation for P, and that Φ's being a formally adequate regimentation of P in PLI is somehow incompatible both with Φ_{LPT-1} in PLI being a formally adequate regimentation of P and with Φ_{LPT-2} in PLI being a formally adequate regimentation of P (as will be the case if the alternative proposed answer has an importantly different logical form, which of course must be the case if it is a proposed solution instead of a non-solution). And so, the majority of the literature has centered around the search for alternative proposed answers to the LPT to supplant LPT_1 and LPT_2.

But if one wants to replace LPT_1 and LPT_2... *what alternative answers could one propose?*

3 Proposed Solutions

Thinking on this issue goes back to the earliest centuries of Christianity. And not just any way of understanding the "three-ness" and "one-ness" of God has been received as within the bounds of orthodoxy. Certain views, though consistent, were rejected as heretical during the course of the Trinitarian controversies of roughly the late 3rd through early 5th centuries AD. I will refer to these as the "Classical Trinitarian Heresies" (CTHs). CTH's may have interpretted S in consistent ways, but they do so only by being at odds with the orthodox doctrine of the Trinity. Thus, they in some sense count as proposed answers to the LPT, even "solutions," but ones that are not available to the Trinitarian. So, for completeness' sake, we will discuss the CTH's in some detail. However, contemporary views may be easier to understand and easier to regiment in a standard way. Also, some of that discussion will help to shed light on the CTHs. So, we will begin with contemporary proposed solutions to the LPT.

Our purpose at the moment is to collect various proposed solutions to the LPT. And what concerns us most at the moment is the matter of formal consistency.

---

[11]There is another approach, labelled "mysterianism" by Tuggy [27], which does take precisely the approach of avoiding the issue of consistency, but arguing for the epistemic acceptability of accepting a set of propositions that appears to be inconsistent. Addressing that approach is beyond the scope of the current paper, however, which has an eye only towards those who would offer a "defense" of the doctrine.

So we will not try to give exhaustively detailed discussions of any of these views, but only so much as to give us a clear enough idea of its *logical form* that we can represent it in a formal language and determine its consistency or inconsistency.

3.1 Contemporary Proposed Solutions

3.1.1 Social Trinitarianism (ST)

Probably the easiest contemporary proposal to understand is Social Trinitarianism (ST). Paradigmatic versions of ST hold that Father, Son and Holy Spirit are straightforwardly numerically distinct persons, each of whom is fully divine. Instances of the phrase "is God" in reference to the persons individually are read as *predications* ("is divine" or "is (a) god") rather than as *identifications* to an individual called "God." But ST (attempts to) escape(s) tritheism by claiming it is the Trinity *as a whole* – the collective or "community" or "society" they compose – to which the term "God" is properly applied when we speak of "the one God" (whether we treat this as a *name* for the collective, or as a predicate that is not, at least not precisely, univocal with "is (a) god" when applied to the persons).

Both proponents and critics of ST tend to focus on its taking the divine "persons" to be fully *"persons"* in our modern, post-Cartesian sense – fully aware centers of consciousness, reason, will, etc. This is thought to be its distinctive feature. But from the point of view merely of logical form, the issue is irrelevant. The "persons" could be *beans* as far as the LPT is concerned. But if there are three of them, and each is a bean, yet there is only one bean, LPT$_2$ would provide a formally adequate regimentation of the view, and the doctrine would be inconsistent.

So what features of ST *are* relevant to our concerns?

First, it is clear that Social Trinitarians insist on making a very strong, real distinction between the persons. But classical non-identity ($\neq$) is the weakest (real) distinction one can make.

It's clear then that Social Trinitarians will agree with LPT$_1$ and LPT$_2$ on their regimentation of P4 through P6. (Indeed, Social Trinitarians often want to go even *further* in distinguishing the persons, but they must *at least* admit the non-identity of the persons.) And in so doing they will (they may as well) take PLI to be a formally adequate language for P. In keeping with this emphasis on the distinctness of the persons, it is also clear that Social Trinitarians will want to treat "is god" in P1 through P3 not as identity claims to some individual, but as predications. Thus, Social Trinitarians will deny the formal adequacy of 1$_{\text{LPT-1}}$ through 3$_{\text{LPT-1}}$ in PLI.

It is also clear that Social Trinitarians make no distinctions *between* the persons as to their divinity. That is, each person is divine in exactly the same sense as either of the other two persons. So, there will be no equivocation here. And while Social Trinitarians will deny the formal adequacy of 1_{LPT-1} through 3_{LPT-1} in PLI, they will admit to the formal adequacy of 1_{LPT-2} through 3_{LPT-2} in PLI (or something relevantly similar, in a sense that will become clear later.)

ST, then, so far *agrees* with LPT_2 on the logical form of P. If ST is to count as a *solution*, then, it must regiment P7 differently. But there is no indication in ST literature that Social Trinitarians have any problem with standard logical regimentations of counting statements in general or with the classical identity relation ($=$) in particular. (Indeed, one of the motivations for adopting ST is precisely to avoid having to give up on analyzing counting statements with classical identity. See the discussion of Relative Identity Trinitarianism below for more.) The only way, then, that ST could possibly avoid contradiction would be to equivocate on "is god," not among its applications to the persons themselves, individually (in S1 through S3) but between its application there on the one hand and in S7 on the other. But it is this purely *formal* feature that lies at the heart of a major criticism of ST. Brian Leftow writes:

> But even if Trinity monotheism avoids talk of degrees of deity, it faces a problem. Either the Trinity is a fourth case of the divine nature, in addition to the persons, or it is not. If it is, we have too many cases of deity for orthodoxy. If it is not, and yet is divine, there are two ways to be divine – by being a case of deity, and by being a Trinity of such cases. If there is more than one way to be divine, Trinity monotheism becomes Plantingian Arianism. But if there is in fact only one way to be divine, then there are two alternatives. One is that only the Trinity is God, and God is composed of non-divine persons. The other is that the sum of all divine persons is somehow not divine. To accept this last claim would be to give up Trinity monotheism altogether.
>
> I do not see an acceptable alternative here. So I think Trinity monotheism is not a promising strategy for ST.[12]

Leftow here uses "Trinity monotheism" for what he takes to be just one *version* of ST. But as we've seen, if all versions of ST admit the non-identity of the persons, and if all versions of ST treat "is god" as univocal across S1 and S3, and if no versions of ST take issue with standard logical regimentations of counting statements, then all versions of ST will have to confront the problem Leftow raises. (At least, they will have to confront the purely *formal* problem Leftow's argument relies on.) Namely,

---

[12][14, p. 221].

first, that ST must equivocate on "is god" in S1 through S3 on the one hand and "is God" in S7 on the other hand (otherwise we end up with *four* gods instead of *one*). But then it follows that either (1) there is more than one "way" of being divine or being "a god" (a position Leftow calls "Plantingian Arianism," see below, section 3.2.1, for more on Arianism), or else (2) the persons are not legitimately divine or "god," or else (3) the "one God" (i.e., according to ST, the Trinity as a whole) is not legitimately divine or "(a) god."

So, although, again, both proponents and critics tend to characterize ST in terms of its taking the divine "persons" to be distinct centers of consciousness and so forth, it is more useful for our purposes to characterize it in terms of the formal feature Leftow's criticism relies on. For even if "x is god" means *that x is a bean*, we can run essentially the same argument to the effect that one will have to equivocate on "is god." If the persons satisfy *any* predicate, and they are all non-identical, yet there is only one thing that satisfies that predicate, then LPT_2 is formally adequate, regardless of what the predicate in quesiton is, or what it means.

So, if ST is to offer a solution, it must reject the formal adequacy of 7_{LPT-2} and replace it with an equivocation on "is god," which we can represent formally by using "G_1" for one sense of "is god," and "G_2" for another sense. (The precise semantic content can be filled in however a particular proponent of ST likes. The important fact from a formal point of view is simply that there are *two* senses, whatever they might be.) Thus, we can pin down a formal regimentation for ST and give an ST proposed solution to the LPT as follows:

1. PLI is a formally adequate language for P.

2. Φ_{ST} in PLI is a formally adequate regimentation of P:

   Φ_{ST}:

   (1_{ST}) $G_1 f$

   (2_{ST}) $G_1 s$

   (3_{ST}) $G_1 h$

   (4_{ST}) $f \neq s$

   (5_{ST}) $f \neq h$

   (6_{ST}) $s \neq h$

   (7_{ST}) $(\exists x)(\forall y)(G_2 x \ \& \ (G_2 y \rightarrow x=y))$[13]

---

[13]It might be objected that this treats "is god" in P7 as another predication, whereas Social Trinitarians might claims it should be treated as a name in P7, thus: (7_{ST}) $(\exists x)(\forall y)(x=g \ \& \ (y=g \rightarrow$

3. Φ_{ST} is formally consistent in PLI.[14]

3.1.2 ("Pure") Relative Identity Trinitarianism (Pure RI)

The major strand of Relative Identity Trinitarianism (RI) in contemporary philosophy of religion, called "pure" RI by Mike Rea,[15] began with Peter Geach's discussions of relative identity, and his application of it to the doctrine of the Trinity.[16] A. P. Martinich also endorsed an RI view a few decades ago,[17] as did James Cain.[18] But probably the clearest, fullest and most influential statements of the view are van Inwagen's.[19] In his earlier statement of the view, van Inwagen does not answer the question whether classical identity exists or not.[20] But in his later statement, he explicitly rejects the existence of classical identity.[21]

Pure RI may be, in some sense, the most difficult proposed solution to the LPT to wrap one's head around, given that it rejects the existence of classical identity altogether, and given how intuitive classical identity seems to most of us. But in another sense (happily, the sense that will matter for us), it is among the easiest. This is especially so as it appears in van Inwagen's work, which, also happily, is what we might call the canonical version of Pure RI.

First, Pure RI explicitly rejects the very existence, or intelligibility, of classical identity, and so explicitly rejects PLI as a formally adequate language for P (PLI being "predicate logic *with identity*"). Van Inwagen has given his own preferred formal language for this purpose, Relative Identity Logic, which he shortens to "RI-logic,"[22] and which I will shorten even further to "RIL." So, Pure RI does not

---

x=y)). However, that is still an equivocation, and so, when we give a more general characterization of a "Family" of views into which ST will fall, such a version of ST will be included in our "Family" anyway. See Section 4.5 below.

[14]It should be obvious that there is a model for Φ_{ST}, and the proof is left as an exercise for the reader.

[15]The distinction begins in [19] p. 433 and *passim*.

[16]See [11, pp. 43–48 and 69–70]; [10] and [9], both reprinted in [12]; and his chapter, [13].

[17][15] and [16].

[18][7].

[19][28], and [29] in [21, pp. 61–75].

[20]In [28], p. 241, van Inwagen considers three arguments concerning classical identity and its relation to relative identity, and says "I regard these arguments as inconclusive. In the sequel, therefore, I shall assume neither that classical identity exists nor that it does not exist." Thus, strictly speaking, in this paper, van Inwagen counted as an adherent of "impure" Relative Identity theory, to be discussed below.

[21]In [29, p 70], he says, "I deny that there is one all-encompassing relation of identity... there is no relation that is both universally reflexive and forces indiscerniblility."

[22][28, p. 231].

accept PLI as a formally adequate language for P, but claims that RIL is a formally adequate language for P.

Second, Pure RI replaces the classical (non-)identity predicate "$\neq$" in the regimentations of P1 through P6 with various relative (non-)identity predicates, the two relevant for our purposes being: "is the same being as" in its equivalents of P1 through P3, and "is (not) the same person as" in its equivalent of P4 through P6.[23] It can then use the "is the same being as" predicate in its equivalent of P7 without generating inconsistency. Although van Inwagen uses the English "is the same being as" and "is (not) the same person as," I will shorten these to "$=_B$" and "$\neq_P$," respectively.

One might think we could now state a Pure RI proposed solution to the LPT as:

1. RIL is a formally adequate language for P.

2. $\Phi_{\text{Pure-RI}}{}^*$ in RIL is a formally adequate regimentation of P:

$\Phi_{\text{Pure-RI}}{}^*$:

$(1_{\text{Pure-RI}}{}^*)$ $f =_B g$

$(2_{\text{Pure-RI}}{}^*)$ $s =_B g$

$(3_{\text{Pure-RI}}{}^*)$ $h =_B g$

$(4_{\text{Pure-RI}}{}^*)$ $f \neq_P s$

$(5_{\text{Pure-RI}}{}^*)$ $f \neq_P h$

$(6_{\text{Pure-RI}}{}^*)$ $s \neq_P h$

$(7_{\text{Pure-RI}}{}^*)$ $(\exists x)(\forall y) (x =_B g \ \& \ ((y =_B g) \rightarrow (y =_B x)))$

3. $\Phi_{\text{Pure-RI}}{}^*$ is formally consistent in RIL.

However, this would not be accurate. At least, not without some qualifications about the uses of "f," "s," and "h" in RIL. As van Inwagen points out,

> The philosopher who eschews classical, absolute identity must also eschew singular terms, for the idea of a singular term is – at least in currently orthodox semantical theory – inseparably bound to the classical semantical notion of reference or denotation; and this notion, in its turn, is inseparably bound to the idea of classical identity. It is a part of the orthodox semantical concept of reference that reference is a many-one relation. And it is a part of the idea of a many-one relation – or of a

---

[23]It will become clear why I say its "equivalents" shortly.

one-one relation, for that matter – that if x bears such a relation to y and bears it to z, then y and z are absolutely identical.[24]

To cut a long story short, RIL must replace singular reference with *relative* singular reference, and this boils down to certain kinds of general or quantified statements employing relative identity relations. Thus, a Pure RI proposed solution to the LPT would instead come to something like this:

1. RIL is a formally adequate language for P.

2. $\Phi_{\text{Pure-RI}}$ in RIL is a formally adequate regimentation of P:

       $\Phi_{\text{Pure-RI}}$:

   $(\exists x)\ (\exists y)\ (\exists z)$

   $(Gx\ \&\ Gy\ \&\ Gz\ \&$ (cf. P1 to P3)

   $x \neq_P y\ \&\ x \neq_P z\ \&\ y \neq_P z\ \&$ (cf. P4 to P6)

   $(\forall v)\ (\forall w)\ ((Gv\ \&\ Gw) \rightarrow (v =_B w)))$ (cf. P7)

3. $\Phi_{\text{Pure-RI}}$ is formally consistent in RIL.[25]

$\Phi_{\text{Pure-RI}}$ is just one long formula. I have split it onto different lines for ease of reading. Obviously the first line is just the initial three quantifiers, which we must use in the place of singular terms. With that in place, the second line corresponds in a way to P1 through P3. The third line corresponds in a way to P4 through P6. And the fourth line corresponds in a way to P7. Thus, the different parts of $\Phi_{\text{Pure-RI}}$ are in some sense the "equivalents" of different parts of P. (One can usefully compare $\Phi_{\text{Pure-RI}}$ to other proposed answers by taking the conjunction of their regimentations of P1 through P7 in order, and then "Ramsifying" away the names of the persons.)

3.1.3 "Impure" Relative Identity Trinitarianism (Impure RI)

The final contemporary proposal we will look at has been defended by Mike Rea and Jeff Brower. In the Rea-Brower account of the Trinity, the persons stand in a "constitution" relation to one another, and the word "God" is systematically ambiguous between the persons.[26] The constitution relation does not entail classical identity,

---

[24][28, p. 244].

[25]It is easy enough to see that this will be consistent, but for more, one can see [28, pp. 249–250].

[26]The view is explicated, defended, and developed in more detail over the course of a number of articles. See [19], [5], [6], [20], and [22]. See also Rea and Michael Murray's discussion of the Trinity in [17].

but the account does not deny the existence or intelligibility of classical identity as on the "pure" RI view. It simply holds that *our ordinary counting practices* rely not on classical identity, but on various relative identity relations. The constitution relation either is, or at least entails, a species of relative identity between the persons, such that we should count them as three persons but one god. (For the time being, we will follow Rea's terminology in calling this "impure Relative Identity" (Impure RI) as distinguished from "pure" RI. We will see later, Section 4.6, why there may be a more useful term to cover both of these views.)

Since Impure RI accepts classical identity, it can (it may as well) accept PLI as a formally adequate language in which to regiment P. Furthermore, it can regiment P4 through P6 as classical non-identity claims just as in LPT_1 and LPT_2. However, like Pure RI, it rejects classical identity as the relation by which we *count*, and instead analyzes counting statements as operating by way of relative identity relations. So, it will regiment P7 differently.

To claim that we count by *classical identity* is to claim that we count one or two (...or n) Fs when there are one or two (...or n) terms (t_1, t_2, ... t_n) of which "F" is true and the appropriate claims of classical non-identity involving those terms ($t_1 \neq t_2$, ...) are all true, and any other term t_{n+1} of which "F" is true is such that at least some claim of classical identity involving t_{n+1} and one of the previous terms is true (thus, $t_{n+1} = t_1$ or $t_{n+1} = t_2$, or ... $t_{n+1} = t_n$).

To claim that we count by *relative identity* is to claim that we count one or two (...or n) Fs when there are one or two (...or n) terms (t_1, t_2, ... t_n) of which "F" is true and the corresponding claims of *relative* non-identity involving those terms and that predicate ($t_1 \neq_F t_2$, ...) are all true, and any other term t_{n+1} of which "F" is true is such that at least some claim of relative identity involving t_{n+1} and one of the previous terms and the appropriate predicate is true (thus, $t_{n+1} =_F t_1$ or $t_{n+1} =_F t_2$, or ... $t_{n+1} =_F t_n$).

Thus, Impure RI's regimentation of P7 will look much like Pure RI's in a way, but stated in PLI instead of RIL. But how does Impure RI analyze P1 through P3?

Over the course of several papers, the Rea-Brower view becomes fairly complex, involving the sharing by the persons of a trope-like divine nature that "plays the role of matter" for the persons, each of which is constituted by the divine nature plus its own hypostatic property (Fatherhood, Sonship, Spiritude). But the deeper importance of that theoretical machinery lies in its licensing of a relative identity claim involving the term "God" (here used as a name or other singular term again) and each of the names of the persons. We can symbolize this relative identity relation as "$=_G$," which allows us to regiment the view more simply, and give an Impure RI proposed solution to the LPT as follows:

1. PLI is a formally adequate language for P.

2. $\Phi_{\text{Impure-RI}}$ in PLI is a formally adequate regimentation of P:

   $\Phi_{\text{Impure-RI}}$:

   ($1_{\text{Impure-RI}}$) f $=_{\text{G}}$ g

   ($2_{\text{Impure-RI}}$) s $=_{\text{G}}$ g

   ($3_{\text{Impure-RI}}$) h $=_{\text{G}}$ g

   ($4_{\text{Impure-RI}}$) f $\neq$ s

   ($5_{\text{Impure-RI}}$) f $\neq$ h

   ($6_{\text{Impure-RI}}$) s $\neq$ h

   ($7_{\text{Impure-RI}}$) $(\exists x)(\forall y)(x =_{\text{G}} g \ \& \ (y =_{\text{G}} g \to y =_{\text{G}} x))$

3. $\Phi_{\text{Impure-RI}}$ is formally consistent in PLI.[27]

Is it really OK to just ignore whatever more intricate logical structure might, given Rea and Brower's fuller account, be entailed by the "$=_{\text{G}}$" relation, such as a reference to the divine nature and the constitution relation? Yes. How so?

Whatever the "same god as" relation might entail, as long as "x is the same god as y":

1. is not in itself formally inconsistent, and

2. does not entail (classical) identity between x and some other term t_i,[28]

then ($1_{\text{Impure-RI}}$) through ($7_{\text{Impure-RI}}$) is still consistent.

On the other hand, if "x is the same god as y" *does* entail a (classical) identity between x and some other term t_i, then ($1_{\text{Impure-RI}}$) through ($6_{\text{Impure-RI}}$) will be inconsistent without even appealing to ($7_{\text{Impure-RI}}$). But not for any reasons interestingly related to Impure RI. It will be inconsistent for the same reasons ($1_{\text{LPT-1}}$) through ($6_{\text{LPT-1}}$) were.

More precisely, for any formula ϕ, where $\phi^{t1,t2}_{x,y}$ is the result of replacing every occurrence of the variables x and y in ϕ with the terms t_1 and t_2, respectively, if:

$$\phi^{t1,t2}_{x,y} \models t_1 = t_i \text{ for some } t_i \neq t_1$$

---

[27]It should be obvious that there is a model for $\Phi_{\text{Impure-RI}}$, and the proof is left as an exercise for the reader.

[28]I include 1 merely to aid comprehension. Given 2, 1 is in fact redundant.

then

$$\phi^{f,g}_{x,y} \ \& \ \phi^{s,g}_{x,y} \ \& \ \phi^{h,g}_{x,y} \ \& \ f \neq s \ \& \ f \neq h \ \& \ s \neq h$$

is inconsistent anyway, but if:

$$\phi^{t1,t2}_{x,y} \nvDash t_1 = t_i \text{ for any } t_i \neq t_1$$

then

$$\phi^{f,g}_{x,y} \ \& \ \phi^{s,g}_{x,y} \ \& \ \phi^{h,g}_{x,y} \ \& \ f \neq s \ \& \ f \neq h \ \& \ s \neq h \ \&$$
$$(\exists x)(\forall y)(\phi^{g}_{y} \ \& \ (\phi^{y,g}_{x,y} \rightarrow \phi^{y,x}_{x,y}))$$

is consistent.

So, as long as "x is the same god as y" doesn't entail a classical identity claim between x and some other term, we are safe. And it doesn't seem that it would on the Rea-Brower account. The only other term that might be involved would be "the divine nature." But on the Rea-Brower account, the divine nature is definitely *not* classically identical to any of the persons. So, we needn't go into more detail on the precise logical structure, or further semantic content, of the "same god as" relation. The above will do to show the Rea-Brower account is at least formally consistent.

3.2 Classical Trinitarian Heresies

3.2.1 Arianism

Although not the first chronologically, the CTH of all CTHs was Arianism. It was Arianism that occasioned the First (and Second) Ecumenical Council(s) and the heated controversies of the 4th century. Historically, Arianism was not *motivated* by the search for a solution to the LPT. Nor was its rejection by the orthodox motivated by concerns about the LPT. Still, the logical problem of the Trinity did have a role in the debate, albeit a minor one. To the central question of whether the *Logos*, i.e., the "Angel of the LORD," i.e. Christ, was created or uncreated, the LPT was tacked on as an after-thought or "back-up" argument to other scriptural and metaphysical arguments.

Gregory Nazianzen in his *Fifth Theological Oration* (On the Holy Spirit) discusses an Arian argument:

> "If," they say, "there is God, and God, and God, how are there not three gods? Or how is that which is glorified not a poly-archy?"[29]

---

[29] [25], Fifth Theological Oration (31), *On the Holy Spirit*, section 13. Translation mine.

But why did those Arians not think the LPT was a problem for *them*? What was *their* proposed solution to the LPT?

For the first part of the answer, we must go back to Gregory's *Third Theological Oration (On the Son)*. Arians took the position that Father and Son have different natures (that they were not "consubstantial"). Second, they took the position that "is god" as applied to the Father predicates the divine nature. It follows directly from these two views that applying "is god" to the Son could only be done equivocally (regardless of concerns about the LPT).[30]

And this is a consequence they themselves acknowledged. We read in Gregory's *Third Theological Oration*:

> And when we advance this objection against them, "What do you mean to say then? That the Son is not properly God, just as a picture of an animal is not properly an animal?[31] And if not properly God, in what sense is He God at all?" They reply, "Why should not these terms be [both] ambiguous, and yet in both cases be used in a proper sense?"

> And they will give us such instances as the land-dog and the dogfish; where the word "dog" is ambiguous, and yet in both cases is properly used,[32] for there is such a species among the ambiguously named, or any other case in which the same appellative is used for two things of different nature.[33]

So there is step one in the Arian solution to the LPT: equivocate on "is god." Not between P7 on the one hand and P1 through P3 on the other, as in ST, but among P1 through P3 themselves.

---

[30]I should emphasize that this semantic claim, that "is god" predicates *the divine nature*, rather than a kind of *activity*, was, originally, a specificially *Arian* claim. It was not a part of the mainstream Christian tradition prior to that point, and was forcefully rejected by St. Gregory of Nyssa and others, while those church fathers who did not specifically reject it, at least refrained from affirming it. Only later was Augustine to be the first church father to actually accept this semantic claim that "is god" predicates divinity, rather than an activity, and it is not clear that his attempt to incorporate this originally Arian semantic claim into a Trinitarian theology was completely successful. See 4.4, below for more.

[31]In Greek, ζῷον means either an animal or a painting.

[32]τὸν κύνα, τὸν χερσαῖον, καὶ τὸν θαλάττιον. In Greek, κύνη, "dog," refers to either a dog or a dog-fish, and neither is a metaphorical or secondary use of the term. A better example in English would be the word "bank," which is ambiguous for either a financial institution or the edge of a river, but neither is so only in a figurative sense. Both are perfectly proper and literal uses of the word "bank." Arians are saying that, just like the English "bank," the word "God" predicates two completely different natures, though neither is a metaphorical or improper sense of the word.

[33][25] Third Theological Oration (29), *On the Son*, section 14. Translation from [24, p. 306].

Step two is that they paired this characteristically Arian equivocation on "is god" with a related view about counting statements involving ambiguous count nouns. Gregory continues a little later in the *Fifth Theological Oration*, speaking in the voice of his Arian opponents:

> "Things of one essence," you [=Arians] say, "are counted together," and by this "counted together," you mean that they are collected into one number. "But things which are not of one essence are not thus counted; so that *you* [=orthodox Trinitarians] cannot avoid speaking of three gods, according to this account, while *we* [=Arians] do not run any risk at all of it, inasmuch as we [=Arians] assert that they are not consubstantial."[34]

So the accusation made against Trinitarians by Arians is something like this. When we count by a count-noun F, for example "dog," that noun must express some essence or nature, in this case dog-hood. And the number of Fs will be the number of things instantiating this essence or nature. So, if there are three things that all instantiated dog-hood, then there are three dogs.

Applied to the Trinity, the Arian argues as follows. The orthodox Trinitarian holds precisely this sort of view with respect to the persons of the Trinity. That is, the orthodox Trinitarian holds that each of the persons instantiates god-hood (or "the Godhead," to use the old-fashioned word). So, given the Arian view of counting, the orthodox Trinitarian will have to say that there are three gods.

On the other hand, if we have a count-noun that is ambiguous between two essences or natures, then we have to precisify (whether explicitly, or tacitly, given a certain context), and only given that precisification can we answer the question how many Fs there are. For example, if "dog" is ambiguous between a kind of mammal and a kind of fish, and there is one land-dog and one dog-fish in the vicinity, and we ask "how many dogs are there?" the Arian will say that we have to precisify. In this context, there are two admissible precisifications. On one, the question comes to, "how many land-dogs are there?" and the answer is "one." On the other, the question comes to, "how many dog-fish are there?" and the answer is "one." So, on every admissible precisification in this context, the answer is "one." And on no admissible precisification in this context is the answer anything other than "one." So, it is right to answer "one" in a context like that.

Applied to the Trinity, the Arian argues that the three persons do *not* exemplify a single essence or nature, but three distinct natures. However, the count-noun "god" is ambiguous, and can predicate any of these three natures. So, in this context,

---

[34] [25], Fifth Theologian Oration (31), *On the Holy Spirit*, section 17. Translation from [24, p. 323].

there are three admissible precisifications of the predicate "is god," which we can represent formally by using "G_1" for one sense of "is god," "G_2" for the second sense, and "G_3" for the third sense. (The precise semantic content of these predicates can be filled in however the Arian likes. The important fact from a formal point of view is simply that there are *three* senses, whatever they might be.) Then, on any admissible precisification of the question "how many gods are there?" in this context, the answer will be "one." (I.e., there is only one god in the sense of G_1, only one god in the sense of G_2, and only one god in the sense of G_3.) And on no admissible precisification of the question in this context is the answer anything other than "one." So, it is right (*for the Arian*) in a context like this to answer "one" to the question "how many gods are there?" (Likewise for, how many gods they believe in, worship, etc.)

So, we can state a proposed Arian solution to the LPT as follows:

1. PLI is a formally adequate language for P.

2. Φ_{AR} in PLI is a formally adequate regimentation for P:

   Φ_{AR}:

   (1_{AR}) G_1f

   (2_{AR}) G_2s

   (3_{AR}) G_3h

   (4_{AR}) $f{\neq}s$

   (5_{AR}) $f{\neq}h$

   (6_{AR}) $s{\neq}h$

   (7_{AR}) $(\exists x)(\forall y)(G_ix \,\&\, (G_iy \to x{=}y))$

   (for every admissible precisification of G_i in this context)

3. Φ_{AR} is formally consistent in PLI.[35]

3.2.2 (Naïve) Modalism

Modalism, also known as monarchianism, patripassianism or Sabellianism, was an early Trinitarian heresy, or family of heresies, that in some way denied the *distinctness* of the divine "persons" or "hypostases."

---

[35]Proof is left as an exercise for the reader.

We are in a more difficult position to determine precisely the content of Modalist doctrine, as compared to Arianism or orthodox Trinitarianism, due to lack of evidence. No complete modalist writings survive; what we have are fragments quoted by the church fathers and descriptions of their views by the church fathers. And the Fathers may not always have shared our concern for charitably interpreting one's opponents. Perhaps because of this, or perhaps for some other reasons, a certain interpretation of modalism has been quite popular. I have misgivings about the historical accuracy of that account, but since we will be able to do well enough with the standard account, I will not explore the issue, but will simply label the standard account of modalism "Naïve Modalism" (NM) and merely note that, in my opinion, there were probably at least some versions of modalism that were more sophisticated.

Now, what seems to me the less charitable interpretation (or perhaps a perfectly good interpretation of a much less plausible *version* of modalism) can be seen in passages such as this one from St. Basil:

> For they get tripped up [thinking] that the Father is the same as the Son, and that the Son is the same as the Father, and similarly also the Holy Spirit, so that there is one person, but three names.[36]

Similar statements can be found in other patristic descriptions of Sabellianism (as well as the related heresies of Praxaeus, Noetius, etc.)

If we today were to say that "Samuel Clemens" and "Mark Twain" are two names for the same person, then we would express that in PLI by making, say "s" in PLI have the same semantic value as "Samuel Clemens" in English, "m" in PLI have the same semantic value as "Mark Twain" in English, and asserting "s=m" in PLI. (At least, those of us who accept classical identity probably would.) So, if "Father," "Son," and "Holy Spirit" (in English, or their equivalents in Greek) are just three names for the same person, then, the persons of the Trinity are related in the way we would express using the "=" sign in PLI. So, if a Naïve Modalist accepts PLI (and he could), his view might be regimented as either of:

$\Phi_{NM\text{-}1}$:		$\Phi_{NM\text{-}2}$:	
$(1_{NM\text{-}1})$	$f=g$	$(1_{NM\text{-}2})$	Gf
$(2_{NM\text{-}1})$	$s=g$	$(2_{NM\text{-}2})$	Gs
$(3_{NM\text{-}1})$	$h=g$	$(3_{NM\text{-}2})$	Gh
$(4_{NM\text{-}1})$	$f=s$	$(4_{NM\text{-}2})$	$f=s$

---

[36] [23, pp. 308–310]. Translation mine.

$(5_{\text{NM-1}})$ f=h $\qquad\qquad$ $(5_{\text{NM-2}})$ f=h
$(6_{\text{NM-1}})$ s=h $\qquad\qquad$ $(6_{\text{NM-2}})$ s=h
$(7_{\text{NM-1}})$ $(\exists x)(\forall y)(x=g$ & $(y=g \rightarrow y=x))$ $\quad$ $(7_{\text{NM-2}})$ $(\exists x)(\forall y)(Gx$ & $(Gy \rightarrow y=x))$

And we can give a proposed NM solution to the LPT as:

1. PLI is a formally adequate language for P.

2. At least one of $\Phi_{\text{NM-1}}$ in PLI or $\Phi_{\text{NM-2}}$ in PLI is a formally adequate regimentation for P.

3. Both $\Phi_{\text{NM-1}}$ and $\Phi_{\text{NM-2}}$ are formally consistent in PLI.[37]

Similar considerations to those discussed in reference to Impure RI[38] show that it doesn't matter what further logical content might be packed into the Naïve Modalist understanding of "is god" in a regimentation of P1 through P3 as long as "x is god" doesn't entail x $\neq$ f, x $\neq$ s, or x $\neq$ h. More precisely, if:

$$\phi^{t1}{}_x \models t_1 \neq f \vee t_1 \neq s \vee t_1 \neq h$$

then

$$\phi^f{}_x \ \& \ \phi^s{}_x \ \& \ \phi^h{}_x$$

is inconsistent anyway. On the other hand, if:

$$\phi^{t1}{}_x \nvDash t_1 \neq f \vee t_1 \neq s \vee t_1 \neq h$$

then

$$\phi^f{}_x \ \& \ \phi^s{}_x \ \& \ \phi^h{}_x \ \& \ f=s \ \& \ f=h \ \& \ s=h \ \& \ (\exists x)(\forall y)(\phi x \ \& \ (\phi y \rightarrow y=x))$$

is consistent.

But although both of these regimentations are consistent (given the caveat in the preceding paragraph), neither is much in the way of a regimentation of P, because however P4 through P6 ought to be analyzed, *this isn't it*. NM avoids the inconsistency of LPT_1 and LPT_2, not by so much by offering legitimate alternative regimentations of P4 through P6, but by simply *denying* them. So NM is heretical by the lights of historical orthodoxy.

---

[37]It should be obvious that there is a model for $\Phi_{\text{NM-1}}$ as well as a model for $\Phi_{\text{NM-2}}$, and each proof is left as an exercise for the reader.

[38]Section 3.1.3, above.

3.3 The Big Question

This completes our discussion of representatives of the "major" answers to the LPT that have actually been proposed, both in ancient times and in our own. The question that faces us is whether these are the *only* ways one could *possibly* solve the LPT. And if not, *what other options could there be* for the Trinitarian? If there are no other options, *how could we know that?*

Some philosophers find fault with all of the on-offer solutions to the LPT, but hold out hope for new avenues in "Trinitarian theorizing." They hold that the "business of Trinitarian theorizing" is simply "unfinished," and that there may be fresh, new ways of creatively answering (and hopefully solving) the LPT. For example, Dale Tuggy in [26] explores a few proposed Trinitarian theories, and finds fault with all of them. However, at least at the time of writing that paper, he still held out hope. "We Christian theologians and philosophers came up with the doctrine of the Trinity; perhaps with God's help we will come up with a better version of it."[39]

I think that sentiment is not atypical of many philosophers in the field. But could there really be any *importantly different* solution to the LPT? Something that is neither a form of RI nor of ST? Is there hope that further "Trinitarian theorizing" may someday pay off in a creative, new way of understanding the Trinity, heretofore undreamt of, and that avoids the anti-Trinitarian's criticisms in some previously unimagined way? Is "the business of Trinitarian theorizing" really "unfinished" in this sense?

In the next section, I will argue that this is not possible. I will show that, despite the fact that there are infinitely many possible answers to the LPT, they can all be grouped together into a finite taxonomy of "Families" based on certain salient logical features. The ultimate result will be (1) a "Family" all of the members of which are logically inconsistent, (2) a "Family" all of the members of which would be either heretical or not relevant to the LPT, and (3) and (4) two "Families" that would avoid those problems, and which closely, though not precisely, map onto ST and RI, but all of which will suffer from one or the other (or both) of the difficulties with those views we have already explored. I.e., they will either (3) equivocate on "is god" between P7 on the one hand and P1 through P3 on the other, or else (4) count in a non-standard way.

Thus, the Trinitarian who hopes that further "Trinitarian theorizing" might help is out of luck. Those who find fault with the on-offer solutions for the reasons we have discussed should simply close up the shop. Those who are willing to live with one or the other (or both) of those difficulties, are already in a position to claim victory, at least with reference to the purely *logical* problem. In either case, no

---

[39][26, p. 179].

real work remains to be done on any purely *logical* problem for the doctrine of the Trinity.

4 Taxonomy of Possible Solutions

Method, Briefly

In this section, we will be grouping all of the infinitely many possible answers to the LPT together into a finite, and thus manageable, taxonomy. Here is how we will proceed. First, we will note certain key logical features of the already proposed answers to the LPT. Second, we will use these features to create a *jointly exhaustive* (though *not* mutually exclusive) taxonomy of sets, or "Families," of answers to the LPT.

Of course, there are infinitely many possible languages in which to regiment P, and within many of those languages, infinitely many sets of formulae with which to regiment P. But for the purposes of showing there to be a formally adequate solution to the LPT, it would be "overkill" to map out all of them.

For example, once we see how Pure RI avoids inconsistency by eschewing classical identity and positing alternative, relative identity relations in its place, it doesn't matter whether we go on to equivocate on "is god" among P1 through P3 or not. Once we see what minimal set of logical features of Pure RI allows it to avoid formal inconsistency, we can group together all proposed answers to the LPT that share those features into one set, or "Family," of answers to the LPT. Then we can go on to consider only other proposed answers that *do not* share those features.

We will proceed in 7 steps, plus three initial caveats.

Three Caveats

First, aside from the Pure RI-er, everyone involved in the debate seems to accept some version of PLI as a formally adequate language for P. Or in any case, they may as well. Therefore, we will continue with our "prejudice" towards PLI. Specifically, we will assume (or pretend) that: PLI is a formally adequate language for P if and only if there is such a thing as classical identity. And if we accept that PLI is a formally adequate language for P, PLI is what we will use to regiment P.[40]

---

[40] Again, nothing substantive hangs on this methodological choice. See footnote 6 at 2.1 above. Also, as I note below, even if one does find one of these three caveats problematic, we can always take answers to the LPT that exhibit one of the qualities discussed here and treat them as another "Family" in our taxonomy. See below.

Second, almost nobody involved in the debate takes it to be legitimate to equivocate on the terms "the Father," "the Son," or "the Holy Spirit." Likewise, almost nobody takes them to be anything other than singular terms, *if* there are such things as singular terms.[41] So, we will also adopt the policy that, so long as we are working within a language in which there are such things as singular terms, we will insist on treating "the Father," "the Son," and "the Holy Spirit" as singular terms, and on regimenting them univocally wherever they appear.[42] (RIL, as we have seen, has its own way of analyzing what appear to be singular terms in natural languages that gets around the too-cozy relation between singular terms and classical identity.)

Third, while both Pure and Impure RI-ers count by a relation other than classical identity, neither they nor anybody else rejects the general *schema* with which logicians typically analyze counting statements. In other words, nobody denies that a formally adequate regimentation of "There is exactly one God" would have the *schema*:

$$(7_{\text{SCHEMA}}) \quad (\exists x)(\forall y)(\phi x \;\&\; (\phi y \to y \; \mathbb{R} \; x))$$

(where $\mathbb{R}$ is a meta-linguistic variable to be filled in with a predicate standing for whatever relation we count by).

Further, it's hard to see what other schema one *could* count by. So, we will only consider answers to the logical problem of the Trinity where P7 is regimented as *some* instance of (7_{SCHEMA}), whether those instances give $\mathbb{R}$ the value of classical identity, some relative identity relation, or whatever.

It should be noted that, even if one were to disagree with *all three* of these provisos, it would by no means wreck the attempt to create a complete taxonomy of possible answers to the LPT. It would only mean that there would be, at most, an additional three Families of answers to the LPT – one Family of answers that does not treat "Father," "Son" and "Holy Spirit" as singular terms (despite accepting the formal adequacy of a language that includes singular terms) and/or equivocates on those terms, one Family that acknowledges classical identity but that for some reason

---

[41]Of course, there is an exception to every rule. See [1].

[42]In what follows, we shall always let those singular terms be, respectively, "f," "s," and "h," when we are using PLI. Strictly speaking, then, we are leaving out formulae that use other terms, other logical names, in PLI, such as "a," "b," "c," etc., to refer to the persons. To be more logically precise, we should instead use meta-linguistic variables such as "α," "β," and "γ" to range over all possible terms in the language, with the stipulation that $\alpha \neq \beta \neq \gamma$ (i.e., that the values of these meta-linguistic variables, the *terms* or "logical names," be distinct, *not* necessarily that their *bearers* be distinct, which would be the substance of P4 through P6 in all non-NM regimentations). But while this latter course is the more logically precise, it would introduce needless complexity in what will already be a complex taxonomy. So, we will simply choose always to use "f," "s," and "h," in PLI as the terms for the persons.

does not find PLI formally adequate, and one Family that regiments P7 according to some schema other than the usual one. I don't find any of those suggestions plausible enough to warrant attention, but even if I am wrong in ignoring these possibilities, we could still give a complete taxonomy of all possible answers to the LPT by simply grouping all answers to the LPT that have any of these three features into a "Bastard Step-Child Family." In what follows, appropriately enough, I will ignore the members of this family.

4.1 The LPT$_1$ Family

As we did in Section 1, suppose that in P1 through P3 we take "is God" to be univocal, treat "God" as the name of an individual, and treat "is" as the "is" of (classical) identity. Then suppose we take "is not" in P4 through P6 as univocal claims of (classical) non-identity. In this case, there is such a thing as classical identity, so we take PLI to be a formally adequate language for P, and we use it. The result is, or at least entails, LPT$_1$, or something just like LPT$_1$ except for 7$_{\text{LPT-1}}$.

But since 7$_{\text{LPT-1}}$ is not necessary in order to derive a contradiction, we will group together any proposed answers to the LPT that share the problematic features of its regimentation of P1 through P6. What exactly are those problematic features?

It might seem that the most salient feature of LPT$_1$ is that it treats "God" as a logical name instead of a predicate. But of course, a contradiction would arise even if there were another name being used besides "God." And a contradiction would arise even if we treated P1 through P3 not as identity claims, but in a way that *entailed* a certain kind of identity claim.

For example, suppose I regiment "x is God" as a predication meaning "x is divine," but then analyze "x is divine" as meaning "x is identical to Lucifer." I will still have a contradiction, and for essentially the same reasons, logically speaking, as LPT$_1$. Indeed, if there is any term t_i such that $t_i \neq$ x and my analysis of "x is God" entails "x = t_i" I will end up with a contradiction. That is because "The Father is God" will now entail "The Father = t_i" and "The Son is God" will entail "The Son = t_i." And those together will entail "The Father = the Son," and that will contradict 4$_{\text{LPT-1}}$, or anything that entails 4$_{\text{LPT-1}}$. So, we can group together any answers to the LPT that:

(1) use PLI, and

(2) give some univocal regimentation ϕ to "is God" in P1 through P3, such that

(3) $\phi\alpha \models \alpha = t_i$ for some term t_i such that $t_i \neq \alpha$, and

(4) either regiment "is not" in P4 through P6 univocally as $\neq$, or for any other reason entails $4_{\text{LPT-1}}$, $5_{\text{LPT-1}}$, and $6_{\text{LPT-1}}$

into the "LPT_1 Family."[43] Any member of the LPT_1 Family will be a non-solution to the LPT, since its analyses of P1-P3 versus P4-P6 will yield a contradiction.

So, from here on, we will only consider proposed answers to the LPT that do at least one (or more) of the following:

(1) use a language other than PLI (and so, given our "prejudice" in favor of PLI, must reject the existence of classical identity), *or*

(2) fail to give a univocal regimentation ϕ to "is god" in P1 through P3, *or*

(3) give a univocal regimentation ϕ to "is god" in P1 through P3 such that $\phi\alpha \not\models \alpha = t_i$ for any term t_i such that $t_i \neq \alpha$, *or*

(4) regiment "is not" in any of P4 through P6 in some way other than $\neq$, and do not for any other reason entail $4_{\text{LPT-1}}$, $5_{\text{LPT-1}}$, or $6_{\text{LPT-1}}$.

4.2   The Non-PLI (Pure RI) Family

We've seen how Pure RI escapes inconsistency by rejecting classical identity, and with it PLI (option (1) immediately above). This means that, *perforce*, classical identity cannot be the relation by which we count gods in P7. This is *both* a feature that allows it to escape inconsistency *and* a feature that makes it controversial.

Since we are assuming (or pretending) that PLI is a formally adequate language for P if and only if there is such a thing as classical identity, we will group together all answers to the LPT that reject classical identity, and with it PLI, into the "Non-PLI Family" of answers – the family of answers all of which choose option (1) above. Since we have already seen at least one member of the Non-PLI Family that has a logically consistent regimentation of P (our Pure RI proposed solution), we know that the Non-PLI Family contains solutions to the LPT.[44]

---

[43] 1 is strictly speaking redundant, given 3 and our "prejudice" that, as long as there is such a thing as classical identity, PLI is a formally adequate language for P, and the language we will use to regiment P.

[44] It also contains non-solutions, but that will not matter for our concerns, since our taxonomy provides a kind of "process of elimination" proof. And if one rejects a particular proposed answer to the LPT as not formally adequate *because* that answer eschews classical identity and PLI, then one should reject *all* proposed answers to the LPT that eschew classical identity and PLI as not being formally adequate, and thus one should reject all proposed answers that fall within this Family.

So, from here on, we will only consider proposed answers to the LPT that accept the existence of classical identity and that (therefore, given our "prejudice" towards PLI) use PLI as the language in which to regiment P.

4.3 The Naïve Modalist Family (and Cousins)

We've seen how NM escapes inconsistency by analyzing P4 through P6 in such a way as to essentially *reject* them. Again, this is *both* a feature that allows it to escape inconsistency *and* a feature that makes it controversial (actually, in this case, heretical).

A related move would be to regiment P4 through P6 in a a non-committal way that simply *does not entail* any of the relevant classical identity claims, i.e. $4_{\text{LPT-1}}$, $5_{\text{LPT-1}}$, or $6_{\text{LPT-1}}$, despite accepting that there is such a thing as classical identity, thus falling into option (4) above.

We've seen that orthodox Trinitarians intend to draw a strong, real distinction between the persons. And, assuming classical non-identity exists, it is the *weakest* real distinction that can be drawn. So, if the orthodox Trinitarian accepts the existence of classical (non-)identity, he himself will insist on regimenting P4 through P6 as classical non-identity claims ($4_{\text{LPT-1}}$, $5_{\text{LPT-1}}$, and $6_{\text{LPT-1}}$). And if the orthodox Trinitarian wanted to analyze P4 through P6 as drawing an *even stronger* distinction than classical non-identity, he would still at least *accept* $4_{\text{LPT-1}}$, $5_{\text{LPT-1}}$, and $6_{\text{LPT-1}}$. Indeed, if his preferred analysis involved a stronger distinction, he would no doubt insist that, in some way or another, his preferred analysis at least *entails* $4_{\text{LPT-1}}$, $5_{\text{LPT-1}}$, and $6_{\text{LPT-1}}$. Thus, we will group together all proposed answers to the LPT that (a) accept the existence of classical (non-)identity, but (b) do *not* entail all of $4_{\text{LPT-1}}$, $5_{\text{LPT-1}}$, and $6_{\text{LPT-1}}$, into the "Naïve Modalist Family" ("NM Family") of answers.[45] Since we have already seen at least one member of the NM Family that has a logically consistent regimentation of P, we know that the NM Family contains solutions to the LPT.[46]

---

[45] A bit of logical housekeeping is in order. What about an answer to the LPT that, say, entails $5_{\text{LPT-1}}$ and $6_{\text{LPT-1}}$, but fails to entail $4_{\text{LPT-1}}$? Thus, the Holy Spirit would be distinct from the Father and from the Son, but the Father aned Son could be identical, a possibility St. Photios calls "a semi-Sabellian monstrosity" in his arguments against the *filioque*, [18, p. 73]. As we've defined the NM Family (any regimentation that does not entail $4_{\text{LPT-1}}$, $5_{\text{LPT-1}}$, *and* $6_{\text{LPT-1}}$ – all three), it includes such "semi-Sabellian monstrosities." And this seems like a reasonable grouping. Clearly the orthodox Trinitarian wants to understand P4 through P6 univocally. Any kind of semi-Sabellian view is just about as bad, from the point of view of orthodoxy, as all-out Sabellianism.

Of course, this will mean some members of the NM Family will still be inconsistent, and for just the same reasons (at least some subset of the same reasons) as LPT_1 is. But that is fine. All we are claiming here is that *some* members of the NM Family are consistent – not that all of them are.

[46] Again, it also contains non-solutions, but that will not matter for our concerns, since the

Note that defining the NM Family this way means there will be certain "cousins" of Naïve Modalism included in the NM Family that will regiment, for example, "the Father is not the Son" simply as some "ho-hum" relation, "f R s," that neither commits us to the classical identity of the persons (characteristic of NM), *nor* the classical non-identity of the persons (characteristic of orthodox Trinitarianism). Is it right to include such non-committal answers in the NM Family?

I think so. Again, the *intent* of the orthodox Trinitarian in saying that "the Father is not the Son," is to draw a strong, real distinction between the two, and, at least within a framework that accepts classical non-identity in the first place, classical non-identity will be the weakest real distinction there is. Thus, any regimentation of "is not" that does not even *entail* classical non-identity (within a framework that admits the existence of classical non-identity) clearly subverts the intent of the claim. Or in any case, it clearly fails to say what the orthodox Trinitarian wants to be saying when he says "the Father is not the Son." On the other hand, regimentations of "is not" in P4 through P6 that are *not* classical non-identity statements but that *do* entail them will still be inconsistent with anything that $4_{\text{LPT-1}}$, $5_{\text{LPT-1}}$, and $6_{\text{LPT-1}}$ are inconsistent with anyway (since they will entail $4_{\text{LPT-1}}$, $5_{\text{LPT-1}}$, and $6_{\text{LPT-1}}$).

So, from here on, we will only consider proposed answers to the LPT that do not reject P4 through P6 and that either *do* regiment them univocally as classical non-identity claims between the persons, or else as some formula χ that in some other way at least *entails* those classical non-identity claims.

That means that at this point we can "lock in" our regimentation of P4 through P6 as:

$(4_{\text{LPT-2-FAMILY}})$ χ_1 such that $\chi_1 \models f \neq s$
$(5_{\text{LPT-2-FAMILY}})$ χ_2 such that $\chi_2 \models f \neq h$
$(6_{\text{LPT-2-FAMILY}})$ χ_3 such that $\chi_3 \models s \neq h$

4.4 The Equivocation₁ Family

We've seen how Arianism escapes inconsistency by equivocating on "is god" among P1 through P3 (option (2) above). Again, this is *both* a feature that allows it to escape inconsistency *and* a feature that makes it controversial or problematic, though not in exactly the same way as NM.

In the case of NM, it is clear that the same formal feature that allows it to escape inconsistency makes it (unavoidably) heretical. That is to say, NM avoids inconsistency by admitting the strict identity of the persons, but there is no way

orthodox Trinitarian must reject *all* answers in this Family as heretical. Being a non-solution to the LPT is only *more* reason for the orthodox Trinitarian to reject a proposed answer to the LPT.

one could strictly identify the divine persons (in the sense of classical identity) and not fall into the heresy of Modalism. And strict identity (at least within PLI) is part of the purely *formal* apparatus of the language. Thus, here a purely formal, logical feature lands us in heresy, regardless of how we interpret the non-logical vocabulary.[47] Is the same the case with the characteristic equivocation that allows Arianism to escape inconsistency?

Trinitarians clearly want to say that the Father and Son share the same divine nature. However, if we are considering purely *formal* features, we cannot assume any particular semantic value for "god" or "divine." In particular, we cannot assume that "god" or "divine" must mean "a thing with the divine nature." Supposing it did, the equivocation here would certainly yield a heretical result. But, for one thing, a long line of Christian authors, from St. Justin Martyr up through St. Gregory of Nyssa, and beyond, deny that "god" means "thing with the divine nature."[48] We are thus in fact in a quite different situation with respect to the non-logical vocabulary "god" or "divine" that relates to Arianism, as opposed to the "is" and "is not" that relates to Modalism, since "is" counts as "logical" vocabulary, regardless of which sense of "is" it is, whereas "god" and "divine" are obviously part of the non-logical vocabulary, and thus take us into substantive questions of semantics, rather than purely formal questions. It is also the case that there is a sense in which many even of the pro-Nicenes would say that the Father alone is "the One God."[49] On the other hand, no orthodox Trinitarian would say that the persons are strictly identical. However, we can say that, in the sense in which the Father alone is "the One God," the Son and Spirit are simply *other than* the One God.[50] And in that case, the LPT simply does not arise in the first place. Thus, it is only in senses of the word "god" such that each person *does* count (univocally) as "(a) god" that the LPT even becomes an issue. And the fact that there may be *some* sense in which the Father alone is "the One God" does nothing to solve the LPT, so long as there is *any* sense

---

[47]Of course, strictly speaking it is not *purely* a matter of logical form that makes the propositions heretical! Rather, it is the fact that we are holding constant our uses of "Father" or "f," "Son" or "s," and "Holy Spirit" or "h." That bit of non-logical content *plus* the purely logical machinery of classical identity is what gives us heresy. But again, we are ignoring interpretations of P that treat these names in any other way.

[48]See [2, pp. 134–151]. Available at www.beaubranson.com/research.

[49]The Nicene Creed itself begins, "I believe in One God, the Father," and statements can be found in St. Athanasius and all three Cappadocian fathers to the effect that the One God is the Father. For a fuller explanation of this sort of view, see [4].

[50]E.g., Gregory Nazianzen, *Carmina Dogmatica* 1, *On the Father* says, "There is one God without source, without cause, uncircumscribed...the mighty Father of a mighty, Only-Begotten, and faithful Son...The Logos of God is *other than* the One God, but not other *in divinity*." (PG 37. Translation mine; emphasis mine.)

of the term "god" that applies to all of the persons univocally. And certainly any Trinitarian would say that there is *some* such sense.

Thus, what we can say is not that there is *no* sense in which one can equivocate on the predicate "is god" among P1 and P3 and remain within the bounds of orthodoxy, but that *there is some sense* in which the predicate "is god" applies univocally to the persons in P1 through P3 (at least, by the lights of orthodox Trinitarianism). And it is this sense (or these senses, if there are multiple such senses), which give rise to the LPT and which we therefore have in view when discussing the LPT. Any sense of the predicate "is god" which would apply only to the Father simply would not give rise to the LPT in the first place. It is only those senses of "is god" that should apply to all of the persons equally, if they apply to them at all, that we have in view here. Thus, while not all analyses of P that equivocate on the predicate "is god" among P1 and P3 are necessarily heretical, they are all *either* heretical *or* irrelevant to the LPT (since they would not be the sense(s) that give rise to the LPT in the first place).

So, we will group together all answers to the LPT that equivocate on the predicate "is god" among P1 through P3 into the "Equivocation$_1$ Family" of answers. Since we have already seen at least one member of the Equivocation$_1$ Family that has a logically consistent regimentation for P, we know that the Equivocation$_1$ Family contains solutions to the LPT.[51]

So, from here on, we will only consider proposed answers to the LPT that do *not* equivocate on "is god" among P1 through P3.

Thus, we can now "lock in" at least the univocality of our regimentation of P1 through P3 as follows:

($1_{\text{LPT-2-FAMILY}}$) ϕf such that $\phi \alpha \nvDash \alpha = t_i$ for any term t_i such that $t_i \neq \alpha$
($2_{\text{LPT-2-FAMILY}}$) ϕs such that $\phi \alpha \nvDash \alpha = t_i$ for any term t_i such that $t_i \neq \alpha$
($3_{\text{LPT-2-FAMILY}}$) ϕh such that $\phi \alpha \nvDash \alpha = t_i$ for any term t_i such that $t_i \neq \alpha$

Why will ϕ be such that $\phi \alpha \nvDash \alpha = t_i$ for any term t_i such that $t_i \neq \alpha$? After Step 1 we decided to only consider answers to the LPT that do one of the following:

(1) use a language other than PLI (and so reject the existence of classical identity), *or*

(2) fail to give a univocal regimentation ϕ to "is god" in P1 through P3, *or*

---

[51] Again, it also contains non-solutions, but that will not matter for our concerns, since the orthodox Trinitarian must reject *all* answers in this Family as *either* heretical *or* as pertaining to an interpretation of "god" that is not relevant to the LPT. Being a non-solution to the LPT is only *more* reason for the orthodox Trinitarian to reject a proposed answer to the LPT.

(3) give a univocal regimentation ϕ to "is god" in P1 through P3 such that $\phi\alpha \nvDash \alpha = t_i$ for any term t_i such that $t_i \neq \alpha$, *or*

(4) regiment "is not" in any of P4 through P6 in some way other than $\neq$, and do not for any other reason entail $4_{\text{LPT-1}}$, $5_{\text{LPT-1}}$, or $6_{\text{LPT-1}}$.

After Step 2 we decided only to consider proposed answers to the LPT that do use PLI (so, option (1) is no longer open). After Step 3 we decided only to consider proposed answers to the LPT that *do* regiment "is not" in P4 through P6 as $\neq$ (or at least for some other reason entail $4_{\text{LPT-1}}$, $5_{\text{LPT-1}}$, and $6_{\text{LPT-1}}$) (so, option (4) is no longer open). And after Step 4, we decided to no longer consider answers to the LPT that equivocate on their regimentation of "is god" among P1 through P3 (so, option (2) is no longer open).

But since we are only considering answers to the LPT that choose at least *one* of the above four options, we can from now on only consider answers that take option (3), that is, that give a univocal regimentation ϕ to "is God" in P1 through P3, but such that $\phi\alpha \nvDash \alpha = t_i$, for any term t_i such that $t_i \neq \alpha$.

Since $\phi\alpha \nvDash \alpha = t_i$, for any term t_i such that $t_i \neq \alpha$, it will not contradict any of:

($4_{\text{LPT-2-FAMILY}}$) χ_1 such that $\chi_1 \vDash f \neq s$
($5_{\text{LPT-2-FAMILY}}$) χ_2 such that $\chi_2 \vDash f \neq h$
($6_{\text{LPT-2-FAMILY}}$) χ_3 such that $\chi_3 \vDash s \neq h$

simply on the basis of the non-identity claims. That is, whatever other logical form may be buried within χ_1, χ_2, and χ_3, could still generate a contradiction, but the non-identity claims themselves will not.

So, from here on out, we know we are dealing with families of answers to the LPT such that their regimentations of P1 through P6 will be consistent barring any problematic logical features that might be tucked away in the regimentation of "is not" beyond mere non-identity. Their regimentations of P1 through P6 will certainly be consistent if "is not" in P4 through P6 is simply analyzed univocally as classical non-identity.

So, our focus now will be on the regimentation of P7. It is here that we will see why ST and RI have seemed intuitively like the only options or the "major" options. Aside from the Non-PLI Family, the Families we have considered so far have all been either inconsistent, heretical, or irrelevant to the LPT. The remaining two Families will map onto ST and Impure RI in a certain sense. We will later consolidate these into just two Families that roughly map onto ST and (Pure or Impure) RI.

4.5 The Equivocation$_2$ Family (Social Trinitarian)

We've seen how Social Trinitarianism escapes inconsistency by equivocating on "is god" between P7 on the one hand, and P1 through P3 on the other. Again, this is *both* a feature that allows it to escape inconsistency *and* a feature that makes it controversial.

So we will group together all such answers to the LPT into the "Equivocation$_2$ Family" of answers.[52]

Proposed solutions of this variety, therefore, will give regimentations of the form:

$(1_{\text{LPT-2-FAMILY}})$ ϕf such that $\phi\alpha \not\models \alpha = t_i$ for any term t_i such that $t_i \neq \alpha$
$(2_{\text{LPT-2-FAMILY}})$ ϕs such that $\phi\alpha \not\models \alpha = t_i$ for any term t_i such that $t_i \neq \alpha$
$(3_{\text{LPT-2-FAMILY}})$ ϕh such that $\phi\alpha \not\models \alpha = t_i$ for any term t_i such that $t_i \neq \alpha$
$(4_{\text{LPT-2-FAMILY}})$ χ_1 such that $\chi_1 \models$ f $\neq$ s
$(5_{\text{LPT-2-FAMILY}})$ χ_2 such that $\chi_2 \models$ f $\neq$ h
$(6_{\text{LPT-2-FAMILY}})$ χ_3 such that $\chi_3 \models$ s $\neq$ h
$(7_{\text{SCHEMA-}\psi})$ $(\exists x) (\forall y) (\psi x \ \& \ (\psi y \rightarrow y \ \mathbb{R} \ x))$

That is, the regimentation ϕ of "is god" for P1 through P3 will be different from the regimentation ψ of "is god" in P7. As we said earlier, not all such answers to the LPT will involve anything particularly "social." Equivocation is the salient *logical* feature of ST that allows it to escape contradiction.

Since we have already seen at least one member of the Equivocation$_2$ Family that has a logically consistent regimentation, we know that the Equivocation$_2$ Family contains solutions to LPT.[53]

So, from here on, we will only consider proposed answers to the LPT that do *not* equivocate on "is god" between P7 on the one hand, and P1 through P3 on the other.

---

[52]Note that, as we are defining the Equivocation$_2$ Family, it *is* necessary that a member of the Equivocation$_2$ Family family equivocate on "is god," but it is *not* necessary that it employ classical identity. A view that *both* equivocates in this way *and* employs a relation other than classical identity here would still fall into the Equivocation$_2$ Family as we are defining it. Of course, if one finds it more useful, one could have a separate "hybrid" family, the members of which would both equivocate on "is god" and count by a relation other than classical identity, then have a "pure" Equivocation$_2$ Family, the members of which equivocate on "is god" and *do* count by classical identity. For now, I will find it more convenient simply to group these all together into one Equivocation$_2$ Family, albeit a family, like Joseph's, that is "splittable" into the half-tribes of "Pure Equivocation$_2$ Family" and "Hybrid Equivocation$_2$ Family."

[53]Again, it also contains non-solutions, but that will not matter for our concerns, since anyone who objects to the characteristic equivocation involved here must reject *all* of the proposed answers in this Family. Being a non-solution to the LPT is only *more* reason for the orthodox Trinitarian to reject a proposed answer to the LPT.

But we have already "locked in" regimentations of P1 through P6. And we are no longer considering proposed answers to the LPT that equivocate on "is god" between P7 on the one hand, and P1 through P3 on the other. So, however we regiment "is god" in P1 through P3, it will have to be the same as our regimentation of "is god" in P7. And since we are assuming that counting works according to the usual schema (only the precise relation may be disputed), we can now "lock in" regimentations of all of P1 through P7 as:

$(1_{\text{LPT-2-FAMILY}})$ ϕf such that $\phi\alpha \not\models \alpha = t_i$ for any term t_i such that $t_i \neq \alpha$
$(2_{\text{LPT-2-FAMILY}})$ ϕs such that $\phi\alpha \not\models \alpha = t_i$ for any term t_i such that $t_i \neq \alpha$
$(3_{\text{LPT-2-FAMILY}})$ ϕh such that $\phi\alpha \not\models \alpha = t_i$ for any term t_i such that $t_i \neq \alpha$
$(4_{\text{LPT-2-FAMILY}})$ χ_1 such that $\chi_1 \models$ f $\neq$ s
$(5_{\text{LPT-2-FAMILY}})$ χ_2 such that $\chi_2 \models$ f $\neq$ h
$(6_{\text{LPT-2-FAMILY}})$ χ_3 such that $\chi_3 \models$ s $\neq$ h
$(7_{\text{SCHEMA-}\phi})$ $(\exists x)(\forall y)(\phi x \,\&\, (\phi y \rightarrow y\,\mathbb{R}\,x))$
  (such that $\phi\alpha \not\models \alpha = t_i$ for any term t_i such that $t_i \neq \alpha$)

leaving open only the question of precisely what relation "$\mathbb{R}$" will represent in $(7_{\text{SCHEMA-}\phi})$.

4.6   The Non-Classical-Identity-Counting Family

We've seen how Impure RI escapes inconsistency by claiming that our counting practices (at least sometimes) employ some relation(s) other than classical identity. Again, this is *both* a feature that allows it to escape inconsistency *and* a feature that makes it controversial.

We are assuming that the logical form of "is god" is not itself formally contradictory and that it does not entail a classical identity claim to some single individual.[54] Thus, as long as the relation we give for $\mathbb{R}$ in $(7_{\text{SCHEMA-}\phi})$ is not classical identity and as long as y $\mathbb{R}$ x does not *entail* y=x, no contradiction will be derivable.

So, we will group together all answers to the LPT that analyze counting statements *via* a relation other than classical identity, and that do not entail classical identity, into the "Non-Classical-Identity-Counting Family" ("NCIC Family") of answers.[55] Since we have already seen at least one member of the NCIC Family that

---

[54] Again, the assumption that the logical form of "is god" is not in itself contradictory is redundant, given the assumption that it doesn't entail a certain kind of identity claim. A contradiction entails anything.

[55] Note that this means that Pure RI will fall into *both* the Non-PLI Family *and* the NCIC Family. That is fine, since this is only intended to be a jointly exhaustive, not mutually exclusive, taxonomy of answers to the LPT. I will have more to say about this below under the heading "Consolidating

has a logically consistent regimentation of P, we know that the NCIC Family contains solutions to the LPT.[56]

So, from here on, we will only consider proposed answers to the LPT that *do* count by classical identity. But since we are assuming that counting works according to the usual schema, and since we are not equivocating on "is god" between P7 on the one hand, and P1 through P3 on the other, if we use classical identity as the relation to count by in P7, we can fill in the variable $\mathbb{R}$ in:

$(7_{\text{SCHEMA-}\phi})$ $(\exists x)(\forall y)(\phi x \mathbin{\&} (\phi y \rightarrow y \mathbb{R} x))$

with "=" and have:

$(7_{\text{LPT-2-FAMILY}})$ $(\exists x)(\forall y)(\phi x \mathbin{\&} (\phi y \rightarrow y = x))$

(And if we used any other relation R such that R *entails* classical identity, then our regimentation of P7, whatever it might be, would still at least *entail* $(7_{\text{LPT-2-FAMILY}})$.)

Thus, we are now out of formally consistent alternatives to LPT_1. We can now "lock in" our entire regimentation of P1 through P7 as:

4.7 The LPT_2 Family

$(1_{\text{LPT-2-FAMILY}})$ ϕf such that $\phi \alpha \nvDash \alpha = t_i$ for any term t_i such that $t_i \neq \alpha$
$(2_{\text{LPT-2-FAMILY}})$ ϕs such that $\phi \alpha \nvDash \alpha = t_i$ for any term t_i such that $t_i \neq \alpha$
$(3_{\text{LPT-2-FAMILY}})$ ϕh such that $\phi \alpha \nvDash \alpha = t_i$ for any term t_i such that $t_i \neq \alpha$
$(4_{\text{LPT-2-FAMILY}})$ χ_1 such that $\chi_1 \vDash f \neq s$
$(5_{\text{LPT-2-FAMILY}})$ χ_2 such that $\chi_2 \vDash f \neq h$
$(6_{\text{LPT-2-FAMILY}})$ χ_3 such that $\chi_3 \vDash s \neq h$
$(7_{\text{LPT-2-FAMILY-SCHEMA}})$ $(\exists x)(\forall y)(\phi x \mathbin{\&} (\phi y \rightarrow y \mathbb{R} x))$
(such that $\phi \alpha \nvDash \alpha = t_i$ for any term t_i such that $t_i \neq \alpha$)
(such that $y \mathbb{R} x \vDash y = x$)

All proposed answers to the LPT that fall into the LPT_2 Family will be non-solutions.[57]

---

our Taxonomy of Proposed Answers," section 5.

[56] Again, it also contains non-solutions, but that will not matter for our concerns, since anyone who rejects the view that counting works by way of some relation other than classical identity must reject *all* answers in this Family anyway. Being a non-solution to the LPT is only *more* reason for the orthodox Trinitarian to reject a proposed answer to the LPT.

[57] Proof is left as an exercise for the reader.

5   Consolidating our Taxonomy of Proposed Answers

Finally, we can usefully reduce the number of options by grouping together some of these families of answers in three steps, as follows.

(1) Anti-Trinitarians need not be picky about whether it is some member of the LPT$_1$ Family or of the LPT$_2$ Family that is formally adequate. If any member of either of these families is formally adequate for P, then P is inconsistent, and the anti-Trinitarians win. So we can combine these Familes into one and talk simply of the "LPT Family."

This leaves only 6 families of answers to the LPT.

(2) Orthodox Trinitarians will want to reject *all* of the answers in the NM Family as heretical and all of the answers in the Equivocation$_1$ Family as either heretical (if "(a) god" is intended to mean a thing with the divine nature, or something else shared by the persons) or else as dealing with a sense of "god" that isn't what gives rise to the LPT in the first place. If any member of either of these Families is formally adequate for P (under an interpretation that is relevant to the LPT in the first place) then the orthodox conception of the Trinity is incorrect, and the heretics win. Thus, we can usefully group all of these answers together into one "CTH Family." (And since we are including the Equivocation$_1$ Family into the CTH Family, we will also now allow ourselves to refer to the Equivocation$_2$ Family simply as "the Equivocation Family.")

This leaves only 5 families of answers to the LPT.

Note that, while we define the LPT Family and the CTH Family as above, we do so with the caveat that while *all* members of the LPT Family are inconsistent, and *all* members of the CTH Family are either heretical or irrelevant, not all inconsistent regimentations of P (all non-solutions to the LPT) go into the LPT Family, and not all heretical views about the Trinity go into the CTH Family. (One can usefully think of the LPT Family, then, as the *Purely* Inconsistent Family, and the CTH Family as the *Purely* Heretical or Irrelevant Family. Regimentations of P found in other families of answers to the logical problem of the Trinity could still be inconsistent for other reasons, or be used to express heretical views about the Trinity once the content is filled in.)[58] The point is simply that the Trinitarian must reject *all* the members of the LPT Family and *all* the members of the CTH Family. Doing so is a necessary, but not a sufficient, condition for the Trinitarian to "win" the debate.

(3) Finally, by rejecting classical identity altogether, Pure RI perforce counts by a relation other than classical identity. That is the characteristic feature of Impure RI that allows it to escape contradiction. But from the point of view of formal

---

[58]"God is good" and "God is evil" have the same logical form. So clearly there is more to heresy and orthodoxy than simply logical form!

consistency, it is really irrelevant whether one then goes on to accept or reject the existence of classical identity and the formal adequacy of PLI. That is, as long as a Pure RI answer agrees with an Impure RI answer in its regimentation of P7,[59] as involving a relation other than classical identity, and which *doesn't entail* classical identity (and Pure RI must agree with Impure RI about that), and as long as whatever formula ϕ it uses in its regimentations of P1 through P3 (or its equivalent of P1 through P3) is such that $\phi\alpha \nvDash \alpha = t_i$ for any term t_i such that $t_i \neq \alpha$ (and Pure RI *must* agree with Impure RI about that as well), then it is irrelevant whether we say that there is such a thing as classical identity or not. And it is irrelevant whether we regiment P4 through P6 as involving classical non-identity or not.[60]

Furthermore, since we grouped together all answers to the LPT that claim that counting works by some relation other than classical identity, and that does not entail classical identity, into the NCIC Family of answers, Pure RI is already included in it anyway.[61]

We can see that the appearance of Pure RI being importantly distinct from Impure RI (in a sense relevant simply to the question of formal consistency at least) is an illusion. Pure RI may have *rhetorical* (or other) advantages over Impure RI. But any advantages it may have are not *formal*.

The rejection of PLI is in itself controversial. And all proposed answers to the LPT that fall into the Non-PLI Family also fall into the NCIC Family. Thus, we can eliminate talk about the Non-PLI Family and simply speak about the NCIC Family.

That leaves only 4 families of answers to the LPT,[62] namely:

(1) the Equivocation Family,

(2) the NCIC Family,

(3) the CTH Family, and

(4) the LPT Family.[63]

All answers in the LPT Family (4) are non-solutions. All answers in the CTH Family (3) will be unusable by the orthodox Trinitarian, or irrelevant to the LPT. So,

---

[59]Or that part of its regimentation that is parallel to P7, see section 3.1.2, above

[60]Or the Pure RI equivalent of P4 through P6.

[61]This is one example of why the categories of our taxonomy are jointly exhaustive, but not mutually exclusive.

[62]Aside from the Bastard Stepchild Family, which we are, appropriately enough, ignoring.

[63]Again, we are ignoring the Bastard Step-Child Family. But if one wants to take these sorts of regimentations seriously, one can simply add them in as a fifth family of answers to the LPT. The features that lead me to ignore them altogether would then simply count as more "controversial" features, since they are at least that.

if the orthodox Trinitarian wants to give an analysis of P, that is, an interpretation of S, that is both (a) non-heretical and (b) offers a *solution* (rather than a non-solution) to the LPT, it must fall into either:

(1) the Equivocation Family, which equivocates on "is god" between P7 on the one hand, and P1 through P3 on the other hand, or

(2) the NCIC Family, which counts by a relation other than classical identity.[64]

So, as promised above (section 1.2), although there are infinitely many logical forms one could attribute to P, we have created an exhaustive taxonomy of all possible logical forms attributable to P based precisely on the logical features of the major proposed answers to the LPT that cause them to be either inconsistent, heretical or controversial. Although the result does not map onto Social Trinitarianism and Relative Identity Trintiarianism precisely, the taxonomy allows one to see why these two approaches might appear to be the only viable ones, as well as the ways in which a possible solution might subtly differ from proposals given so far. (Specifically, there could be other members of the Equivocation Family in which the non-logical content doesn't necessarily have to do with "centers of consciousness," "divine societies," etc., and there could be other members of the NCIC Family that count by various other relations.)

6 Conclusion

Anyone who takes the "business of Trinitarian theorizing" to be "unfinished" in the sense that there may be new solutions to the purely *formal* difficulty with the doctrine of the Trinity is out of luck. Every answer to the LPT must fall into one (or more) of the categories we have discussed. Only two of these categories contain any solutions to the LPT that are non-heretical. These two categories do indeed roughly correspond to the usual divide between Social Trinitarianism and Relative Identity Trinitarianism, though there is room for additional proposals that may differ in the specific content they employ.

However, anyone who rejects ST *on the basis of* its characteristic equivocation must reject *all* answers in the Equivocation Family. And anyone who rejects RI *on*

---

[64]It could fall into both, since, again, these categories are jointly exhaustive but *not* mutually exclusive. If one prefers a mutually exclusive taxonomy here, one could stipulate that the NCIC Family *not* equivocate on "is god," then split the Equivocation$_2$ Family into the "pure" and "hybrid" ST families, and relabel them as the "pure NCIC Family," "pure ST family" and "hybrid family," respectively.

the basis of its analysis of counting must reject *all* answers in the NCIC Family. The Trinitarian speculations of philosophers might help with the *metaphysics* of the Trinity, with establishing the Biblical basis for it, or with some rhetorical or other issue. But from a purely *formal* point of view, they will always be just another member of one of the Families of answers to the LPT we have defined here, and will necessarily share the controversial features that define those families.

References

[1] H. E. Baber. Trinity, filioque and semantic ascent. *Sophia*, 47(2):149 – 160, 2008.

[2] Beau Branson. *The Logical Problem of the Trinity*. Dissertation, University of Notre Dame, 2014.

[3] Beau Branson. Ahistoricity in analytic theology. *American Catholic Philosophical Quarterly*, 92(1):195–224, 2018.

[4] Beau Branson. The neglected doctrine of the monarchy of the father, and its implications for the analytic debate about the trinity. *Ephemerides Theologicae Lovanienses*, forthcoming.

[5] Jeffrey Brower and Michael Rea. Material constitution and the trinity. *Faith and Philosophy*, 22(1):57–76, 2005.

[6] Jeffrey Brower and Michael Rea. Understanding the trinity. *Logos: A Journal of Catholic Thought and Culture*, 8(1):145–157, 2005.

[7] James Cain. The doctrine of the trinity and the logic of relative identity. *Religious Studies*, 25(2):141–152, 1989.

[8] Richard Cartwright. On the logical problem of the trinity. *Philosophical Essays*, pages 187–200, 1987.

[9] Fred Feldman and Peter Geach. Geach and relative identity (with rejoinder and reply). *The Review of Metaphysics*, 22(3):547–561, 1969.

[10] Peter Thomas Geach. Identity. *The Review of Metaphysics*, 21(1):3 – 12, 1967.

[11] Peter Thomas Geach. *Reference and Generality: An Examination of Some Medieval and Modern Theories*. Cornell University Press, Ithaca, New York, 1968.

[12] Peter Thomas Geach. *Logic Matters*. University of California Press, Berkeley, 1972.

[13] Peter Thomas Geach. Ontological relativity and relative identity. In Milton Karl Munitz, editor, *Logic and Ontology*. New York University Press, New York, 1973.

[14] Brian Leftow. Anti social trinitarianism. In Stephen T. Davis, Daniel Kendall, and Gerald O'Collins, editors, *The Trinity : An Interdisciplinary Symposium on the Trinity*, pages 203–249. Oxford Univ Press, 1999.

[15] A. P. Martinich. Identity and trinity. *The Journal of Religion*, 58(2):169–181, 1978.

[16] A. P. Martinich. God, emperor and relative identity. *Franciscan Studies*, 39(1):180–191, 1979.

[17] Michael Murray and Michael Rea. Philosophy and christian theology. In Edward N. Zalta, editor, *The Stanford Encyclopedia of Philosophy*. The Metaphysics Research Lab, Stanford, CA, 2012.

[18] Photius. *On the Mystagogy of the Holy Spirit*. Studion Publishers, 1983. Includes "Saint Photios and the Filioque" by Michael Azkoul and "The Life of Saint Photios the Great" by St. Justin Popovich, translated by Ronald Wertz.

[19] Michael Rea. Relative identity and the doctrine of the trinity. *Philosophia Christi*, 5(2):431 – 445, 2003.

[20] Michael Rea. Polytheism and christian belief. *Journal of Theological Studies*, 57:133–48, 2006.

[21] Michael Rea. *Oxford Readings in Philosophical Theology 1. 1.* Oxford Univ. Press, Oxford, 2009.

[22] Michael Rea. The trinity. In *The Oxford Handbook of Philosophical Theology*, pages 403–429. Oxford, Oxford University Press, 2009.

[23] St. Basil the Great. *Bibliothek der Symbole und Glaubensregeln der Alten Kirche*. E. Morgenstern, Breslau, 3 edition, 1897.

[24] St. Cyril of Jerusalem and St. Gregory Nazianzen. *A Select Library of Nicene and Post-Nicene Fathers of the Christian Church: S. Cyril of Jerusalem. S. Gregory Nazianzen.*, volume 7 of *A Select Library of Nicene and Post-Nicene Fathers of the Christian Church: Second Series*. Christian literature Company, Oxford; New York, 1894.

[25] St. Gregory Nazianzen. *Die Fünf Theologischen Reden; Text und Übersetzung mit Einleitung und Kommentar*. Patmos-Verlag, Dusseldorf, 1963.

[26] Dale Tuggy. The unfinished business of trinitarian theorizing. *Religious Studies*, 39(2):165–183, 2003.

[27] Dale Tuggy. On positive mysterianism. *International Journal for Philosophy of Religion*, 69(3):205–226, 2011.

[28] Peter van Inwagen. And yet they are not three gods but one god. In Thomas Morris, editor, *Philosophy and the Christian Faith*, pages 241–278. University of Notre Dame Press, 1988.

[29] Peter van Inwagen. Three persons in one being: On attempts to show that the doctrine of the trinity is self-contradictory. In Melville Y. Stewart, editor, *The Holy Trinity*, pages 83–97. Springer, 2003.

Received 27 May 2019

What Means 'Tri-' in 'Trinity'? An Eastern Patristic Approach to the 'Quasi-Ordinals'

Basil Lourié

National Research University Higher School of Economics, St. Petersburg
`hieromonk@gmail.com`

The numbers are not connected with order. Each number does not imply itself to be surrounded with other numbers. We discern between arithmetical and natural interaction of the numbers. The arithmetic sum produces a new number; the natural union of numbers does not produce a new number. In the nature, there is no equality. $<\ldots>$ The nature does not make one equal to another. Two trees cannot be equal to each other. They can be equal by their length, by their thickness, by their properties in general. But two trees in their natural wholeness cannot be equal to each other. $<\ldots>$ We think that the numbers are alike to the trees or the grass[1].

Daniil Kharms (1905–1942), 1933[2]

The present study is a part of a larger project no. 16-18-10202, 'History of the Logical and Philosophical Ideas in Byzantine Philosophy and Theology', implemented with a financial support of the Russian Science Foundation. The author is grateful for their help to Lela Aleksidze, Magda Mtchedlidze, Denis Saveliev, Alex Simonov, and two anonymous reviewers.

[1] «Числа не связаны порядком. Каждое число не предполагает себя в окружении других чисел. Мы разделяем арифметическое и природное взаимодействие чисел. Арифметическая сумма чисел дает новое число, природное соединение чисел не дает нового числа. В природе нет равенства. $<\ldots>$ Природа не приравнивает одно к другому. Два дерева не могут быть равны друг другу. Они могут быть равны по своей длине, по своей толщине, вообще по своим свойствам. Но два дерева в своей природной целости, равны друг другу быть не могут. $<\ldots>$ Мы думаем, что числа вроде деревьев или вроде травы».

[2] From an untitled note: Д. Хармс, Неизданный Хармс. Полное собрание сочинений. [Том 4.] Трактаты и статьи. Письма. Дополнения к т. 1–3. Состав. В. Н. Сажин [D. Kharms, *Unpublished Kharms. Complete Works*. Vol. 4. *Treatises and Articles. Letters. Additions to vols. 1–3.* Ed. by Valery N. Sazhin]. St. Petersburg: 'Akademicheskij Proekt', 2001, pp. 15–16.

Abstract

The intuition of number implied in the Byzantine notion of Holy Trinity is inconsistent and, more specifically, paraconsistent. The corresponding paraconsistent numbers can be called 'quasi-ordinals' taking in mind their 'duals', the numbers introduced for paracomplete quantum logics by Newton da Costa et al., which are called 'quasi-cardianls'.

1   Introduction

Is there such thing as the Eastern Patristic Approach to the notion of Trinity applied to God? I would dare to say that, looking from a logical point of view, the answer is positive. There is a substantially invariable approach that is traceable throughout the whole *Byzantinische Jahrtausend*, from Athanasius of Alexandria in the middle of the fourth century to Joseph Bryennios in the 1420s. Meanwhile, the most important names are the Cappadocian Fathers, especially Gregory of Nazianzus, then Dionysius the Areopagite and Maximus the Confessor. These authors form the 'mainstream' we are interested in, whereas, of course, some other authors would have been 'deviant' in a lesser or bigger extent. Anyway, the history of the Byzantine tradition is not our immediate interest, because our purpose is to make explicit the logical 'core' of Eastern Triadology.

The word 'Trinity' implies some notion(s) of number. Our purpose will be to make explicit, in modern terms, what kind of numbers was implied by the Byzantine Fathers when they have said that the Trinity is the Oneness and the Oneness is the Trinity. This approach will lead us to some problems that are now discussed in connexion with inconsistent logics and some new formalisms of quantum theory.

2   The Eastern Trinity is Inconsistent

I will start from a little-known but most explicit quotation from Evagrius Ponticus (345–399), a direct disciple of Gregory of Nazianzus. It is hardly possible that he did not share the faith of his teacher in triadological matters. The text is preserved in Syriac, but the key words are easily translatable back into Greek[3]. Even in the

---

[3] A. Guillaumont, *Les six centuries des 'Kephalaia Gnostica' d'Évagre le Pontique. Édition critique de la version syriaque commune et édition d'une nouvelle version syriaque, intégrale, avec une double traduction française,* Patrologia orientalis, t. 28, f. I, No. 134; Turnhout: Brepols, 1985 [first publ. 1958], 221, 223 (recension S_2; cf. recension S_1, pp. 220, 222). I have partially used the retroversion by Wilhelm Frankenberg incorporated into his translation of Babai the Great's commentary on the later recension S_1: W. Frankenberg, Euagrius Pontikus, Abhandlungen der könglichen Gesellschaft der Wissenschaften zu Göttingen. Philol.-hist. Kl. NF, 13:2; Berlin: Wei-

wording, we will see some striking similarities with the quotation from the Russian avant-garde thinker and absurdist poet Daniil Kharms proposed as the *motto* to this article.

VI, 10. The Holy Trinity [ἡ τριὰς ἁγία] is not as the quaternity, the quintet, and sextet, because the latter are a number [ἀριθμός, *possibly to restore the plural* 'numbers' ἀριθμοί], non-hypostatic [= unreal, imaginable] simulacra [ὁμοιώματα ἀνυπόστατα], whereas the Holy Trinity — the essential knowledge [γνῶσις οὐσιώδης].

11. After the trinity of numbers follows the quaternity [Τῇ τῶν ἀριθμῶν τριάδι ἐπακολουθεῖ ἡ τετράς], but the Holy Trinity is not followed by the quaternity. Therefore, it is not a trinity of numbers [ἡ τριὰς τῶν ἀριθμῶν].

12. The trinity of numbers is preceded by the dyad [Τῆς ἀριθμῶν τριάδος προηγεῖται ἡ δυάς], but the Holy Trinity is not preceded by the dyad. Therefore, it is not a trinity of numbers [ἡ τριὰς τῶν ἀριθμῶν].

13. The trinity of numbers is composed with addition of non-hypostatic [ἀνυπόστατα = imaginable] one by one, but the blessed Trinity is not composed with addition of such ones [units]. Therefore, it is not a trinity of numbers.

'Trinity' means 'three' but in such a way that there is no 'two' and no 'four'. This is some very specific kind of numbers. The Evagrian 'Trinity of numbers' is the same as the 'arithmetical sum' by Kharms—and, in both cases, something different from the union dealt with by the respective author. One can say in advance that the Trinity described here is certainly incompatible with any Trinity respecting the principle of non-contradiction. For instance, this is an answer to the question why no Trinity of our modern analytical philosophers is matching Eastern Patristic Orthodoxy: none of them allows the contradictions[4].

---

dmannsche Buchhandlung, 1912, 367, 371.

[4]Peter van Inwagen, dealing with Triadological doctrines, is especially categorical on this matter: '...nothing that is true can be internally inconsistent'; 'I have said that I could find no theologian who was actually said that inconsistencies were to be believed' (P. van Inwagen, 'Three Persons in One Being: On Attempts to Show that the Doctrine of the Trinity is Self-Contradictory', in: M. Y. Stewart (ed.), *The Trinity. East/West Dialogue*, Dordrecht: Kluwer

3   Gregory of Nazianzus

Gregory of Nazianzus (329–390), unlike most of his commentators, was perfectly aware of the fact that his teaching about the Holy Trinity is paradoxical. He legitimates explicitly such a way of theological thinking against the argumentation of Arians. For this purpose, he refers to the paradoxes of Liar and of Coming to Being (what came to be you was yourself and not yourself); this part of his logical argumentation has been recently analysed by Stamatios Gerogiorgakis[5].

According to Gregory, we need, for Triadology, the reasoning where the two oppositions can be simultaneously true or false, that is, exactly what we call now paraconsistent and paracomplete logics, breaking either the principle of non-contradiction or the principle of the excluded middle.

No wonder that a 'theory of numbers' that he made explicit is also far from classical logics and even from the Neoplatonic parallels to Christian triadological doctrines. I will quote now a passage that became extremely popular in later Greek and Latin authors who proposed many different variants of its interpretation (and it is another matter, in agreement or disagreement with Gregory's theological ideas). Nobody, however, from these mediaeval commentators grasped the original logical (not theological) idea of Gregory. I would argue that the most adequate context of the quotation below is my quote from Evagrius above.

Gregory teaches us[6] how to count to three with skipping two (literally, overstep-

---

Academic Publishers, 2003, pp. 83–97, at pp. 86, 87). See, for a general overview, D. Tuggy, 'Trinity', *The Stanford Encyclopedia of Philosophy* (Winter 2016 Edition), Edward N. Zalta (ed.), URL = <https://plato.stanford.edu/archives/win2016/entries/trinity/>.

[5]S. Gerogiorgakis, 'The Byzantine Liar', *History and Philosophy of Logic* 30 (2009), pp. 313–330. Gerogiorgakis, however, did not discuss Gregory's theological point that required this recourse to the logical paradoxes neither paid much attention to Gregory's interpretation of the paradox of Coming to Being. A detailed study of both paradoxes in Gregory's thought remains a *desideratum*.

[6]Sermon 23, 8; J. Mossay, Grégoire de Nazianze, *Discours 20–23*; Sources chrétiennes, 270; Paris: Cerf, 1980, 298. Since the seventh century, a rich tradition of exegesis of these words by Gregory has developed in Byzantium. Despite the variety of exegetical attitudes, the Byzantine authors were agree that the second element of the 'dyad' was not the Son. All these interpretations, however, were remote from the fourth-century context. Unlike Evagrius, the Byzantine authors were considering a normal counting from one to three. Therefore, all of them denied applicability of this Gregory's passage to the ontology of the intra-Trinitarian relations. Namely, some of them insisted that the movement of the 'monad' is limited to our comprehension of God and has no place in God himself (thus Maximus the Confessor and many later authors) or interpreted the movement from the henad to the triad as the process of actualisation having nothing to do with the Triadology: οὐσία–δύναμις–ἐνέργεια (essence–power/potency–actualisation/energy; thus, e.g., Photius). See an almost comprehensive review by Arkady Chouffrine in: Г. И. Беневич (сост.), Преп. Максим Исповедник: Полемика с оригенизмом и моноэнергизмом. Изд. 2-е испр. и доп. [G. I. Benevich (ed.), *St. Maximus the Confessor: Polemics against the Origenism and the Monoenergism*. 2nd ed., corrected

ping):

...Τριάδα τελείαν ἐκ τελείων τριῶν, μονάδος μὲν κινηθείσης διὰ τὸ πλούσιον, δυάδος δὲ ὑπερβαθείσης — ὑπὲρ γὰρ τὴν ὕλην καὶ τὸ εἶδος, ἐξ ὧν τὰ σώματα —, Τριάδος δὲ ὁρισθείσης διὰ τὸ τέλειον, πρώτη γὰρ ὑπερβαίνει δυάδος σύνθεσιν, ἵνα μήτε στενὴ μένῃ θεότης, μήτε εἰς ἄπειρον χέηται. Τὸ μὲν γὰρ ἀφιλότιμον, τὸ δὲ ἄτακτον· καὶ τὸ μὲν ἰουδαϊκὸν παντελῶς, τὸ δὲ ἑλληνικὸν καὶ πολύθεον.

...the perfect Triad (Trinity) from the perfect three, in such a way that the Monad would be moving because of richness, whereas the Dyad would be **overstepped** – because (the Trinity) is above the matter and the form, from which are the bodies, – to limit itself to the Triad because of (its) perfectness. Because it (Monad) being the first overcomes the composition of the Dyad, in a way that the divinity neither remains constrained nor overflows into limitlessness. Because the first (alternative) is unworthy, whereas the second one is out of order: the first is completely Judaic, whereas the second is Hellenic and polytheistic.

In a parallel place in a different homily, he is a bit less explicit but explicit enough[7]:

......ὥστε κἂν ἀριθμῷ διαφέρῃ, τῇ γε οὐσίᾳ μὴ τέμνεσθαι. Διὰ τοῦτο μονὰς ἀπ' ἀρχῆς εἰς δυάδα κινηθεῖσα, μέχρι τριάδος ἔστη. Καὶ τοῦτό ἐστιν ἡμῖν ὁ Πατήρ, καὶ ὁ Υἱός, καὶ τὸ ἅγιον Πνεῦμα·

...in such manner that (the persons of the Trinity) if even differ (from each other) by number are not divided by the essence. Therefore, the Monad, after having been moved from the beginning to the Dyad, stayed at the Triad. And this is what are for us the Father, the Son, and the Holy Spirit.

Many later readers of this text understood the Monad as the Father, the Dyad as the Son, and the Triad as the third element, the Spirit, as if Gregory used here the ordinal numbers 'first', 'second', and 'third'. It is not the case, however. He deals with the numerical notions that are not ordinal numbers and are not other words for naming hypostases. He said what means 'Trinity' as such, without going to the details related to the Father, the Son, and the Spirit.—I have just repeated the clarification made by the late Byzantine theologian Joseph Bryennios in the 1420s[8].

---

and augmented]; Библиотека христианской мысли; Византийская философия, т. 16; Σμάραγδος φιλοκαλίας; St. Petersburg: Oleg Abyshko Publishing House, 2014, pp. 326–330 (note 5) and to add Magda Mtchedlidze, 'The Commentaries of Michael Psellus and John Italus on Gregory the Theologian's Expression: 'Therefore the Monad, Moved from the Beginning to the Dyad, Stood until the Triad' [in Georgian, with 4-page English summary], in: humanitaruli kvlevebi. c'elic'deuli [*Studies in Humanities. Yearbook*] 2 (2011), 203–220.

[7] Sermon 29, 2; P. Gallay, Grégoire de Nazianze, *Discours 27–31 (Discours théologiques)*; Sources chrétiennes, 250; Paris: Cerf, 1978, pp. 178, 180.

[8] See, e.g., his *Logos 1, On the Holy Trinity*, in his series of the twenty-one triadological homilies

The implied logic here is the following.

The Dyad is unavoidably connected with the 'composition' (σύνθεσις). According to the most important axiom of the Christian monotheism in antiquity, the unique God is 'simple', that is, not composed from any kind of parts. Thus, the 'composition' is to be excluded, even though it cannot be completely excluded from our manner to speak about God. Thus, it is clear that the unique God could not be a Dyad.

This idea of skipping the Dyad is an innovation peculiar to the Greek patristics. An earlier scheme, already Jewish, was called by Daniel Boyarin 'Binitarianism' exactly because it has represented the unique God as a Dyad, even though this Dyad was paraconsistently implying both identity and non-identity[9]. Compare, in an often-quoted Second Temple Jewish text, 'I and the Father are one' (John 10:30): the identity is proclaimed, whereas the opposition is not forgotten.

For Gregory, however, the Dyad was the constructive principle of the material world composed from the matter and the forms. Thus, on these somewhat 'Hellenic' grounds, the Dyad was excluded from the notion of God. It was 'skipped'.

However, the next and the final station of the Monad is the Triad. The Dyad is not *completed* to the Triad, but *eliminated*: our Triad is without any Dyad at all.

4   Teaching Trichotomy: the Ternary Exclusive OR and the n-Opposition

In Gregory's Triad, we are dealing with an object that Kant considered unthinkable: a trichotomy *a priori*: '...dichotomy is the only division from principles *a priori*, hence the only *primitive* division. For the members of a division are supposed to be opposed to one another, but for each A the opposite is nothing more than *non* A. Polytomy cannot be taught in logic, for it involves *cognition of the object*. Dichotomy requires only the *principle of contradiction*...'[10] Indeed, if only we leave behind us the principle of contradiction, polytomy becomes open to us.

delivered before the Emperor Manuel Palaiologus and Patriarch Joseph ca. 1420: [Eugenius Boulgaris (ed.)], Ἰωσὴφ μοναχοῦ τοῦ Βρυεννίου Τὰ εὑρεθέντα, τόμος Α'. Leipzig: Ἐν τῇ Τυπογραφίᾳ τοῦ Βρεϊτκόπφ, 1768, pp. 10–11; cf. passim in this cycle.

[9]D. Boyarin, 'The Gospel of the Memra: Jewish Binitarianism and the Prologue to John', *The Harvard Theological Review* 94 (2001), pp. 243–284. Cf. also *idem, Border Lines: The Partition of Judaeo-Christianity*, Divination: Rereading Late Ancient Religion; Philadelphia: University of Pennsylvania Press, 2004.

[10]I. Kant, *Lectures on logic*. Translated and edited by J. M. Young; The Cambridge Edition of the Works of Immanuel Kant; Cambridge: Cambridge University Press, 1992, p. 637, cf. p. 624 (*The Jäsche logic*); cf. in other courses: pp. 368 (*The Vienna logic*); 437, 494–495 (*The Dohna-Wundlacken logic*).

In the light of modern logics, it is more difficult to see how the dichotomy could be primary, given that any opposition implies something third as the border between the two. As Chris Mortensen has formulated it, 'natural logic is paraconsistent'[11]. Considering the opposition formed by two elements, we have, at least, one more element factored out. In this way, the binary opposition and the Boolean algebra turns out to be a particular case of a more general structure: it is located in the middle between the Heyting paracomplete and the Brouwer paraconsistent algebras[12].

In Gregory's Trinity, we see three and not two objects opposed to each other. Such kind of opposition was first described by Emil Post in his 1941 monograph containing a comprehensive classification of the logical connectives[13]. It is a different kind of exclusive disjunction, distinct from the binary exclusive disjunction $\oplus$.

If we need to choose out of plurality of objects, we can either to iterate the choosing out of two or to choose directly out of this plurality. In the latter case, we will have a different kind of exclusive disjunction, now often called 'ternary' (although it could be, of course, n-ary)[14]. If our plurality has an even number of elements, the result will be the same in both cases. However, if it has an odd number of elements, the corresponding functions will have different truth-values. Thus, for two elements these two kinds of the exclusive disjunction are extensionally coinciding, even though intentionally different, whereas for three elements they become to be different extensionally as well. Three is the minimal number of arity corresponding to specific behaviour of the connective, thus called 'ternary'.

In Tables 1 and 2, are shown in comparison the truth-values of the two exclusive disjunctions corresponding to the arities $n = 2$ and $n = 3$ respectively. For the arity 2, the truth-values coincide, whereas, for the arity 3, they differ.

---

[11] The title of a paragraph in his book: Ch. Mortensen, *Inconsistent Geometry*. Studies in Logic, 27; London: College Publications, 2010, pp. 5–10.

[12] *Ibid.*

[13] E. L. Post, *The Two-Valued Iterative Systems of Mathematical Logic*, London: Oxford University Press, 1941. Reprinted within M. Davis (ed.), *Solvability, Provability, Definability: The Collected Works of Emil L. Post*; Contemporary Mathematics; Boston–Basel–Berlin: Birkhäuser, 1994.

[14] F. J. Pelletier, A. Hartline, 'Ternary Exclusive OR', *Logic Journal of the IGPL* 16 (2008), pp. 75–83.

φ_1	φ_2	$\varphi_1 \oplus \varphi_2$	$\varphi_1 \underline{\vee}^2 \varphi_2$
T	T	F	F
T	F	T	T
F	T	T	T
F	F	F	F

Table 1

φ_1	φ_2	φ_3	$(\varphi_1 \oplus \varphi_2) \oplus \varphi_3$	$\underline{\vee}^3(\varphi_1, \varphi_2, \varphi_3)$
T	T	T	T	F
T	T	F	F	F
T	F	T	F	F
T	F	T	F	F
T	F	F	T	T
T	T	T	T	F
F	T	T	F	F
F	T	F	T	T
F	F	T	T	T
F	F	F	F	F

Table 2

One can see that only the ternary exclusive disjunction forbids the situation where all the three hypostases would be called with the name of any one from them (e.g., 'Father'). This is not a sophism but a proof by contradiction that the Byzantine Trinity does not contain pairs. To be a triad without dyads is the unique feature of our Byzantine Trinity making it sharply different from all other Trinities of Christian theologies. All other Trinities are internally connected with the iterated binary exclusive disjunction, whereas the Byzantine Trinity is internally connected with the ternary exclusive disjunction[15].

The existence of the ternary exclusive disjunction as a connective irreducible to any other connectives is enough to prove that Kant was wrong saying that the dichotomy is 'the only primitive division'. Now we see that, at least, not the only one.

---

[15]For a survey of different Triadologies of the Byzantine epoch (but not only Byzantine ones), see B. Lourié, 'Nicephorus Blemmydes on the Holy Trinity and the Paraconsistent Notion of Numbers: A Logical Analysis of a Byzantine Approach to the *Filioque*', *Studia Humana* 5 (2016), pp. 40–54.

For our present purpose, there is no need to consider the 'ternary' exclusive disjunction with the arity more than 3. However, one note should be in order. In the recent works on generalisation of the notion of opposition from three kinds (contrary, subcontrary, contradictory) to n, the corresponding notions are introduced with a geometrical method, as generalisations of Blanché's hexagon of oppositions. This procedure includes a generalisation of the connectives 'or' and 'and'[16]. I would like to point out that the corresponding n-ary OR is the 'ternary' exclusive OR we are dealing with. Emil Post who described this connective is, therefore, also a predecessor of the modern n-opposition theories.

The concept of n-opposition is not necessary for our particular case of the Byzantine Trinity, whereas it would be necessary for understanding the Byzantine notion of God in general—the doctrine of uncreated energies-*logoi* of God, that is, for understanding the divine multiplicity in the divine unity and trinity.

5 Neither Order Nor Consistency in the Trinity

The three elements are not ordered according to the schemes $2 + 1$ or $1 + 2$, which are presupposed by some later Triadological concepts, including both Latin *Filioque* and the extreme Greek anti-Filioquism. The principle of the so-called μοναρχία of the Father (that the Father is the only 'cause' in the Trinity) does not mean that there exists, between the hypostases, any order according to which the Father is the first. To be the first as the 'cause' does not mean to be the first according to some order, because there is no 'order' in the Trinity. In the respect to the 'cause' as the first both Son and Spirit are the second, and there is no 'third' at all. Even if we wish to call these relations 'order', we need to realise that such order is not an order of the Trinity itself, because it implies only two positions and not three, without allowing discerning between the Son and the Spirit. In the Byzantine technical language, these relations were never called 'order'.

The Byzantine authors never call the Father 'the first hypostasis of the Trinity', the Son 'the second hypostasis', and the Spirit 'the third hypostasis'. The question of the 'cause' in the Trinity was not a question of its logical structure formed with three elements; it is a question of another logical structure formed with two elements, the 'cause' and the 'caused'. In the polemics against the Latin *Filioque*, the Byzantine

---

[16]Cf. the seminal paper by Alessio Moretti, 'Geometry for modalities? Yes: Through n-opposition Theory', in: J.-Y. Béziau, A. Costa-Leite, and A. Facchini (eds.), *Aspects of Universal Logic*, Travaux de logique, 17, Neuchâtel: Université de Neuchâtel, 2004, pp. 102–145, as well as R. Pellissier, "'Setting' n-Opposition", *Logica Universalis* 2 (2008), pp. 235–263; H. Smessaert, 'On the 3D Visualisation of Logical Relations', Logica Universalis 3 (2009), pp. 303–332; J.-Y. Béziau, 'The Power of the Hexagon', *Logica Universalis* 6 (2012), pp. 1–43.

authors constantly protested against confusing these two logical structures. From a historical viewpoint, I would consider the difference between the 'cause' and the 'caused' as the 'afterlife' of the Jewish Second Temple binitarianism, still without its logical development into the Christian Triadology.

Already in the early fifth century the reason why there is no 'first', 'second', and 'third' among the hypostases has been formulated by Severian of Gabala whose homily became mostly known under the name of John Chrysostom: Οὐ γὰρ ἔχει τάξιν ὁ Θεός, οὐχ ὡς ἄτακτος, ἀλλ᾿ ὡς ὑπὲρ τάξιν ὤν 'Because God does not have an order — not as if he is unordered but as being above the order'[17]).

If there is no order, there could be no row of natural numbers. Indeed, we have been already told by Evagrius that there is no numbers in the Holy Trinity, which is not a 'trinity of numbers', but now we can see why. Not only in the modern set-theoretical conceptions but also in the antique ones, the row of natural numbers has been derived using the notions of order and pair[18]. We see, however, that both are absent in this Byzantine Triadology. If we take the side of Couturat and Zermelo in their discussion with Poincaré on the nature of numbers, we must say that our 'tri-' in 'Trinity', which is not preceded by two and not followed by four, is not a number at all[19]. However, if we prefer the side of Poincaré, we can see that our Triad is still in agreement with his 'intuition du nombre pur'[20], even though its interpretation along with von Neumann's set-theoretical line is impossible.

6 Trichotomy: Paraconsistency and Non-extensionality

Even though the hypostases of the Trinity do not form pairs, we can consider them per two in our mind. In this case, we will see neither a set of disconnected pairs nor a chain of two pairs formed from two links with the common intermediary (this chain would correspond to the Latin *Filioque*) but something more complicated. This scheme has been fully explained and even represented in a graphical form in the 1270s by hieromonk Hierotheos and eventually 'canonised' for Byzantine theology

---

[17] *Hom. in Gen.* 24:2, ch. 2; *PG* 56, 555.

[18] Cf., for antiquity, especially R. Waterfield, *The Theology of Arithmetic. On the Mystical, Mathematical and Cosmological Symbolism of the First Ten Numbers Attributed to Iamblichus.* Grand Rapids, MI: Phanes Press, 1988; S. Slaveva-Griffin, *Plotinus on Number.* Oxford: Oxford University Press, 2009.

[19] Cf. W. Goldfarb, 'Poincaré against the logicistics', in: W. Aspray and P. Kitcher (eds.), *History and Philosophy of Modern Mathematics.* Minneapolis: University of Minnesota Press, 1988, 61–81.

[20] H. Poincaré. Du rôle de l'intuition et de la logique en mathématiques, *Compte-rendu du deuxième Congrès international des mathématiciens* — Paris 1900. Paris: Gautier-Villars, 1902, 115–130, at 122.

in the 1420s by Josephus Bryennios (see Fig. 1: a 18th-cent. etching based on the picture in a Byzantine manuscript[21]).

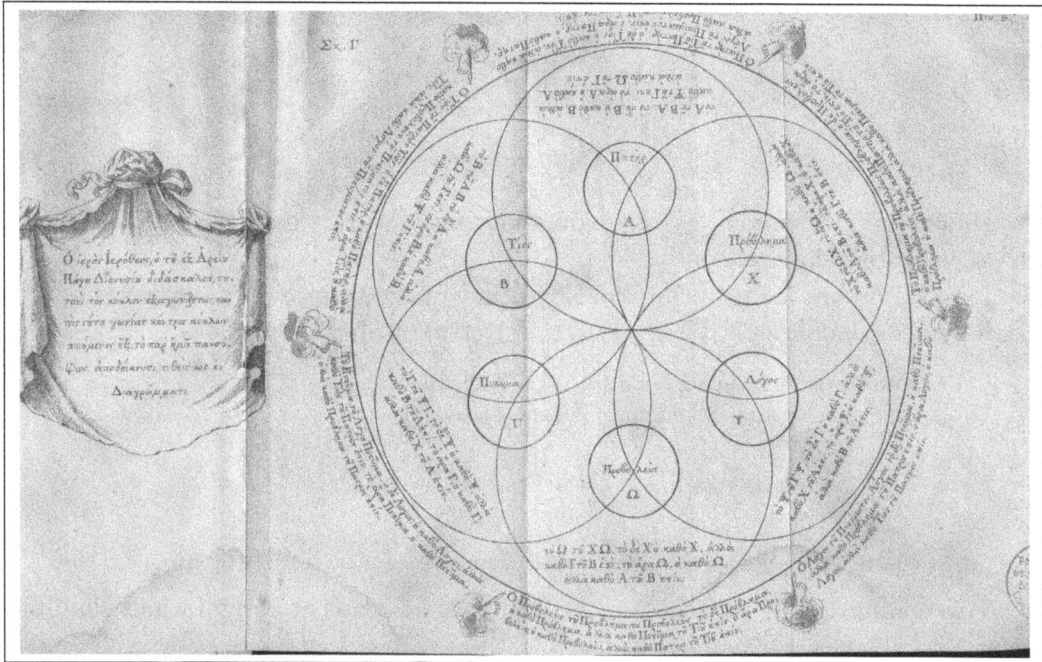

Figure 1: The Orthodox (Byzantine) Trinity according to Joseph Bryennios, 1420s. An eighteenth-century etching based on a Byzantine manuscript

Hierotheos and Joseph Bryennios used graphic schemes for comparing the Patristic Byzantine Trinity with the Latin Catholic one. I provide only one of such schemes, the one that explains what we see in fact when we try to deal with pairs in the Trinity of Byzantine Patristics.

Instead of three, we see here six elements. Why the Triad looks as a Sextet?— Because there is no pair without participation of a third element. The Father is both the Father of the Son but the *Proboleus* ('Proceeder') of the Spirit. The Son is both the Son of the Father but the Word (Logos) of the Spirit. The Spirit is both the Spirit of the Son and the *Problema* ('What is proceeded') of the Father.

---

[21] From [Eugenius Boulgaris (ed.)], Ἰωσὴφ μοναχοῦ τοῦ Βρυεννίου Τὰ εὑρεθέντα, τόμος Α', σχῆμα Γ' (a chart at the end of the volume, no pagination). Cf., for a detailed analysis of this scheme, B. Lourié, 'A Logical Scheme and Paraconsistent Topological Separation in Byzantium: Inter-Trinitarian Relations according to Hieromonk Hierotheos and Joseph Bryennios', in: D. Bertini and D. Migliorini (eds.), Relations: Ontology and Philosophy of *Religion*; Mimesis International. Philosophy, n. 24; [Sesto San Giovanni (Milano)]: Mimesis International, 2018, pp. 283–299.

Thus, we are dealing not with unordered pairs, which are combinations by two from three (the number of which would be three) but with ordered pairs, that is, permutations, the number of which is six, according to the formula of combinatorics:

$$P_n^m = \frac{n!}{(n-m)!}$$

$$P_3^2 = \frac{3!}{(3-2)!}$$

Unlike the Kuratowski ordered pairs, however, our ordered pairs imply all kinds of permutations simultaneously.

Let us compare the two definitions of ordered pairs, that of Kuratowski and that of Hierotheos and Joseph Bryennios (the latter in our reconstruction):

> Kuratowski's ordered pair: $(a, b) := \{\{a\}, \{a, b\}\}$
> Hierotheos's and Bryennios's paraconsistent ordered pair:
>
> $$\bigwedge_{i,j}(a_i, a_j) = \bigwedge_{i,j}(a_i, a_j) = \{\{a_i\}, \{a_i, a_j\}\},$$
>
> where $i \neq j$, both i and j are natural numbers.

This conjunction is paraconsistent. It implies all kinds of permutations simultaneously.

Thus, despite the order in the Trinity is conceivable, this is not an order in any ordinary sense. This is a paraconsistent order breaking the axiom of Extensionality and the law of identity.

> Axiom of Extensionality:
>
> $$\forall a \, \forall b \, [\forall x \, (x \in a \leftrightarrow x \in b) \to a = b]$$
>
> In words: if, for any sets a and b, is true that, for any set x, it is an element of the set a if and only if it is an element of the set b, then the sets a and b are identical. In other words: if all elements of some sets are identical, these sets themselves are identical.

Indeed, according to the axiom of Extensionality, we cannot have a numerical row looking as

$$1, \ 2, \ 2, \ 2, \ 2, \ 2, \ 2, \ 3,$$

where the six '2' are equal but different, in the same manner as the Kharms's non-extensional numbers in the *motto* to the present article.

In the Trinity, however, if we prefer not to 'skip' two, we should pass through six different 'twos'. They are different but equal. In other words, they are not identical but identical. Using Bryennios's terms, we can formulate that the Father is identical but not identical to the *Proboleus*, the Son is identical but not identical to the Logos, the Spirit is identical but not identical to the *Problema*.

These three pairs (combinations by two from three) form six permutations (ordered pairs by two from three). All of these six permutations are valid simultaneously.

Evagrius's saying that our Triad is not preceded with a Dyad could be reinterpreted as it is preceded with a paraconsistent conjunction of six mutually exclusive Dyads.

7 Non-reflexive vs Super-reflexive Logics

Our description of Triadological problems in Byzantine Patristics has a close parallel in the mathematical formalisms proposed for the Quantum mechanics.

At first, according to the Correspondence Principle by Niels Bohr, the mathematical formalism was following that used in the classical mechanics. Therefore, the quantum objects became considered 'in correspondence' with the elements of classical sets of Zermelo-Fraenkel or similar. These elements are crisp (having no vagueness) and identical to themselves and only themselves (their relation of identity is reflexive). In fact, the quantum objects do not have such kinds of identity. They are non-individual. This is why, in 1974, Yuri Manin formulated the so-called Manin's problem[22]: to elaborate a mathematical formalism adequate to the real nature of the quantum objects[23]. Newton da Costa met this claim. Since 1979, he and other scholars, especially Décio Krause, proposed the so-called non-reflexive logic for the specific kinds of sets formed with the non-individuals[24].

---

[22]The term 'Manin's problem' belongs to Steven French and Décio Krause, *Identity in Physics: A historical, philosophical and formal analysis*, Oxford: Oxford University Press, 2006, pp. 239–240 *et passim*.

[23]Yu. I. Manin, 'Foundations', in: F. E. Browder (ed.), *Proceedings of the Symposium in Pure Mathematics of the American Mathematical Society held at Northern Illinois University, Dekalb, Illinois, May 1974*; Proceedings of Symposia in Pure Mathematics, 28; Providence, RI: American Mathematical Society, 1976, p. 36.

[24]The bibliography became ample; I limit my references to several publications (see them for further bibliography): French, Krause, *Identity in Physics*; J. R. B. Arenhart, D. Krause, 'Classical logic or non-reflexive logic? A case of semantic underdetermination', *Revista Portuguesa di Filosofia* 68 (2012), pp. 73–86; N. C. A. da Costa, C. de Ronde, 'Non-reflexive Logical Foundation for Quantum Mechanics', *Foundations of Physics* 44 (2014), pp. 1369–1380. It is interesting in itself but does not concern us now that da Costa put forward an alternative formalism apparently avoiding inconsistency (whereas, in fact, perhaps only concealing it): N. da Costa, O. Lombardi, M. Lastiri, 'A modal ontology of properties for quantum mechanics', *Synthese* 190 (2013), pp. 3671–3693.

For the non-individuals, the relation of identity does not work: they are not identical to themselves. Therefore, the permutations are impossible: no ordered pairs and no numbers in any consistent sense of the word. However, they are still countable, and the corresponding kind of numbers is called quasi-cardinals. The non-individuals form a contrary opposition, which breaks the principle of the excluded middle. The quantum superposition is the 'middle' that would to be excluded in the logics respecting the rule of *tertium non datur*.

In his remarkable 1974 one-page paper, Manin said also the following: 'The twentieth century return to Middle Age scholastics taught us a lot about formalisms. Probably it is time to look outside again. Meaning is what really matters'[25]. I think that the modern physics and logics could improve our understanding of Scholastics and especially Patristics, and *vice versa*.

Thus, I would dare to say that the late Byzantine theologians and especially hieromonk Hierotheos and Joseph Bryennios resolved 'the Manin problem' of their time. To the earlier language of Gregory of Nazianzus based on the Correspondence Principle they added a non-classical logical system. I would dare to call it super-reflexive logic.

In the non-reflexive logic of da Costa and Krause, the non-individual elements were not identical to themselves. In our super-reflexive logic, the elements are identical not only to themselves but to all others. In the first case, the reflexivity of identity does not work. In our case, it works with an excess. In the first case, the permutations are impossible. In our case, they are perfectly possible but only all of them simultaneously: the elements are different (therefore, the permutations are possible) but identical (therefore, all possible permutations are identical).

This is why, in analogy with French's and Krause's numbers which are called 'quasi-cardinals', our numbers in the Holy Trinity could be called 'quasi-ordinals'. Our elements form a kind of ordered row, but this row is not unique. We have several different rows breaking the rule of extensionality.

Our quasi-ordinal numbers are based on the subcontrary opposition and, therefore, are paraconsistent, whereas the quasi-cardinals are based on the contrary opposition and are paracomplete.

8 Conclusion

Regardless of theological usage, we can say that the 'theory of numbers' elaborated by Byzantine Fathers is one half of the whole theory of quasi-cardinal and quasi-ordinal numbers, whose another half is described by da Costa and his followers. The

---

[25] Manin, 'Foundations'.

relevant Byzantine intuition appeared after having been called for by theological discussions but it was not theological *per se*. Daniil Kharms apparently 'absurdist' reasoning about the numbers is merely an example of similar intuitions in a secular context. I think that the role of both quasi-cardinals and quasi-ordinals in the human thinking operating with quantities and in the logic of the natural language is still to be discovered.

Received 27 May 2019

THE ÉMINENCE GRISE OF CHRISTOLOGY: PORPHYRY'S LOGICAL TEACHING AS A CORNERSTONE OF ARGUMENTATION IN CHRISTOLOGICAL DEBATES OF THE FIFTH AND SIXTH CENTURIES

ANNA ZHYRKOVA

Jesuit University Ignatianum in Cracow, Dept of Philosophy, ul. Kopernika 26, 31-501, Kraków, Poland

Anna.zhyrkova@ignatianum.edu.pl

Abstract

The scope of the paper is to show the role of Neoplatonic logic, especially of Porphyry's logical account of substance, in Christological debates of fifth and sixth centuries AD. I argue that those conceptions were employed in Christology of Cyril of Alexandria, as well as in Trinitological writings of Gregory of Nyssa that were widely referred to in debates over Christological solutions propounded by the Chalcedon Council. In this claim, I deviate from the opinion, frequently adopted in history of theology, that Christological teaching of Cyril and Chalcedon involved incorporation of elements of Aristotelian metaphysics. I strengthen my thesis by showing how the two parties in post-Chalcedonian debates, miaphysite anti-Chalcedonians and so-called Neochalcedonias (the latter including John Grammarian and Leontius of Byzantium), also relied, quite explicitly, on tenets of Neoplatonic logic. Alongside, I show how those logical claims were being given ontological interpretations and discuss some reasons for which an ontology was looked for in Neoplatonic logical works, in spite of the fact that Neoplatonics emphasized divergences between logical and metaphysical approaches, both with respect of their methodologies and objects they study.

Keywords: Christology, Cyril of Alexandria, Gregory of Nyssa, Porphyry, Neochalcedonism, Neoplatonic Logic.

The article presents some results of the author's research carried out within the framework of the project "Neochalcedonian Philosophical Paradigm", financed by Poland's National Science Center (grant UMO-2016/22/M/HS1/00170).

1   Introduction

In the fifth and sixth centuries AD, debates took place on the union of human and divine natures in Christ that were both fiery in tone and far-reaching in their consequences. Prior to this point in time, ontological solutions based on different conceptions of composition and mixture had arisen within Christological discourse. However, none of these had resolved a deep logical problem, this being that one had to make contradictory statements about one and the same entity, to the effect that an individual known as Jesus Christ was simultaneously created and uncreated, eternal and mortal, and, most obviously, both divine and human — in short, that Christ was both p and *not-p*.

A new kind of solution emerged in the fifth century out of discussions inaugurated by the Nestorian crisis. The two key conceptual innovations that made it possible to outline the orthodox doctrine, and which determined, in its main lines, the later Christological debates, were Cyril of Alexandria's theory of the union of natures in one hypostasis, and the Cappadocians' distinction between substance *vel* nature, understood as what is common, and hypostasis, interpreted as what is particular. While almost all commentaries to date have focused on the ontological presuppositions and developments that these theological advances implied and/or involved, my research points to the fact that Cyril and the Cappadocians proposed solutions rooted in the Neoplatonic logical stance of Porphyry. My focus in this paper will mainly be on showing that this was indeed the case. However, I also intend to address the implications of the fact that in this way Porphyry's own more narrowly conceived logical conception came to receive, in the writings of Cyril and the Cappadocians, a metaphysical reading. In that regard I shall be emphasizing some of the theoretical repercussions of Cyril's and the Cappadocians' proposals, while at the same time pointing in passing to later theological controversies that one can, in my view, explain as natural developments of those proposals.

Prior to this, though, it will be necessary to explicate very briefly why the solutions that made use of ontological conceptions of the Ancient thought were untenable. The theological vision of the Church needed a different philosophical apparatus in order to express (but not necessarily to explain) what was accepted as doctrinal truth without straying into any unorthodox interpretations such as might follow necessarily from the philosophical premises of earlier solutions. It seems that Porphyrian logic provided the theologians of the era with an imperfect, but in some respects promising and useful, vehicle for uttering theological truths.

2   Christ as a Theoretical Problem

Until the mid-fifth century, Christian thinkers confronting the ontological paradox of Christ tried to apply conceptions developed by either the Stoic, Aristotelian or Platonic schools. Those models tried to account for things that could be considered as unifying within themselves some essentially dissimilar substances through different theories of mixture and composition. However, no matter which conception of mixture they applied, it did not allow, on either ontological or conceptual levels, for any possible explication or justification of a being which, while existing as one single being, would simultaneously be of two distinct and essentially different natures, without their being altered and mixed together, and without producing out of them at least a temporal *tertium quid*, or, indeed, without the annihilation of one of the two natures united together or the acceptance that such a union is not an ontological one (in the sense that it that it would not result in one truly united and really existing entity).

We should mention here that it was Nestorius who, through his comprehensive analyses, pointed to the theologically unorthodox consequences of elucidating Christ through different kinds of mixture. His solution to the problems he exposed consisted, however, in abandoning as rationally impossible the idea of the ontological unity of two natures in Christ and developing a two-subject Christology.

In consequence, Nestorius' main adversary and defender of the orthodox doctrine, Cyril of Alexandria, had no choice but to seek out a form of explication or exposition that would not rely on some kind of mixture or composition. Cyril's formula of "one incarnate nature of God the Word" emphasized the unity of Christ. This way of putting it aimed to preclude the possibility of a separation of human and Divine natures in Christ after His Incarnation. Cyril did recognize the distinctness of the two natures in Christ, and their differences, but characterized this distinctness as obtaining "in knowledge" only. Thus, we were to regard the two natures as being distinct in respect of the mind's perception of them. However, they cannot be separated in reality, and do not constitute two independent substances. Neither are they blended or fused together into one substance.[1] While they are united, they do remain two distinct natures and do preserve their properties and differences. This is possible thanks to a union that is described as obtaining "καθ᾽ ὑπόστασιν" —

---

[1]Cyril of Alexandria, *Contra Nestorium* [hereafter *CN*] II.33.6–9; III.5.72.2–6; II.52.31–3; V.4.99.29–32; IV.6.90.21–3. Texts of the authors discussed in the article are cited according to standard editions defined in the *Clavis Patrum Graecorum* or included in the *Thesaurus Linguae Graecae*. Abbreviations follow those defined in the *Oxford Classical Dictionary* or the custom of the majority of scholars working in the field. For the convenience of the reader, each abbreviation is explained in the first reference made to a given work.

"according to" or "as pertaining to hypostasis." While Cyril did not define "hypostasis" when proposing the formula and did not offer an elucidation of what a union "pertaining to" hypostasis is, his *usus* of the word in Christological discourse itself makes it possible to conclude that what he had in mind was an "independently established particular entity."[2]

The word was offered a more in-depth elucidation and a comparative definition, along Neoplatonic lines, in Cyril's *Dialogues on the Trinity*. In contrast to the term "substance", it was shown to express the notion of an individual of a certain kind, of which a common substance is predicated.[3] The unity of natures was not explained by any kind of mixture or composition, although Cyril did not refrain from comparing the unity of natures in Christ with the unity obtaining between the soul and the body in humans. The latter so-called "human paradigm" in Christology is in itself an example of a Platonic account of the union of the intelligible with the sensible, and is understood in Neoplatonism to be possible due to the intelligible nature of the soul. But even if he did compare the unity of natures in Christ to the unity of the soul and the body in humans, Cyril did not seek to elucidate the unity of Christ in terms of the intelligible nature of one of its composites. The core of his contention was that this union is achieved not as some kind of mixture, but according to hypostasis. Cyril's teaching became the foundation for the doctrinal formulation produced at the Council of Ephesus and the Council of Chalcedon. The famous Chalcedonian *Horos*, in which Christ is elucidated as "acknowledged in two natures" that "come together into one person and one hypostasis," reflected Cyril's Christological teaching.[4]

It is widely assumed that Cyril's formulation relies on the fact that he adopted and adjusted such Aristotelian metaphysical notions as those of primary and secondary substance, and that it is against this background, in terms of the Aristotelian notion of substance, that one should approach the task of presenting and understanding his idea of hypostasis. Nevertheless, I shall argue that all those terms, even if instigated by Aristotle, actually appear in Cyril in their Neoplatonic reinterpretation, where it is the Porphyrian logical reading of Aristotle that they exhibit the strongest affinities with.

---

[2]The expression "καθ᾽ ὑπόστασιν," which occurs in various writings of Cyril, became the core technical expression in his *Second Letter to Nestorius* (ACO 1.1.1.26–28). It is used in its technical sense on many occasions in *CN*. For "hypostasis" in the meaning of particular entity, see *CN* II.34.37–39, 35.2–13; 46.28–31. The term "person" is used with a similar meaning, occurring in most cases together with "hypostasis," see *CN* II.34.37–39.35.16, 48.30–31, III.60.31–33, 72.4, 72.39–73.14.

[3]See Cyril of Alexandria, *De sancta Trinitate dialogi* [*Dial. Trin.*] I.408.29–409.14. Cf., for instance, Porphyry, *Isagoge* [*Isag.*] 7.24–7.

[4]See Richard Price [13, 78]; Richard Price and Michael Gaddis [14, 2:117–18].

3 Porphyry and the Key Notions of Christology

By the fifth century, Porphyry had become an undeniable philosophical authority. His *Isagoge* and his commentary *On the Categories* had both become extremely popular and widely known, offering intellectuals of the time a clear and concise work of reference. (Analogously, in the 1960 and 1970s, people from various areas of the humanities read Roland Barthes' *Eléments de Sémiologie*, frequently without studying the philosophical and linguistic investigations that made this little, apparently self-contained synthesis possible.) The clear and concise exposition of difficult logical issues in both the *Isagoge* and the commentary would have had the capacity to convince readers that these texts were presenting a set of self-evident claims that pertained to both logic and ontology. Boethius, for instance, showed no indication of feeling a need to restrain himself from delving into deeper ontological questions, such as the nature of genera, while commenting on Porphyry's logical texts, and this in spite of the clear warning from Porphyry that both the *Isagoge* and *On the Categories* were introductory works discussing subjects that, in themselves, were also to be considered merely introductory with respect to the larger framework of philosophy. Boethius went so far as to correct Porphyry's explanation of his theoretical approach in the *Isagoge*: Porphyry's characterization of this approach as "more logical" (λογικώτερον) was rendered by Boethius as "probabiliter," with the latter being explained as having been used in his translation in the sense of "verisimilitude." Boethius suggested that Porphyry's aim in the *Isagoge* had been merely to dwell on such issues as the Peripatetics would have been "very likely" to dispute.[5]

Even so, if we believe such Neoplatonists as Ammonius, who was certainly closer to Porphyry than Boethius, then the term "λογικώτερον" was used in the *Isagoge* to designate "logical activities" (τῇ λογικῇ πραγματείᾳ), which consisted in the analyzing of categorical propositions.[6] Porphyry's intention in the *Isagoge* was to address issues surrounding the terms and conceptions that would need to have been correctly understood by someone attempting a reading of Aristotle's *Categories* from a logical rather than an ontological point of view. Besides, he defined the theoretical aim, or *skopos*, of the *Categories* itself as being concerned with meaningful expressions that designate things, and not with things as such. Thus, one may characterize his introduction to and commentary on the*Categories* in contemporary terms as giving an account of a theory that seeks to classify terms according to their syntactic and semantic roles in propositions, taking the latter as belonging to the propositional

---

[5]Porphyry, *Isag.* 1.14–16. For Boethius' justification of his rendering and interpretation of Porphyry's text, see *In Isagogen*, editio secunda I.12, 167.24–169.5.

[6]See Ammonius, *In Aristotelis Categorias commentarium[in Cat.]* 43.10–24; 44.11–45.22. Cf. Sten Ebbesen, [4, 146]; Steven K. Strange, [17, 961–2].

network of everyday language. And yet — probably because it was not an ontological treatise but a logical one — it contained an element that Christological discourse lacked: in spite of the fact that in the *Isagoge* Porphyry reaffirms the Platonic stance that particular entities evade our cognition,[7] his logic makes it possible to speak about a particular individual subject. While little is actually said in the *Isagoge* about the latter, what Porphyry did put there in due course turned out to be of the utmost importance for the development of the core Christian doctrine itself.

3.1   Cyril: a Porphyrian rather than an Aristotelian

At first glance, one might well be tempted to surmise that Cyril's Christology is philosophically grounded in Aristotle's view of substance: after all, the referential scope of the term "substance" in Cyril would seem to be in conformity with the Aristotelian view that there are so-called primary and secondary substances, equally deserving of the name "substance," albeit on somewhat different grounds.[8]

In point of fact, however, Cyril's usage of the term "substance" diverges from the one that can be found in Aristotelian teaching, and rather adheres to the senses and usages defined by Aristotle's Neoplatonic commentators for the purposes of their logic. We should remind ourselves at this juncture that in Aristotle's *Categories* substance is, in fact, a homonymous notion (similar in this respect, for instance, to the notion of being). "Substance" primarily stands for particulars understood as individual things of a kind ("τὸ τί" — literally, "a given something"), and only secondarily refers to the genera and species of things: i.e. to forms abstracted from particulars. The primary substances are neither said of nor are in subjects, while secondary substances are said of subjects, but are not in subjects.[9] Thus, the category of substance embraces predicates that are said in essence of things and also things that are subjects of predication. In that sense, "substance" as it appears in Aristotle's logic is a homonymous term describing two aspects of how we speak about particular realities. In the *Metaphysics*, in turn, especially in Book Z, where substance is considered from an ontological point of view, Aristotle concludes that genuine substance is nothing else but enmattered form: i.e. εἶδος.[10]

The way in which Cyril speaks about substance corresponds to neither of these two originally Aristotelian uses. His own employment of the term seems to have

---

[7]Porphyry, *Isag.* 6.11–16, cf. Plato, *Philebus* 16c5–18d2; *Sophist*, 266a–b; *Politicus* 262a–c.

[8]In this respect theology scholars considered as authoritative and appear to relay on the studies by Hans van Loon, [10, 68–122, 27–44, 89–90, 297–8, 505–6]. See also Ruth Mary Siddals, [16, 344–5].

[9]Aristotle, *Categories* [*Cat.*] 2a11–19, 2b17–18, 2b37–3a1. See Joseph Owens, [12, 470].

[10]Aristotle, *Metaphysics* [*Metaph.*] Z, 1041b9–33. See Lambertus Marie de Rijk, [15, 2:244–9].

been inspired to a much greater extent by the Neoplatonic reinterpretation of the meaning of "substance"[11] that had been formulated as a consequence of Plotinus' crushing critique of Aristotle's conception of substance as genus.[12] According to the Neoplatonists, there are two meanings associated with the term substance. What they call "primary substance" is the correlate of a meaning that points to an individual understood as a collection of qualities, which always is such and such and not, as in Aristotle, a something. "Secondary substance," meanwhile, refers to definable forms that determine primary substances: i.e. to genera and species.[13]

Cyril's usage in his Trinitarian works is closer to the Neoplatonists than to Aristotle, especially in that he understands "substance" in the meaning of genus not as something abstracted, but as a real entity, common to individuals of the same kind. Alongside those "common substances" closely related to Neoplatonic genera, he also applies the term "substance" to individuals of a species, in a manner broadly in line with the Neoplatonic definition of "primary substance."[14] This pattern is also adhered to in Cyril's Christology, with one important difference: "substance" is replaced there by "nature," as Cyril considered the latter to be completely synonymous with the former. In those texts, consequently, "nature" in most cases designates essential content which individuals of the same species have in common, and thanks to this fact, when applied to Christ, that same term indicates the secondary substances of divinity and humanity. Nevertheless, "nature" is also employed with reference to individuals, making it possible for one to think that Cyril allows for "individual natures." Still, such a "nature" as Cyril's famous μία φύσις is equivalent to a primary, i.e. particular, substance.[15]

Most obviously, this identity of nature and substance cannot be found in Aristo-

---

[11]Cyril's familiarity with Neoplatonic teaching is broadly acknowledged. Some scholars ascribed to him advanced knowledge of Aristotle's and Neoplatonic philosophies, see Robert M. Grant, [6]; Marie-Odile Boulnois, [1, 181–209]. However, a few, with whom I tend to agree, are less enthusiastic about his expertise, and ascribed to him only a limited use and understanding of philosophical terminology. See de Durand, [3, 1, 378 n. 3 to *Dial. Trin.* II.419]; Lionel R. Wickham, [18, xxxiv].

[12]Cf. Anna Zhyrkova, [21]; [20].

[13]See Porphyry, *in Cat.* 89.10–90.11; Ammonius, *in Cat.* 36.2–21, 37.22–40.5; Dexippus, *in Cat.* 45.3–46.29; Simplicius, *in Cat.* 80.15–85.33.

[14]In the meaning of secondary substance, in *Dial. Trin.* I.407.18–20, I.408.29–409.14; in the meaning of primary substance, in *Thes.* 36.19–22; 444.13–16; in the meaning of both, in *Thes.* 316.12–38.

[15]See, for instance, Cyril of Alexandria *Thes.* 152.19–52, 485.38–41, 521.50–54; *Dial. Trin.* I.411.4–5, II.423.16–31, VI.587.1–23; *De incarnatione unigeniti* 690.31–691.4, 696.11–24. In those passages "nature" is just used to mean common or secondary substance, whereas in *CN* II and III, the term occurs in both meanings: as common and as individual nature (especially in the famous passage II.33.6–9). One may say the same of the *Second Letter to Nestorius*. See Jürgen Hammerstaedt, [7]; Jean-Marie Labelle, [8, 36–9]; van Loon, [10, 127–37, 43–52, 78–9].

tle. "Nature" is invested by the latter with a multiplicity of well-defined meanings, such as "origin of movement and rest," "the principle of what things are," the very "τὸ τί" of something, or "the realm of all things-that-there-are."[16] Thus, even though Cyril viewed particular natures as individual manifestations of common natures, his terminological choice was ambiguous and misleading. It was not obvious what he meant by "nature" when applying the term to separate individual realities. Used in this way to designate an individual of a certain kind, of which, as Cyril emphasized, a common substance is predicated, "nature" could be understood as referring to that common substance and as being synonymous with "hypostasis."

Nonetheless, the distinction between hypostasis and nature was already established in the writings of the Cappadocian Fathers in the context of the Trinitological debates. It is to the Cappadocians that the followers of Cyril's teaching turned in order to clarify the conception of a union of natures in one hypostasis.

3.2   The Cappadocian Reception of Porphyry

All sides in the Christological debates adopted, as their key principle, a terminological decision introduced by the Cappadocians within (and for the purposes of) their Trinitology. Specifically, Gregory of Nyssa, in *Letter 38* (preserved in the collection of letters attributed to Basil of Caesarea, and numbered within this collection), established the distinction between "substance/nature" on the one hand, and hypostasis on the other. Both substance and nature were construed there as that which is common and predicated of what is proper: i.e. of hypostases. Hypostasis itself, though, was defined as a subsisting thing, which is revealed according to its proper mode through its name, and in which a certain nature is subsistent.[17] This kind of distinction, marking out on the one side nature and substance construed as what is common and universal, and on the other hypostasis and persons characterized as what is proper and particular, can be found in several of the writings of the Cappadocians, and particularly in the works of Gregory of Nyssa.[18] Yet this seems just to implement, by means of a terminological demarcation, the well-known Neoplatonic account of universals, such as genera and species — the latter elucidating

---

[16]See, respectively, *Physics* 2.1, 192b20–23; Aristotle, *Metaph.* A1, 993a30–b7; Δ4, 1015a 13–9 (the word is used there in the meaning of "eternal nature," as opposed to γένεσις). See de Rijk, [15, 2:22, 2:39 n. 95.].

[17]Gregory of Nyssa, *Epistula* [*Ep.*] *38* 2–3, especially 3.1–12.

[18]See for instance Gregory of Nazianzus, *Oratio* [*Or.*] 21 (35.1124.44-7); *Or.* 39 (36.345.41-4); Basil *Ep.* 214.4.6–15; Gregory of Nyssa, *Contra Eunomium* [*CE.*] 205; *Ep.* 38.3, passim in *ad Ablabium, ad Graecos*. Cf. Joseph T. Lienhard, [9]; Anthony Meredith, [9, 44].

these as denoting what is common to the particulars of which they are predicated.[19]

To be sure, in speaking of substance and nature, Gregory prefers the term "common" (κοινόν), broadly recognized as belonging to Stoic logical discourse, over the term "universal" (καθόλου).[20] Yet when he applies it to clarify the terms "substance" and "nature," he uses it in a sense that accords with Porphyry's definition of "common," explained by the latter as what is in simultaneous use by many while remaining undivided.[21] Secondly, for Gregory the terms "substance" and "nature" are synonymous, and also identical, with their meaning being tantamount, furthermore, to what is captured by the notion of species/form (εἶδος).[22] Ostensibly, Gregory construes species/form as equivalent to the lowest species in Porphyry, for he describes it as possessing features that meet the criteria that the latter establishes for specific differences, while such differences combine to form the definition of a substance and constitute the species.[23] This formulation parallels a tenet (not mentioned hitherto) of Porphyry's logical interpretation of Aristotle's categorical doctrine of substance, according to which one predicates a certain substance (in the sense of a substance of a certain kind) as a universal of a particular or an individual.[24]

Besides, it is necessary to point out that in *Letter* 38, in *Ad Ablabium*, as well as in *Ad Graecos* — that is, in the works where Gregory sets up the distinction between substance/nature and hypostasis/person — the manner in which he approaches issues such as substance, nature, hypostasis, etc., resembles the methodological stance adopted by Porphyry in the *Isagoge*, and in *Commentaries on the Categories*, in which works the latter sets out to explain such Aristotelian conceptions as primary and secondary substance. Just as with Porphyry, Gregory discusses the aforemen-

---

[19]See Ammonius, *in Cat.* 49.5–11; Simplicius, *in Cat.* 53.6–9; 55.32–56.4. See Ammonius, *in Cat.* 49.5–11; Simplicius, *in Cat.* 53.6–9; 55.32–56.4. In Plotinus, the opposition common vs. proper occurs in descriptions of the intellect as such and in us in *Enn.* 1.1.8.1–8. It occurs also in his elucidation of how "living being" in its completeness as whole is composed of parts. See *Enn.* 6.7.10.

[20]There are 37 applications of the term "common" to substance and nature in his writings, in contrast to one direct application of the term "universal" to nature, occurring in *De opificio hominis*, 204.48.

[21]Porphyry, *in Cat.* 62.29–33.

[22]For synonymous usage of "substance" and "nature" as both signifying universal human, see Gregory of Nyssa, *Ad Graecos* 31.26–32.7; *ad Ablabium* 40.20–21; *Ep.* 38.3.1. For substance being the same as nature, see *CE* 3.4.3. On identification of substance with species, see *Ad Graecos* 30.19–31.11.

[23]Gregory of Nyssa, *Ad Grecos* 31.5–7. On accounts of the lowest species, see Porphyry, *Isag.* 4.11–13; 5.1–5; 5.14–16; 6.12–13. On specific differences, see Porphyry, *Isag.* 8.20–9.1; 9.11–15; 10.9–14; 12.9–10; 18.24–19.3, etc.

[24]Porphyry, *in Cat.* 71.30–37; 72.7–9; 73.30–5; 74.7–9; 14–20, etc. Universal and particular substance are equivalents of secondary and primary substance, respectively. See *in Cat.* 90.5–10; 88.33–89.17.

tioned notions in terms of predication (τὸ λεγόμενον— i.e. what is said). Accordingly, the term "hypostasis" is the name given to predications made in the mode of particularity, as opposed to generic predications of such terms as "substance" or "nature."[25]

It is not incorrect, then, to surmise that Gregory, in his account of substance and its correlation with hypostasis, draws on a Neoplatonic, and in particular the Porphyrian, logical account of universals. The Cappadocians' terminology was in all probability founded — just as was the case with Cyril — on premises acquired from Porphyry's logic. Key conceptions and definitions, such as they put to a theological use, match closely with what Porphyry puts forward as the elements of an account of predication. However, the very fact that they were invoked in the context of Trinitology and Christology lay them open to a reading with a more ontological bent.

4   Debates after Chalcedon:
The Ontological Consequences of the Adoption of
Porphyrian Logical Terminology

Two interpretations, broadly speaking, were given to the Cyrilian doctrine, read through the lens of the terminological decisions of the Cappadocians. The so-called anti-Chalcedonian party construed it as referring directly to reality, rather than to a manner of speaking about things. With the so-called Neo-Chalcedonians, though, matters are somewhat more complicated.

Anti-Chalcedonians took for granted that what subsists is a hypostasis, while no universal (that is, no nature or substance) subsists separately from its particular subject — namely, from a hypostasis or person.[26] Those assumptions, whose truthfulness they considered warranted by tradition, led them to claim that there are entities of the sort they called "particular natures." However, in order to draw

---

[25] In his paper "Porphyry and Cappadocian Logic" Mark Edwards pointed to similarities between Gregory's way of interpreting the conception of substance, nature, etc., in *Ep.* 38, and Porphyry's treatment of categories as such. See Mark Edwards, [5, 61–74]. However, we should point out that there are quite significant differences between Gregory's and Porphyry's accounts. Richard Cross, in [2] and Johannes Zachhuber, in [19, 124], have quite rightly highlighted some of these, which one should certainly not neglect, but which I have had to pass over in this paper due to its limited aims. I can only assert that on those points where Gregory differs from Porphyry, he seems rather to accept, in my opinion, certain elements of the thought of Porphyry's great teacher Plotinus, which better suited his Trinitological vision.

[26] Such a reading can be found, for instance, in Philoponus' *Arbiter* [*Arb.*]. For him it is already a part of traditional ecclesiastical doctrine. See *Arb.* VII. 21; 27.24.19–25.4.

such a conclusion, they needed to accept yet another premise, which they drew from Cyril and perceived as equally authoritative: that the term "nature" pertains both to common natures and to natures of particulars. If that is so, then whenever we encounter a nature, we encounter both a common nature and a nature in a particular. This makes sense only if the nature in question amounts to all of what a given thing is — the entirety of what is common and particular in a subject. For this reason, the expression "nature of a subject" is equivalent to the expression "particular nature."

The intent behind drawing this conclusion was obviously not merely to promote a philosophical vision of nature as existent only in and through particular natures. The ultimate conclusion of the argument was that Christ has one particular nature, and that such a nature is identical with his being a singular entity of one particular nature. The anti-Chalcedonians believed that rejecting this argument would result in the assertion that Christ is more than one entity. They contended that such an assertion actually followed from the Chalcedonian teaching that there are two natures of Christ. It is precisely for this reason that they opposed the doctrine of Chalcedon. For, if one posits two natures of Christ, one has to ascribe to Him two hypostases or persons, thereby committing oneself to the errors of Nestorius. Rather than falling into this fallacy, the Chalcedonians should have instead asserted that He has just one nature, which would be consistent with their positing one hypostasis of Christ. This was the gist of the charges levied against the doctrine of Chalcedon by Philoxenus, Severus, and other anti-Chalcedonians.[27]

The defenders of Chalcedonian doctrine that formed the theological movement known as Neo-Chalcedonism placed special emphasis on terminological clarity and the correctness of the lines of argumentation employed in Christology. On their view, all Christological errors were rooted in the indiscriminate employment of such terms as "substance," "nature" and "hypostasis."[28] The synonymy of "substance" with "nature" appeared at this point in the Christological debates to have been sanctioned by Church tradition.[29] The Neo-Chalcedonians embraced this synonymy as a broadly valid intuition, but also tried to refine the meaning of "substance/nature." In so doing, such important figures of the Neo-Chalcedonian movement as John the Grammarian and Leontius of Byzantium relied on Porphyry's logic to an even greater extent than their predecessors and adversaries.

John the Grammarian, in line with Porphyry's *Isagoge*, stresses that both "sub-

---

[27]See for instance Severus, *Ep.* 6; Philoponus, *Arb.* VII.27.24.19–25.4.

[28]Severus, *Ep. 3 ad Sergium*: CSCO 119 [120].

[29]John Grammarian, *Apologia Concilii Chalcedonensis*[*Apol.*], 1.1.2.15–16; 1.1.6; 1.2.1.9–10; *Contra Monophysitas* 7.86–89; Leontius of Byzantium, *Contra Nestorianos et Eutychianos* [*CNE*], 1273A 1–2 (5.5–6)

stance" and "nature" point to that which is common to a multiplicity of things.[30]
He offers a conception of "substance/nature" that corresponds to Porphyry's lowest
species, understood as that which is predicated essentially of individuals.[31] Leontius, meanwhile, adheres to John's Neoplatonic interpretation of "substance/nature"
as "that which is common."[32] While developing this, he becomes even more depen-
dent on the Neoplatonic logical account of substance, and distances himself both
from Aristotle's identification of substance with some particular or other possessing
a given essence and from treating substance as the manner of being of particulars.
Leontius understands "substance" as denoting the existence of something, whether
it be the genus and species of existing entities, or particular entities as such. Thus
"substance" can refer to all that is — even if "substance" as such signifies the peculiar features of "a something." In its broad scope, and in its relationship to the names
that designate given genera, species, and particular instances of a species, Leontius'
"substance" very closely resembles the Neoplatonic "highest genus" of substance.
Porphyry's *Isagoge* gives an account of the latter, as being predicated synonymi-
cally (in the Aristotelian sense of "synonymy") of, and encompassing, subsequently
coordinated genera, species and individuals. After having defined "substance", Leontius refers his readers to what one can easily recognize as the "Porphyrian tree" of
predication. He shows how "substance" can be predicated synonymously and in a
definitional way of each subsequent member of this tree — as things referred to by
the term "that which is corporeal" are neither more nor less substances than an
individual horse.[33]

"Nature," according to Leontius' account, can be treated as being interchange-
able with "substance," since one can predicate it, too, of coordinated genera and
species. Yet it does not point to the existence of a something, but rather reveals the
ontological completeness of an entity. One cannot equate its meaning with "a given
existent someone or something" — it being focused, instead, on what this given
someone or something is "made of." Leontius' complex analyses lead, ultimately,
to a view of nature that requires, for its completeness, all constitutive and specific
differences. In its fundamental sense, "nature" therefore seems to differ from "substance" understood as "the highest genus." If one seeks to elucidate it in this way,
"nature" corresponds to the lowest Porphyrian kind of universal predicate: i.e. to

---

[30]John Grammarian, *Apol.* 1.2.1.1–2. Cf. understanding of the five basic notions (i.e. genus, species, differentia, etc.) as common in Porphyry, *Isag.*2.18–24; 13.10–17.

[31]See Porphyry, *Isag.* 4.11–12; 13.10–17; 21.5. The same relates to essential characteristics of individuals belonging to the same species. See John Grammarian, *Apol.* 1.2.2.22–25. Compare with Porphyry, *Isag.* 7.23–8.1; 9.16–17; 18–23.

[32]Leontius of Byzantium, *CNE* 1288D; *Epilyseis* [*Epil.*], PG86, 1917D.

[33]Leontius of Byzantium, *Epil.* PG86, 1921C–D, Porphyry, *Isag.* 4.21–27.

"species."[34]

It is in the context of these definitions of "substance" and "nature" inspired by Neoplatonic logic that the Neo-Chalcedonians formulated what amounted to their greatest achievement: a redefinition of "hypostasis". Yet their solution not only differed from that of their adversaries, but also went far beyond the proposals of Neoplatonic logic. They elucidated hypostasis as an underlying factor through which the ontological complements of particular entities exist. Nature and substance became such ontological en-hypostasized elements: i.e. realities that are actualized only through a hypostasis and only as such are real, contributing to the being of sensible particulars. At least, this is, in my opinion, the best way of condensing the principal intuition behind the complex discussions of hypostasis in the Neo-Chalcedonian writings. It is impossible here to go into details concerning those lengthy discussions, as attempting to give an adequate account would unavoidably lead one to the writing of a new philosophical story about the discoveries, influences and consequences at work there. Let me therefore just confine myself to noting that while the Neo-Chalcedonian vision of hypostasis morphed into a theory of individual entities, its development was triggered by the necessity of dealing with Porphyry's elucidation of the individual as a collection of qualities. Most obviously, this theoretical advancement required slipping from logic into ontology.

5 Conclusions

From a philosophical point of view, one can see both anti-Chalcedonian and Neo-Chalcedonian approaches as resulting from — or at least involving — a confusion of logic with ontology. For Porphyry, at least, the two domains were, however, separate: he described all categories — in the sense of "predications", for this is the meaning of the word κατηγορία— as simple significant expressions[35] just inasmuch as they served to designate things, and only insofar as they differed from each other in respect of the ten genera (rather than merely in respect of number).[36]

Of course, Porphyry did not treat substance construed as a category as anything different from this. Thus, the category of substance encompasses significant expressions referring to sensible individual things.[37] To be sure, Porphyry stated clearly that categories were concerned primarily with simple significant expressions

---

[34]See Leontius, *Epil.* PG86, 1921A–B; *Epil.*1945A–C; *Epap.* 22–23; 25 PG86, 1908C; 1909A; 1909C. Cf. Porph. *Isag.* 9.2–10.21.

[35]The term "significant expression" is accepted within Neoplatonic studies as rendering of "λέξις σημαντική" / "φωνή σημαντική."

[36]Porphyry, *in Cat.* 58.3–20.

[37]Porphyry, *in Cat.* 91. 19–27.

qua their being significant.[38] However, expressions belonging to categories are expressions of first imposition: i.e. they refer directly to things. Considered as an expression of first imposition, an expression in the category of substance will be viewed as representing the thing it refers to. A person lacking the necessary philosophical education may easily then conflate different aspects of Porphyry's logic of meaningful expressions and assume that he is speaking about actual entities.[39]

We may also surmise that the very inner make-up of Porphyry's logic, which discusses expressions qua their being *significant* without separating out syntactic and semantic considerations, facilitates this kind of confusion. Yet there are some other reasons that may be pointed to, thanks to which I am not obliged to conclude this article with a denouncement of the philosophical ignorance of Christian theologians. It is a fact that both parties to the post-Chalcedonian theological debates eventually moved beyond logic. The Miaphysite theologian and Neoplatonist philosopher Philoponus gave the anti-Chalcedonian stance a philosophical underpinning through his consistent theory of what he called "particular nature." To be sure, this theory was hardly Neoplatonic in its core, and was rather influenced by Alexander of Aphrodisias' account of universals. Likewise, one cannot characterize as Neoplatonic the Neo-Chalcedonian response offered by Leontius of Jerusalem through his detailed elucidation of hypostasis as the bedrock of individual being, irreducible to any kind of ontological structure but nevertheless such as to allow for an ontological structure to make up a truly independent and separate being of a given nature. Even so, the two opposing theologies could not have erected their contrary ontologies without preserving an impulse that they had explicitly taken from Porphyrian logic. Referring his readers to Plato's *Philebus*, Porphyry seeks to remind us in the *Isagoge* that there is no theoretical knowledge of individuals. His logic, however, by its very focus on significatory meaning, made it possible to speak of and analyze individual entities.

One may therefore contend that the Christological controversies of the fifth and sixth centuries are very much a consequence of Porphyry's logic having been entwined in Christological discourse. Since what Porphyry had offered were in fact only some rules concerning the use of significant expressions, various metaphysical interpretations could be given to those rules. In this way, a philosopher and metaphysician whom Augustine ranked amongst the most remarkable and dangerous adversaries of Christianity also came to be one of the greatest authorities for

---

[38] Porphyry, *in Cat.* 58.27–29; cf. 58.5–6.

[39] As regards the group I have chosen to designate as the "anti-Chalcedonians", I would certainly not wish to include there John Philoponus, who, as a professional philosopher, produced an ontology for the Miaphysite theology itself, rather than conveniently adopting some philosophical tools just for the sake of their usefulness for Christological discourse.

Christian thought itself.

References

[1] Boulnois, Marie-Odile. *Le paradoxe trinitaire chez Cyrille d'Alexandrie: Herméneutique, analyses philosophiques et argumentation théologique.* Collection des Études Augustiniennes, Série Antiquité 143. Paris: Institut d'Études Augustiniennes, 1994.

[2] Cross, Richard. "Gregory of Nyssa on Universals." *Vigiliae Christianae* 56, no. 4 (2002): 372–410.

[3] de Durand, Georges Matthieu. "Introduction; Notes." In Cyril of Alexandria, *Dialogues sur la Trinité*, edited by Georges Matthieu de Durand, vol. I, *Dialogues I et II.* Sources chrétiennes 231. Paris: Cerf, 1976.

[4] Ebbesen, Sten. "Philoponus, 'Alexander' and the Origin of Medieval Logic." In *Aristotle Transformed: The Ancient Commentators and Their Influence*, edited by Richard Sorabji, 445–61. Ithaca: Cornell University Press, 1990.

[5] Edwards, Mark. "Porphyry and Cappadocian Logic." *Greek Orthodox Theological Review* 61 (2016): 61–74.

[6] Grant, Robert M. "Greek Literature in the Treatise *De Trinitate* and Cyril *Contra Julianum.*" *Journal of Theological Studies* 15 (1964): 265–79. http://dx.doi.org/10.1093/jts/XV.2.265.

[7] Hammerstaedt, Jürgen. "Das Aufkommen der philosophischen Hypostasisbedeutung." *Jahrbuch für Antike und Christentum* 35 (1992): 7–11.

[8] Labelle, Jean-Marie. "Saint Cyrille d'Alexandrie témoin de la langue et de la pensée philosophiques au Ve siècle." *Revue des sciences religieuses.* Parts 1 and 2. 52 (1978): 135–158; 53 (1979): 23–42.

[9] Lienhard, Joseph T. "Ousia and Hypostasis: The Cappadocian Settlement and the Theology of 'One Hypostasis.'" In *The Trinity*, edited by Stephen T. Davis, Daniel Kendall, and Gerald O'Collin. Oxford: Oxford University Press, 2002. http://dx.doi.org/10.1093/0199246122.003.0005.

[10] van Loon, Hans. *The Dyophysite Christology of Cyril of Alexandria.* Supplements to *Vigiliae Christianae* 96. Leiden; Boston: Brill, 2009.

[11] Meredith, Anthony. *The Cappadocians.* Outstanding Christian Thinkers. London: Chapman, 1995.

[12] Owens, Joseph. *The Doctrine of Being in the Aristotelian Metaphysics: A Study in the Greek Background of Mediaeval Thought.* 3rd ed. Toronto: Pontifical Institute of Mediaeval Studies, 1978.

[13] Price, Richard. "The Council of Chalcedon (451): A Narrative." In *Chalcedon in Context: Church Councils, 400–700*, edited by Richard Price and Mary Whitby, 70–91. Translated Texts for Historians, Contexts 1. Liverpool: Liverpool University Press, 2011.

[14] Price, Richard and Michael Gaddis. *The Acts of the Council of Chalcedon.* Translated Texts for Historians 45. Liverpool: Liverpool University Press, 2005.

[15] de Rijk, Lambertus Marie. *Aristotle: Semantics and Ontology.* 2 vols. Philosophia antiqua 91. Leiden; Boston: Brill, 2002.

[16] Siddals, Ruth Mary. "Logic and Christology in Cyril of Alexandria." *Journal of Theological Studies* 38 (1987): 341–67.

[17] Strange, Steven Keith. "Plotinus, Porphyry and the Neoplatonic Interpretation of the Categories." In *Aufstieg und Niedergang der römischen Welt: Geschichte und Kultur Roms im Spiegel der neueren Forschung*, edited by Hildegard Temporini and Wolfgang Haase, II.36.2:955–74. Berlin; New York: W. de Gruyter, 1987.

[18] Wickham, Lionel R. "Introduction." In Cyril of Alexandria, *Select Letters*, edited and translated by Lionel R. Wickham, xi–xlix. Oxford Early Christian Texts. Oxford: Clarendon Press, 1983.

[19] Zachhuber, Johannes. "Gregory of Nyssa, Contra Eunomium III 4 r." In *Gregory of Nyssa Contra Eunomium III: An English Translation with Commentary and Supporting Studies; Proceedings of the 12th International Colloquium on Gregory of Nyssa (Leuven, 14–17 September 2010)*, edited by Andrew Radde-Gallwitz, 313–34. Supplements to *Vigiliae Christianae* 124. Leiden; Boston: Brill, 2014.

[20] Zhyrkova, Anna. "Plotinus' Conception of the Genera of Sensibles." *Dionysius* 26 (2008): 47–59.

[21] Zhyrkova, Anna. "Porphyry's Interpretation of Categories — the Neoplatonic Approach to Nominalism?" *Eos* 95, no. 2 (2008): 253–67.

Received 27 May 2019

THE PROBLEM OF UNIVERSALS IN LATE PATRISTIC THEOLOGY

DIRK KRAUSMÜLLER
Universität Wien

In the late fourth century the Christian writer Gregory of Nyssa famously claimed that one could speak of Peter, Paul and John but was not permitted to speak of three human beings since the human nature was one and the name "human being" should therefore only be used in the singular. In order to support this view, he argued that Peter, Paul and John only came into existence when their individual characteristics were added to the account of being, that is, the set of properties that all members of a species share, which in itself remained undivided. When Gregory developed this conceptual framework he did so primarily because he was looking for an analogy that would help him prove that Father, Son and Spirit were only one God and not three. Yet he was also interested in the human species for its own sake. By insisting that it was one he could make the case that the benefits of the incarnation were not limited to one individual but extended to the entire human race.[1]

In the next two centuries Gregory's arguments found widespread acceptance. This does not, however, mean that there were no dissenting voices. In the middle of the sixth century the Alexandrian philosopher-theologian John Philoponus contended that the human nature in one individual was not the same as the human nature in another individual. Like Gregory, Philoponus was of the opinion that there was no categorical difference between an ordinary species and the divinity. Therefore, he declared that Father, Son and Spirit were three particular natures. This position met with furious opposition from representatives of the ecclesiastical establishment who worried that Christianity might lose its status as a Monotheistic religion.[2] Yet it would be wrong to think that Philoponus' opponents focused exclusively on Trinitarian theology. Quite the contrary, the ontological status of the human species also became a subject of debate.

"This article is part of the project 'Reassessing Ninth Century Philosophy. A Synchronic Approach to the Logical Traditions' (9 SALT) that has received funding from the European Research Council (ERC) under the European Union's Horizon 2020 research and innovation programme (grant agreement No. 648298)."

[1]Gregory's ontology has often been discussed. See e.g. [9, pp. 149–185], and [34, pp. 436–447].
[2]See [30].

This article discusses the contributions of Chalcedonian theologians of the sixth century. It seeks to show that these theologians did not present a united front. Some defended the existence of immanent universals in the created order because they wished to uphold traditional soteriology. Others were prepared to accept Philoponus' position in principle and only demanded that an exception be made for the divinity. This debate has so far attracted little attention from scholars. Richard Cross and Christophe Erismann have studied passages in the oeuvre of John of Damascus that suggest a "nominalist" reading. But they have come to the conclusion that one should not take John's words at face value because he could not possibly have held such a view.[3] Other relevant evidence has not been discussed at all.

1   John Philoponus

When he was already an old man, the philosopher John Philoponus decided to engage in the debate about the proper understanding of the incarnation of the Word.[4] In his treatise *Arbiter* he attempted to show that the solution proposed by the defenders of Chalcedon was untenable and that only his own Monophysite position could withstand scrutiny.[5] One of his targets is the Chalcedonian teaching that there are two different natures in the incarnated Word but that the incarnated Word is nevertheless one. He points out that something cannot be at the same time one and two on the same ontological level, and then explains that oneness always has a higher status: two species can fall under the same genus, and two individuals can belong to one species.[6] He illustrates his argument with the two human beings Peter and Paul who can be said to be one because they share the same account of being, namely "rational and mortal living being", but are two insofar as "this one is Peter and that one is Paul", and then offers the following explanation:

> Ὁ γὰρ κοινὸς καὶ καθόλου τῆς τοῦ ἀνθρώπου φύσεως λόγος, εἰ καὶ αὐτὸς καθ᾽ ἑαυτὸν εἷς ἐστιν, ἀλλ᾽ οὖν ἐν πολλοῖς ὑποκειμένοις γινόμενος πολλὰ γίνεται, ὁλόκληρος ἐν ἑκάστῳ καὶ οὐχ ἀπὸ μέρους ὑπάρχων, ὥσπερ καὶ ὁ ἐν τῷ ναυπηγῷ τοῦ πλοίου λόγος εἷς ὢν πληθύνεται ἐν πολλοῖς ὑποκειμένοις γινόμενος[7].

---

[3]See [5, p.85]; and [10, p. 50]. Late Patristic theology in general see [35].

[4]On Philoponus' philosophical oeuvre there exist a great number of studies. See e.g. [33]; and [31]. On Philoponus as a theologian see [13]. See also the contributions to [26].

[5]See [18].

[6]For a summary see [18, p. 57].

[7][15, 83], addit., [16, p. 50, ll. 5–8].

> For the common and universal account of the nature of man, although
> it is by itself one, nevertheless becomes many when it comes to be in
> many subjects, while existing in each one completely and not partially,
> as the account of a ship in a ship-builder, being one, is multiplied, when
> it comes to be in many subjects.[8]

Here Philoponus declares that the account of being in one individual is different
from the account of being in another individual and that there are therefore as many
human natures as there are individuals. This amounts to an outright rejection of
the conceptual framework that Gregory of Nyssa had created in the late fourth
century when he claimed that the instantiated account of being was undivided.[9]
Philoponus was so insistent on this point because he saw himself confronted with a
Christological problem. He was of the opinion that if immanent universals existed,
all three divine persons would have become incarnate in all human beings. The only
solution he could envisage was to assume the existence of particular natures. Even
so, he could still speak of the oneness of the account of being. However, according
to him this oneness was found outside the instantiations. The comparison with a
shipbuilder who has the building plan of a ship in his mind gives the impression
that Philoponus accepted the existence of *ante rem* universals.[10] However, this
impression is misleading. In another part of his treatise Philoponus declares:

> Εἰ γὰρ καὶ ἴδιον ἔχει τὸν τοῦ εἶναι λόγον τὸ ζῷον, φέρε καὶ ὁ ἄνθρωπος, ὧν
> τὸ μέν ἐστι γένος, τὸ δὲ εἶδος, ἀλλ᾽ ἐν τοῖς ἀτόμοις τὴν ὕπαρξιν ἔχουσιν,
> οἷον Πέτρῳ καὶ Παύλῳ, χωρὶς τούτων οὐχ ὑφιστάμενα.[11]

> For even if the animal has its own account of being, and let us say also
> man, of which the former is genus and the latter species, it is nevertheless
> the case that they have their existence in the individuals, as for example
> in Peter and in Paul, since they do not subsist without them.[12]

This passage shows that for Philoponus the non-instantiated account of being
has no objective reality. He had to take this step because otherwise he would have

---

[8]My translation. I render the Greek term λόγος as 'account'. It indicates the 'content' of a
species, that is, its constituent features. In this sense λόγος corresponds to the scholastic term *ratio
entis*.

[9]See [34, p. 464]; and [8, pp. 285–294]. This was disputed by [18, pp. 56–57]. See, however,
the arguments of M. Rashed in [24, p. 352–357].

[10]For a summary of the argument see [18, p. 56].

[11][15, 83], addit., [16, pp. 51–52, ll. 48–50].

[12]My translation.

introduced a fourth component into the Trinity.[13] Since he argued for a strict parallelism between the divinity and the human species he was then forced to reject the existence of *ante rem* universals in the created order as well. Such a view would have been acceptable to the Cappadocians. Basil of Caesarea, for example, had declared that the three divine persons were not subordinated to an overarching genus (here used in the sense of species).[14] Significantly, however, Philoponus drew his inspiration not from a theological but from a philosophical text. In a later treatise, which had the Trinity as its subject matter, he made the following comment:

> We have shown that the nature that is called common, does not have an existence of its own in any being, but is either altogether nothing – which is true – or exists only in our mind where it is constituted from the particulars.[15]

This is a clear reference to Aristotle's treatise *De anima* where the same two options are proposed.[16] Philoponus chose the former option because he sought to dispel any suspicion that he wished to turn the Trinity into a quaternity. Such a position, however, came at a cost. It meant that there was no longer a unifying bond between individuals. This wrought havoc not only on traditional Trinitarian theology but also on traditional soteriology since it was believed that the immanent universal ensured the transmission of the benefits of the incarnation to the entire human race.

2 Anastasius of Antioch

The conceptual framework that Philoponus had set out in the *Arbiter* and in his treatises about the Trinity met with considerable opposition, not only in his own, Monophysite, church but also among the adherents of the Council of Chalcedon. Indeed, it seems that it was not the Monophysites but the Chalcedonians who were most upset about Philoponus' innovations. This should not come as a surprise. Monophysite theologians had even before Philoponus been willing to regard the Word and the flesh as particular natures. By contrast, their Chalcedonian colleagues had always insisted that the incarnation was a union of two common natures. Anastasius I, the Chalcedonian patriarch of Antioch, declares in his treatise *Doctrinal Exposition*:[17]

---

[13]See [29, 8–9, PG 86, 60]; and [21, X.8.1, pp. 310–311].

[14][4, p. 202]. See [36, p. 96].

[15][25, p. 161].

[16][3, I.1, p. 402b7-8].

[17]On Anastasius see [32].

Ἐπειδὴ γὰρ ὅλον τὸ πεπτωκὸς ἀναστῆναι προέθετο, πεπτώκει δὲ τὸ γένος ἅπαν, ὅλον ἑαυτὸν ὅλῳ τῷ Ἀδὰμ κατέμιξε, ζωὴ ὑπάρχων τῷ θανατωθέντι.[18]

For since he purposed to raise up all that had fallen, and the entire race had fallen, he mixed himself with the entire Adam, being life for the one who had been put to death.

The repeated use of the adjective "entire" in this passage is no coincidence. It is meant to exclude the possibility that the flesh is a particular nature. The formula "entire Adam", which corresponds to "entire race", suggests that the Word in some way united himself with all human beings. Here one would expect Anastasius to explain why Christ nevertheless did not become incarnate in every single individual. Such an explanation, however, is missing. Instead Anastasius contents himself with rejecting Philoponus' position and affirming his own:

Λέγομεν γὰρ αὐτὸν θεόν, οὐ τινὰ θεόν, λέγομεν αὐτὸν καὶ ἄνθρωπον, οὐ τινὰ ἄνθρωπον. Ἐστὶ δὲ θεὸς ἅμα καὶ ἄνθρωπος διὰ τῶν γενικωτέρων ὀνομάτων δηλούμενος τὸ ἐξ ὧν ἐστιν, οὐκ ἐκ μερικῶν ὑποστάσεων ἀλλ᾿ ἐκ γενικῶν οὐσιῶν.[19]

For we call him God, and not a certain god, and we call him man but not a certain man. He is at the same time god and man since the parts out of which he is are indicated through the more generic names, not out of particular hypostases but out of generic substances.[20]

Here Anastasius simply asserts the existence of common natures. It is evident that after Philoponus' intervention into the theological discourse such a response was no longer sufficient. One also had to show why common natures were immanent and real and not extrinsic and mere names as Philoponus had claimed. Significantly, Anastasius' substantial oeuvre does not contain a single discussion of this problem.

3 Leontius of Byzantium

Anastasius was first and foremost a man of action who engaged in speculation very much against his will. His muddled reasoning shows that he lacked the training necessary for an effective response. Yet this does not mean that all Chalcedonian

---

[18] [2, p. 53, ll. 30–32].
[19] [2, p. 54, ll. 15–18].
[20] My translation.

theologians were incompetent. The monks of Palestine were of quite a different calibre. They had a long-standing interest in the speculation of Origen and Evagrius Ponticus and were thus better prepared for the construction of coherent theological positions.[21] Chief among them was Leontius of Byzantium, a contemporary of Philoponus. Leontius may not have known Philoponus' *Arbiter* but his work shows that he was already wrestling with the same problems.[22] At the beginning of his treatise *Solutiones* he lets a Monophysite interlocutor ask whether the Word assumed the human nature in an individual or in the entire species. Leontius replies that the question is nonsensical because the account of being that defines the human nature is the same regardless of whether it is seen in one person or in a collective. Then he continues:

> Τὸ γὰρ ἐν ἑνὶ ἢ ἐν πλείοσι ταύτην (sc. τὴν φύσιν) θεωρεῖσθαι τὰ ἐν οἷς ἐστι πολλὰ ἢ ἓν ποιεῖ, οὐ τὴν φύσιν ἓν ἢ πολλὰ φαίνεσθαι παρασκευάζει. ...
> ὅτι δὲ ταῦτα οὕτως ἔχει, δῆλον ἐξ ὧν ὁ τῆς φύσεως λόγος ἐπί τε πλήθους καὶ ἑνὸς ὁ αὐτὸς ἀποδίδοται· ὃν γὰρ ἀποδῷς λόγον περὶ τῆς ἁπλῶς φύσεως, οὗτός σοι καὶ ἐπὶ τῆς ἔν τινι θεωρουμένης ἀποδοθήσεται, καὶ οὔτε πολλὰς ποιεῖ φύσεις τὴν μίαν τὸ πολλοὺς ταύτης μετέχειν ...[23]

For the fact that it (sc. the nature) is seen in one (sc. item) or in multiple (sc. items) makes those in which it is many or one, and does not cause the nature to be one or many. ... And that this is so is evident from the fact that the same definition of the nature is given for the multitude and for the one. For which definition you give for nature in the absolute sense, it will also be given by you for nature, which is seen in a certain one, and the fact that many participate in it (sc. the one nature) does not make the one (sc. nature) many natures ...[24]

This passage bears a striking resemblance to the statement by Philoponus with which we began the discussion. Here, too, we are told what happens when a common account of nature appears in various subjects. Yet Leontius comes to a radically different conclusion. He claims that the common account of nature is not divided when it is instantiated. Here we thus have an affirmation of universals *in re*, which undergirds traditional Christian soteriology. This does, however, not mean that Leontius merely restates Gregory of Nyssa's position. The following exchange shows that he is prepared to accept the existence of particular natures:

---

[21]See [14, pp. 133–138]; and [17].
[22]See however [20].
[23][19, p. 270, l. 20-p. 271, l. 4].
[24]My translation.

ἈΚΕΦ. Τὴν τινὰ οὖν ἀνέλαβε φύσιν (sc. ὁ λόγος);
ὈΡΘ. Ναί, ἀλλὰ τὴν αὐτὴν οὖσαν τῷ εἴδει.[25]

A. Did he (sc. the Word) then assume a certain nature?
O. Yes, but one that is the same as the species.[26]

Leontius probably made this concession because he did not wish to be told by his adversary that the Word would then become incarnate in all human individuals. For him taking this step posed no problems. He was clearly convinced that the identity of the account of being in all members of a species established an ontological link that was strong enough to ensure that the benefits of the incarnation were passed on to the entire human race. It is, however, doubtful whether this argument would have cut any ice with Philoponus. As we have seen he, too, accepts that the account of being is the same in all individuals but nevertheless concludes that the common nature is broken up into particular natures.

4 Doctrina Patrum

One striking parallel between the arguments of Philoponus and Leontius is the references to the non-instantiated account of being, which had played no role in the speculation of Gregory of Nyssa. This does not mean, however, that they agreed on its ontological status. For Philoponus it could only be a mere name. Leontius, on the other hand, may have considered it to be an *ante rem* universal. Indeed, one gets the impression that it plays an important role in the argument. Leontius insists that immanent universals must exist because the account of being in the individuals is identical with the non-instantiated account of being. The same argument is put forward in a brief anti-Philoponian treatise, which was later incorporated in the *Doctrina Patrum*:[27]

Εἰ χωρίσαντες τῇ ἐπινοίᾳ τὰ συμβεβηκότα ἰδιώματα καὶ ἐφ' ἑαυτὴν τὴν Πέτρου σκοπήσαντες φύσιν ὁριζόμενοι οὕτω λέγομεν, ὅτι ζῷον λογικὸν θνητόν, ὁ αὐτὸς δὲ ὅρος καὶ ἐπὶ τῆς ἁπλῶς φύσεως ἀποδίδοται, ὁ αὐτὸς ἄρα ἔσται λόγος ἐπὶ τῆς ἁπλῶς φύσεως καὶ ἐπὶ τῆς ἔν τινι θεωρουμένης.[28]

---

[25][19, p. p. 271, ll. 6-7].

[26]My translation.

[27]On the author of this text, see [27], who attributes the work to Anastasius Apocrisiarius, a companion of Maximus the Confessor. See also [1, pp. 172–175].

[28]Anonymous (Eulogius of Alexandria?), in [7, p. 72, ll. 10-15].

When we separate in thought the accidental idioms and focus on the nature of Peter itself, we say by way of definition that it is "rational mortal animal", and when the same definition is given in the case of the nature in the absolute sense, then it will be the same account in the case of the nature in the absolute sense and in the case of that which is contemplated in a certain one.[29]

With this argument the author of the treatise seeks to prove that the instantiated nature is common and not divided. This suggests that the non-instantiated account of being has become the linchpin for the entire ontological edifice.

5 Anonymus Rashed

How crucial the notion of an *ante rem* universal was in the Chalcedonian theological discourse is evident from an anonymous treatise, which has recently been edited by Marwan Rashed.[30] The author of this text, which may date to the late sixth or seventh century, seeks to affirm the traditional teaching about soteriology. What makes his task difficult is the objections of a follower of Philoponus:

Ὅταν λέγῃς ὅτι ὁ Πέτρος ἄνθρωπός ἐστι, ποῖον ἄνθρωπον κατηγορεῖς, τὸν καθόλου καὶ τὸν μερικόν; οὐδέτερον. οὔτε τὸν καθόλου μόνον τὸν κοινὸν οὔτε τὸν μερικὸν μόνον, ἀλλὰ τὸν ἐν τῷ νῷ μόνον θεωρούμενον καθόλου, ὑπάρχοντα δὲ ἐν τῷ Πέτρῳ ἀτομωθέντα.[31]

When you say "Peter is a human being", which human being do you mean, the universal one or the particular one? – Neither of the two, neither the universal alone, the common one, nor the particular alone, but the universal one, which is seen in the mind only but exists in Peter where it is individuated.[32]

Here the author is presented with two options: the human nature in an individual is either particular or common. As a Chalcedonian he could not have chosen the first option. Yet had he picked the alternative he would have been told that that the Word would then have incarnated in all human beings. Therefore, he drops the immanent universal and instead introduces a third option, the individuated common nature,

---

[29] My translation.
[30] See above note 7.
[31] Anonymus, [24, p. 367, ll. 28-31].
[32] My translation.

which is divided in itself but one through participation in an extrinsic common nature. How important the common nature was for the author can be seen from the following paragraph. There he asserts that it ensures the consubstantiality of all human beings. However, it is very questionable whether it could really have had this function. After all, we are told that the common nature is only seen in thought. As such it should not have been able to function as a unifying element. The author was clearly unhappy about this outcome. At the end of the text he returns to the topic:

Ἰστέον ὅτι καὶ ἡ θεότης καὶ ἡ ἀνθρωπότης οὐκ ἔστι χωρὶς τῶν ὑποστάσεων, θεωρούμεναι δὲ καθ᾿ ἑαυτὴν ἑκάστη ἄνευ τῶν ὑποστάσεων θεωρεῖται. ἡ δὲ θεωρία οὐκ ἐστὶ κωλυτικὴ τῆς ὑπάρξεως.[33]

One must know that the divinity and the humanity do not exist without the hypostases, but when they are contemplated, each of them is contemplated by itself without the hypostases. Contemplation, however, does not exclude existence.[34]

This is an extraordinarily confused statement. The author first declares that non-instantiated natures have no objective existence but can only be contemplated. Yet then he changes tack and declares that what is contemplated is not necessarily without objective existence. Thus he is insinuating that *ante rem* universals do indeed exist.

6 Arguments Against Particularism

Philoponus was not content with merely asserting that each individual has its own incommunicable account of being. He also presented arguments in support of this view. In the *Arbiter* he points out that when an individual is born, suffers or dies this has no effect on other members of the same species.[35]

Τὸ γὰρ ἐν ἐμοὶ ζῷον λογικὸν θνητὸν οὐδενὸς ἄλλου κοινόν ἐστιν. ἀμέλει παθόντος ἀνθρώπου τινὸς ἢ βοὸς ἢ ἵππου ἀπαθῆ μένειν τὰ ὁμοειδῆ τῶν ἀτόμων οὐκ ἀδύνατον. Καὶ γὰρ Παύλου τεθνεῶτος μηδένα τεθνάναι τῶν λοιπῶν ἀνθρώπων ἐνδέχεται, καὶ γενομένου Πέτρου καὶ εἰς τὸ εἶναι παρενεχθέντος οἱ ἐσόμενοι μετ᾿ αὐτὸν ἄνθρωποι οὔπω τῶν ὄντων εἰσίν.[36]

---

[33]Anonymus, [24, p. 375, ll. 89-92].
[34]My translation.
[35]For a summary of the argument see [18, pp. 61–62].
[36][15, 83] addit., [16, 52, ll. 55-59].

For the rational mortal animal in me is not common to anybody else. Indeed, when a certain man or ox or horse suffers it is not impossible for the individuals belonging to the same species to remain unaffected. For when Paul dies it is possible that none of the other human beings dies, and when Peter is born and brought into existence the human beings that will exist after him do not yet exist.[37]

With these observations Philoponus not only intended to prove the existence of particular natures. He also sought to outmanoeuvre the defenders of immanent universals. According to him their position was untenable because it was manifestly untrue: members of a species do not experience the same things at the same time. Thus he could buttress his argument that the Word could not have assumed the common human nature because otherwise he would have become incarnate in the entire human race. Chalcedonian theologians found this reasoning particularly irksome. The author of the anti-Philoponian treatise in the *Doctrina Patrum* came up with the following counterargument:

Τί γὰρ Πέτρου σταυρωθέντος ἢ Παύλου ἀποτμηθέντος καὶ θατέρου αὐτῶν πλήρη καὶ ὁλόκληρον τὴν κοινὴν ἔχοντος τῶν ἀνθρώπων φύσιν, τοὺς λοιποὺς τοῦτο παρέβλαψε τοὺς ὑπὸ τὴν αὐτὴν ἀναγομένους φύσιν;[38]

What then? When Peter was crucified or Paul beheaded, both of whom had the common nature of the human beings in its fulness and entirety, did this harm the others who are assigned to the same nature?[39]

Here we are told that individuals have a common nature and nevertheless do not suffer at the same time. The author simply takes it for granted that there is a common nature and can therefore come to the conclusion that its existence can be reconciled with the phenomena of which Philoponus had spoken. This, however, is not his last word. In another passage he explains:

Εἰ τὴν κοινὴν φύσιν ὁ λόγος οὐκ ἀνέλαβεν, ἐμὲ οὐκ ἀνέλαβεν. εἰ δὲ λέγουσιν ἐκεῖνοι· οὐκοῦν καὶ τὸν Ἰούδαν ἀνέλαβεν, ἀπολογούμεθα ἡμεῖς, ὅτι τὴν φύσιν εἴπομεν αὐτὸν ἀναλαβεῖν, οὐ μὴν τὰ ὑποστατικὰ ἑκάστου ἰδιώματα. Ταῦτα γὰρ ποιεῖ τὸν Ἰούδαν καὶ τὸν δεῖνα καὶ τὸν δεῖνα.[40]

---

[37] My translation.
[38] [7, p. 73, ll. 4-8].
[39] My translation.
[40] [7, p. 72, ll. 19-23].

If the Word did not assume the common nature, he would not have assumed me. But if those people say "Then he has also assumed Judas", we will respond, "we say that he assumed the nature, but indeed not the hypostatic idioms of each one. For they are what make Judas and this one and that one".[41]

Here the author insists that the nature must be one and indivisible because otherwise the beneficial effects of the incarnation could not be passed on to all human beings. Yet this does not mean that the Word assumes all human individuals because the characteristic idioms remain separate.

This argument is problematic because it loosens the link between the substantial and the accidental dimensions within the individual. Thus it is not surprising that the search for solutions continued. The Anonymus Rashed has the following to say:

Γνῶτε ὅτι μία καὶ ἡ αὐτὴ φύσις Πέτρου καὶ Παύλου, καὶ ἀποθνήσκοντος Πέτρου, ἡ φύσις ἡ ἐν αὐτῷ οὐκ ἀποθνήσκει. ἡ γὰρ ἐν αὐτῷ ἀνθρωπότης τὰ ἰδιώματα δέξεται καὶ οὐ λέγεται φύσις ἀλλ' ὑπόστασις.[42]

Know that there is one and the same nature of Peter and Paul, and that when Peter dies the nature in him does not die. For the humanity in him will receive the idioms and is not called nature but hypostasis.

Here it is claimed that the nature in a particular person does not die because after the characteristic idioms have been added to it it is no longer a nature but an individual. This is a very strange argument. Since the nature only exists in particular persons where it is endowed with accidents it would mean that it never exists as nature when it is instantiated. This would then put paid to the immanent universal. How confused the debate became can be seen from another argument of the Anonymus Rashed.

Καὶ ἕτερον πάλιν ἄτοπον συμβαίνει τοῖς λέγουσιν τὸν μερικὸν ἄνθρωπον κατηγορεῖσθαι τοῦ Πέτρου. εἰ γὰρ μὴ ἔστι ὁ καθόλου ἄνθρωπος ἀτομωθεὶς κατηγορούμενος τοῦ Πέτρου, ἀποθανόντος τούτου ἀποθανεῖται ἡ φύσις καὶ δεῖ πάντας ἀνθρώπους ἀποθανεῖν, ὅπερ ἄτοπον.[43]

And again another absurdity happens to those who say that the particular human being is predicated of Peter. For if it is not the individuated

---

[41] My translation.
[42] Anonymus, [24, p. 375, ll. 102-105].
[43] Anonymus, [24, p. 369, ll. 42-45].

universal human being that is predicated of Peter, the nature will die
when he dies and it is necessary that all human beings die, which is
absurd.[44]

Here we are told that if there are particular natures the entire species would die
if one individual dies. This is clearly a nonsensical argument. Since the author then
goes on to say that the individuation of common natures prevents such a case from
happening one would have expected him to reject not the particular human being
but the common nature that has not been individuated. It is evident that this was a
step that he was not prepared to take, even though his conceptual framework would
have allowed him to do so.

7   Arguments Supporting Particularism

The authors of the texts on which we have focused so far did their utmost to defend
traditional soteriology. This does not, however, mean that everybody was equally
concerned about this topic. Some Chalcedonian theologians contented themselves
with battling particularism in Trinitarian theology. In order not to be encumbered
with a secondary debate they conceded to Philoponus that in the created order
universals were mere concepts. Indeed, they even volunteered arguments to support
such a position.

We encounter this stance for the first time in the *Praeparatio* of Theodore of
Raithou, which dates to the late sixth century.[45] Theodore claims that in creation
oneness only exists in the mind and supports his contention with the division into
two genders:

> Οὐ τὴν τυχοῦσαν διαφορὰν δέδεκται πρὸς ἑαυτὴν ἡ ἀνθρώπου φύσις, αὐτὴ
> καὶ εἰς θῆλυ καὶ εἰς ἄρσεν μεριζομένη· ὧν ἡ παραλλαγὴ κατά τε τῆς ψυχῆς
> τὰ ἤθη κατά τε τὰ μέλη τοῦ σώματος πολλὴ καὶ λίαν ἐναργεστάτη.[46]

> The human nature has admitted of a difference that is not insignificant,
> since it is itself divided into a female and a male part, where the difference
> as regards the habits of the soul and as regards the limbs of the body is
> great and most obvious.[47]

---

[44]My translation.
[45]On Theodore of Raithou see [12, pp. 112-117].
[46][28, p. 210, ll. 26–28].
[47]My translation.

More often, authors juxtapose the real oneness of the divinity with the apparent oneness of the human species. A short text that is incorporated into the *Doctrina Patrum* has the following to say on this topic:

Οὔτε γὰρ τοπικὴν διάστασιν ὥσπερ ἐφ᾽ ἡμῶν δυνάμεθα ἐπὶ τῆς θεότητος κατηγορεῖν τῆς ἀπεριγράπτου, οὔτε θελήματος διαφορὰν ἢ δυνάμεως ἢ γνώμης, ἅπερ τὴν πραγματικὴν ἐν ἡμῖν γεννῶσι διαίρεσιν.[48]

For in the case of the uncircumscribed divinity one cannot speak of spatial distance as one can in our case, nor of a difference in will or power or opinion, which produce in us the real distinction between one and another.[49]

Here it is claimed that accidental differences turn human beings not only into different individuals but also into different particular natures. Significantly, this is not the only argument against immanent universals found in the text. In the concluding section we read:

Οὐκ ἦν ποτε, ὅτε οὐκ ἦν ἐν ταῖς παρ᾽ ἡμῶν πιστευομέναις τρισὶν ὑποστάσεσιν ἡ μία θεότης, οὔτε αὔξησιν ἢ μείωσιν πώποτε ἐδέξατο ἢ δέξεται. ἐφ᾽ ἡμῶν δὲ τοὐναντίον ἅπαν. ἦν γάρ ποτε ὅτε οὐκ ἦν ἐν Πέτρῳ τυχὸν καὶ Παύλῳ καὶ Ἰωάννῃ ἡ κοινὴ φύσις, ἀλλ᾽ ἐν ἑτέρῳ ἢ ἑτέροις, καὶ ἔσται πάλιν ἐν ἄλλοις, καὶ ἦν ποτε, ὅτε ἐν οὐδενὶ ἦν. πῶς γοῦν οὐκ ἐπινοίᾳ μόνῃ θεωρηθήσεται ἡ κτιστὴ καὶ γενητὴ φύσις, ἡ καθόλου φημὶ καὶ κοινὴ ἐκ μὴ ὄντων τε γενομένη καὶ ἐξ ἑτέρου εἰς ἕτερον μεταβαίνουσα; ὧν οὐδὲν ἐπὶ τῆς ἀληθοῦς καὶ ἀγενήτου καὶ ἀκτίστου καὶ ἀναλλοιώτου ἔστιν ἐννοῆσαι θεότητος.[50]

There was never a time when the one divinity was not in the three hypostases in which we believe, and it has never received nor will ever receive augmentation or diminution. In our case the exact opposite holds true. For there was a time when the common nature was not in Peter, for example, or John, but in another one or in other ones, and it will again be in others, and there was a time when it was in nobody. How then will the nature that has been created and has come to be not be contemplated in thought alone, I mean, the universal and common one, which has come to be from nothing and goes from one to another, none of

---

[48][7, p. 189, ll. 9-12].

[49]My translation.

[50][7, p. 189, l. 23-p. 190, l. 8].

which is conceivable in the case of the true and unbegotten and uncreated and unchanging divinity?[51]

Here, too, a clear distinction is made between the divinity and the created order. The author insists that the criteria needed for the existence of the immanent universal are only met by the divinity. He points out that only the divine persons are always of the same number whereas the sum total of human beings varies. Playing with the Arian slogan "there was a time when he was not" he then states that it does not apply to the divine persons but is manifestly true for the human species where individuals constantly disappear and are replaced by new ones. Finally, he emphasises the transience of human beings who are created from nothing and will again dissolve into nothingness.

8 Eulogius of Alexandria

The arguments found in the *Doctrina Patrum* have counterparts in the writings of a known Chalcedonian theologian, the Alexandrian patriarch Eulogius who flourished in the late sixth and early seventh century.[52] Eulogius' treatise, which has only survived in a summary by Photius of Constantinople, contains the following statement:

> Ἀδιαίρετος γὰρ ὁ Πατὴρ πρός τε τὴν ἑαυτοῦ σοφίαν καὶ τὴν ἁγιαστικὴν δύναμιν, ἐν μιᾷ φύσει προσκυνούμενος, οὐκ εἰς ἕνα καὶ ἕνα μεριζόμενος θεός, καθάπερ ἐφ᾽ ἡμῶν, οἳ τῷ ἀκοινωνήτῳ τῶν ἰδιωμάτων καὶ τῷ διαφόρῳ τῆς ἐνεργείας μεριζόμεθά τε καὶ διαιρούμεθα, καὶ τῇ διόλου τομῇ τὴν πρὸς ἀλλήλους διαφορὰν ὑφιστάμεθα.[53]

> For the Father is not divided from his wisdom and sanctifying power, since he is God who is worshipped in one nature, and not divided into one part and another, as is the case with us, who through the incommunicability of the idioms and the difference of activity are divided into parts and suffer the difference from each other through the complete cut.[54]

Here, too, it is claimed that the difference of idioms and activities is proof of the non-existence of immanent universals in creation. By Eulogius' time this had

---

[51]My translation.
[52]On Eulogius see [11, pp. 65–71].
[53][22, p. 485].
[54]My translation.

clearly become a standard argument. Yet in his case this is not the entire story for he continues:

Οὐδὲ γὰρ τὸ ἓν ἐπὶ τῆς θείας οὐσίας ὡς ἐπὶ τῶν κτισμάτων νοοῦμεν, παρ᾽ οἷς οὐδὲ τὸ κυρίως ἓν ἔστι θεωρῆσαι. οὐ γὰρ τὸ ἓν ἀριθμῷ ἐφ᾽ ἡμῶν καὶ κυρίως ἕν. καὶ γὰρ τὸ ἐφ᾽ ἡμῶν λεγόμενον ἓν οὐ κυρίως ἕν, ἀλλά τι ἕν. τοῦτο δὲ ἕν τέ ἐστι καὶ οὐχ ἕν, ἅτε δὴ καὶ τοῦ ἑνὸς φέρον τὴν κλῆσιν καὶ πρὸς τὰ πολλὰ εἶναι μεριζόμενον.[55]

For in the case of the divine substance we do not conceive of the one as we do in our case, where one cannot even see oneness in the strict sense. For in our case the one in number is not one in the strict sense. For that which in our case is called one is not one in the strict sense but a certain one. And this is both one and not one, since it carries the appellation "one" and is nevertheless divided into many.[56]

The juxtaposition of "one in the absolute sense" and "a certain one" and the claim that the latter is one in name only is derived from a philosophical text, most likely Proclus' *Elements of Theology*.[57] Eulogius clearly had looked around for arguments that would support his two contentions, that nature was one in God and multiple in human beings, and lighted on the writings of the Neoplatonists because they, too, were not willing to accept the existence of immanent universals in the material world.[58] Thus the case for particularism, which Philoponus had made through a conceptualist reading of Aristotelian philosophy, was reinforced through recourse to the Platonic tradition.

9 Conclusion

Drawing inspiration from Aristotle's treatise *De anima* John Philoponus declared that hypostases were at the same time particular natures and that the common nature was only a concept or even non-existent. By taking this step he questioned not only traditional Trinitarian theology but also traditional soteriology where the immanent universal was thought to ensure that the benefits of the incarnation were passed on to the entire human race. Thus it is not surprising that he was attacked by

---

[55][22, p. 486].

[56]My translation.

[57]Cf. Proclus, Elements of Theology, prop. 2, 4, [23], prop. 2, p. 2, ll. 15-25, prop. 4, p. 4, ll. 9-18.

[58]See e.g. [6, pp. 375-376].

mainstream theologians not only of the Monophysite but also of the Chalcedonian persuasion. The responses varied greatly. Anastasius of Antioch merely affirmed the traditional teaching and avoided any discussion of the status of universals. Leontius of Byzantium accepted the existence of particular natures but claimed that there was nevertheless an immanent universal because the account of being in each individual was identical, a point that was also conceded by Philoponus. The Anonymus Rashed argued that the human nature in individuals was individuated from the common nature and that the common nature ensured that the human species is one even though he was not able to show that the common nature was more than a mental concept. Some Chalcedonian authors sought to disprove the arguments with which Philoponus had tried to support his position albeit with little success. Others were prepared to accept that there were indeed no immanent universals in creation as long as they could make a case that the divinity was one. They even put forward arguments that were meant to show that created species are one in name only. Most of these arguments seem to have been created ad hoc. Only Eulogius of Alexandria supported his position through recourse to Neoplatonic philosophy.

References

[1] P. Allen and B. Neil. *Maximus the Confessor and his Companions: Documents from Exile, Oxford Early Christian Texts*. Oxford, 2002.

[2] Anastasius of Antioch. Oratio III. In S. N. Sakkos, editor, *Anastasii I Antiocheni opera omnia genuinae quae supersunt*. Salonica, 1976.

[3] Aristotle. *De anima*.

[4] Basil of Caesarea. Epistula 361. In Y. Courtonne, editor, *Saint Basile, Lettres, III*. Paris, 1966.

[5] R. Cross. Perichoresis, Deification, and Cristological Predication in John of Damascus. *Mediaeval Studies*, 62:69–124, 2000.

[6] R. Cross. Gregory of Nyssa on universals. *Vigiliae Christianae*, 56:372–410, 2002.

[7] F. Diekamp (editor). Doctrina patrum 11. In *Doctrina Patrum de Incarnatione Verbi. Ein griechisches Florilegium aus der Wende des 7. und 8. Jahrhunderts (2. Auflage)*. Münster, 1981.

[8] Ch. Erismann. The Trinity, Universals, and Particular Substances: Philoponus and Roscelin. *Traditio*, 63:77–305, 2008.

[9] Ch. Erismann. *L'homme commun. La genèse du réalisme ontologique durant le haut Moyen Age*. Paris, 2011.

[10] Ch. Erismann. Catachrestic Plural Forms. Gregory of Nyssa and Theodore Abu Qurrah on Naming and Counting Essences. *British Journal for the History of Philosophy*, 22:39–59, 2014.

[11] A. Grillmeier and Th. Hainthaler. *Christ in Christian Tradition, II.4: The Church of Alexandria with Nubia and Ethiopia after 451*. London, 1996. Tr. O. C. Dean.

[12] A. Grillmeier and Th. Hainthaler. *Christ in Christian Tradition, II.3: The Churches of Jerusalem and Antioch from 451 to 600*. Oxford, 2013. Tr. M. Ehrhardt.

[13] Th. Hainthaler. Johannes Philoponus, Philosoph und Theologe in Alexandria. In A. Grillmeier, editor, *Jesus der Christus im Glauben der Kirche, II.4: Die Kirche von Alexandrien mit Nubien und Äthiopien nach 451*, pages 109–149. Freiburg, Basel, Wien, 1990.

[14] D. Hombergen. *The Second Origenist Controversy. A New Perspective on Cyril of Scythopolis' Monastic Biographies as Historical Sources for Sixth-Century Origenism*. Rome, 2001.

[15] John of Damascus. *Liber de haeresibus*.

[16] B. Kotter, editor. *Die Schriften des Johannes von Damaskos, vol. 4: Liber de haeresibus. Opera polemica (Patristische Texte und Studien, 22)*. Berlin-New York, 1981.

[17] D. Krausmüller. Origenism in the sixth century: Leontius of Byzantium on the pre-existence of the soul. *Journal of Late Antique Religion and Culture*, 8:46–67, 2014.

[18] U. M. Lang. John Philoponus and the Controversies over Calcedon in the Sixth Century: A Study and Translation of the Arbiter. *Spicilegium Sacrum Lovaniense*, 47, 2001.

[19] Leontius of Byzantium. Solutiones. In B. E. Daley, editor, *Leontius of Byzantium. Complete Works (Oxford Early Christian Texts)*. Oxford, 2017.

[20] B. Lourié. Leontius of Byzantium and His "Theory of Graphs" against John Philoponus. In M. Knezevic, editor, *The Ways of Byzantine Philosophy*, pages 143–170. Alhambra, CA, 2014.

[21] Michael the Syrian. Chronicle'. In J.-B. Chabot, editor, *Chronique de Michel le Syrien, Patriarche Jacobite d'Antioche (1166-1199)*, volume 2. Paris, 1901.

[22] Photius. *Library, codex 230*. Pisa, 2016. Fozio, Biblioteca.

[23] Proclus. *The Elements of Theology. A Revised Text, with Translation, Introduction and Commentary*. Oxford, 2 edition, 1963.

[24] M. Rashed. Un texte proto-byzantin sur les universaux et la Trinité. In M. Rashed, editor, *L'héritage Aristotélicien. Textes inédits de l'Antiquité*. Paris, 2007.

[25] A. Van Roey. Les fragments trithéites de Jean Philopon. *Orientalia Lovanensia Periodica*, 11:135–163, 1980.

[26] R. R. K. Sorabji, editor. *Philoponus and the Rejection of Aristotelian Science*. London, 1987.

[27] J. Stiglmeyr. Der Verfasser der Doctrina Patrum de Incarnatione Verbi. *Byzantinische Zeitschrift*, 18:14–40, 1909.

[28] Theodore of Raithou. Praeparatio. In F. Diekamp, editor, *Analecta patristica. Texte und Untersuchungen zur griechischen Patristik (Orientalia Christiana Analecta, 117)*. Rome, 1938.

[29] Timothy of Constantinople. *De iis qui ad ecclesiam accedunt*. London, 1987.

[30] A. van Roey and P. Allen. Monophysite Texts of the Sixth Century. In R. Chiaradonna and G. Galluzzo, editors, *Orientalia Lovaniensia Analecta, 56*, pages 104–263. Leuven, 1994.

[31] K. Verryken. The development of Philoponus' thought and its chronology'. In R. R. K. Sorabji, editor, *Aristotle Transformed*, pages 233–274. London, 1990.

[32] G. Weiss. Studia Anastasiana, I: Studien zum Leben, zu den Schriften und zur Theologie des Patriarchen Anastasius I. von Antiochien (559-598). In *Miscellanea Byzantina Monacensia, 4*. Munich, 1965.

[33] Ch. Wildberg. *John Philoponus' Criticism of Aristotle's Theodore of Aether*. Berlin, 1988.

[34] J. Zachhuber. Universals in the Greek Church Fathers. In R. Chiaradonna and G. Galluzzo, editors, *Universals in Ancient Philosophy*, pages 425–470. Pisa, 2013.

[35] J. Zachhuber. Christology after Chalcedon and the Transformation of the Philosophical Tradition. In M. Knezevic, editor, *The Ways of Byzantine Philosophy*, pages 103–127. Alhambra, CA, 2015.

[36] J. Zachhuber. Derivative Genera in Apollinarius of Laodicea. In B. Gleede S.-P. Bergjan and M. Heimgartner, editors, *Apollinarius und seine Folgen (Studien und Texte zu Antike und Christentum, 93)*, pages 93–128. Tübingen, 2015.

Received 27 May 2019

Intuitionist Reasoning in the Tri-unitrian Theology of Nicholas of Cues (1401–1464)

Antonino Drago
Formerly at University "Federico II" Naples I, Italy
drago@unina.it

Abstract

The main subject of Cusanus' investigations was the name of God. He claimed to have achieved the best possible one, Not-Other. Since Cusanus stressed that these two words do not mean the corresponding affirmative word, i.e. the same, they represent the failure of the double negation law and therefore belong to non-classical, and above all, intuitionist logic. Some of his books implicitly applied intuitionist reasoning and the corresponding organization of a theory which is governed by intuitionist logic. A comparison of two of Cusanus' short writings shows that throughout his life he substantially improved his use of this kind of logic and ultimately was able to reason consistently within such a logic and recognize some of its basic laws. One important idea developed by him was that of a proposition composed of a triple repetition of "not-other" expressing "the Tri-unity of concordance" i.e. the "best name for the Trinity". I complete his application of intuitionist logic to theological subjects by characterizing the inner relationships within the Trinity in such a way that there are no longer contradictions in the notion. Generally speaking, the notion of the Trinity implies a translation from intuitionist to classical logic, to which Cusanus closely approximated. Moreover, I show that the main aspects of Christian revelation, including Christ's teachings, are represented both by this translation and by some doubly negated propositions of intuitionist logic. Hence, intuitionist logic was introduced into the history of Western theological thinking with Christian revelation, as only Cusanus partly recognized. Appendix 1 summarizes a detailed analysis of Cusanus' second short writing. Appendix 2 shows that the Athanasian creed regarding the Christian Trinity is a consistent sequence of intuitionist propositions provided that some verbal emendations are added, showing that ancient trinitarian thinking was also close to intuitionist reasoning.

I am grateful to both Prof. David Braithwaite and Prof. Michael Braithwaite for having revised my poor English. I have to express my fervent thanks to Jane Spurr for the work of editing my paper.

1 Introduction

Nicholas of Cues' (1401-1464; otherwise called Cusanus) books developed several sorts of arguments in order to give an appropriate name to God and gain insights into the Trinity. Owing to the variety of arguments and also the evolution of Cusanus' thought, some scholars have accused him of inconsistency in his thinking (e.g. [42, pp. 3–28]). As a result, past scholars of his writings tried above all to reconstruct a consistent framework of his thinking in its entirety, through intuitive interpretations of his philosophical writings. This approach seems to have achieved its goal through Flasch's encyclopedic work, [36] which provides a fascinating and consistent framework for Cusanus' thought and its evolution. A new wave, which began some years ago, attempts to achieve a more accurate interpretation of his major works and specific features of his thinking. The present paper indicates a consistent definition of Cusanus' logical thinking.

A century ago Cassirer suggested that Cusanus had intuitively introduced a new logic [13, pp. 15 and 31]. A widespread opinion maintains that Cassirer tended to exaggerate the extent to which Cusanus' thinking anticipated modern philosophical and scientific issues. Against this opinion I will show that Cassirer's appraisal of Cusanus' logic is correct. It is a recognized fact that Cusanus' search for new names of God not only went beyond 'negative theology', which is based on the privative characteristic features of God, but also argued in opposition to the logic of the "*Aristotelis secta*" consistently and logically [20, p. 463, no. 6][1]. Firstly, he introduced and exploited a surprising notion, i.e. a coincidence of opposites, which dramatically departs from classical logic since it reduces Aristotle's square of opposition to a segment representing a logic of two positive predicates only, existential and total. Cusanus then invented several more names which at the present time we recognize as belonging to modal or intuitionist logic. In particular, even the title of his most important book on God [22] announces His "most accurate" name, "*Non Aliud*" (Not-Other). Since "*Aliud*" is a negative word (= not the same) and since "not-other" — as Cusanus stresses — is different from the corresponding affirmative word idem (the same), here the double negation law fails; the non validity of this law is the main difference between classical logic and almost all kinds of non-classical logic, of which the most important is intuitionist logic. This use of a different logic than the usual one appears to be the main reason why Cusanus' illustration of the subjects of his study was so obscure to scholars that they were not able to achieve a common interpretation of any of his major books.

---

[1] All Cusanus' writings have been edited in Latin. For the English translations of almost all Cusanus' philosophical works I refer to precious Jasper Hopkins' site: http://jasper-hopkins.info/

The aim of the present paper is both to recognize his surprising insights into intuitionist logic and try to situate them in a consistent system. I will show that Cusanus made use of intuitionist logic to fashion not only single names of God, but also to organize the complex of all the propositions of some his books in a way that was alternative to the Aristotelian, apodictic organization of a theory; in particular, he avoided deductive reasoning as well as Aristotle's syllogisms. In addition, he conceived the relations of human beings with the Trinity through intuitionist logic. With regard to this I complete Cusanus' innovations by suggesting a new conception of both the inner relationships within Trinity and Its relationship with mankind — i.e. the Christian revelation - as essentially belonging to intuitionist logic.

In sec. 2 I will analyze the author's summary of his book *Non Aliud* [22, Ch 4, pp. 1303–4]. This summary, which is full of doubly negated propositions of intuitionist logic, adheres to the model of organization which is alternative to the apodictic model of organization. In addition, I will show that he reasoned so precisely using intuitionist logic that he was able to define some intuitionist laws and also apply the logical translation between intuitionist and classical logic. In sec. 3, I will investigate the logical features of one of Cusanus' short writings, *De Deo Abscondito* [19], which precedes the former one by twenty years. I will show that this text also closely approximates to the alternative model of organizing a theory. The comparison of the logical analyses of the two texts will show both that, over a period of twenty years, the characteristics of the alternative organization of a theory are persistent features of Cusanus' thinking; and Cusanus' way of reasoning evolved from an approximate to a substantial use of intuitionist logic.

In sec. 4 I will pursue my intuitionist logical analysis by tackling the controversial notion of the Christian Trinity. First I will list the main oxymora originating from the usual conception of Him through classical logic. In sec. 5 I will consider a surprising proposition put forward by Cusanus based on the intuitionist name of God in the title of his above-mentioned book: "The Not-Other is not-other than the Not-Other". According to him, it represents at the same time the Trinity and the Unity of God, i.e. a precise logical definition of the "Tri-Unity". After pointing out the defects of this formula, I suggest how to improve it through double negations in order to obtain a new consistent conception of the Tri-Unity. By means of a diagram I will represent His logical structure, composed both by the relationships between one Element of the Tri-unity with the Unity and the relationships between each two Elements. Furthermore, I will illustrate the dynamics of this complex notion of Tri-Unity as represented by the translation from intuitionist to classical logic. This essential role of intuitionist logic in representing the relations within the Trinity is confirmed by the essential role that this logic also plays in the revelation made by Christ of the Trinity's relations outside, with men. Thus from the logical point of view this revelation constitutes the introduction of intuitionist logic into Western theological thought.

In Appendix I will present the Athanasian creed on the Christian Trinity; with some emendations of the original text I will obtain a consistent version of it according to intuitionist logic, thus showing that also the tradition of negative theology on the Christian Trinity closely approximated to reasoning according to intuitionist logic.

An understanding of the following does not require previous knowledge of intuitionist logic; the few laws I will refer to will be presented in so far as they will be useful and explained as far as is necessary.

2 An analysis of the logical features of Cusanus' summary of his book *De Non Aliud (1460)*

Let us recall the following words of St. Augustine:

> Have we spoken or announced anything worthy of God? Rather I feel that I have done nothing but wish to speak: if I have spoken, I have not said what I wished to say. Whence do I know this except because God is ineffable? If what I said were ineffable, it would not be said. And for this reason God should not be said to be ineffable, for when this is said, something is said. And a contradiction in terms is created, since if that is ineffable which cannot be spoken, then that is not ineffable which can be called ineffable. This contradiction is to be passed over in silence rather than resolved verbally. (quoted by Miller [51, p. 10]

Cusanus, very familiar with Augustine's thought, on this point, however, chose to accept the contradiction, or rather to investigate what to others appeared to be contradictions, since he discovered that when he makes use of a doubly negated proposition both the corresponding affirmative and negative propositions do not mutually contradict each other. He thus founded an "eminential theology", which went beyond the two traditions of affirmative theology and negative theology.

In the year 1462 Cusanus wrote the book *De Non Aliud*, which may be considered the apex of his attempt to approach God through a name. Even the title of the book manifests an essential use of the double negations[2] of intuitionist logic;[3] in fact, the

---

[2]Here we have to overcome a deeply rooted prejudice according to which only primitive languages make use of double negations. For a long time Anglo-Saxon linguists ostracised the double negations, which explains why the importance of the DNPs was rarely noticed (Horn [44, pp.79–83], [45, pp. 111–112]).

[3]One more prejudice, supported by most modern logicians, denies that intuitionism has any

two words of the title, _Not Other_,[4] constitute a double negation which, as Cusanus himself stresses, is not equivalent to the corresponding affirmative word, _Idem_, "the Same" [22, p. 1304, n. 41]. The consequence of this is that the name represents a failure of the double negation law and hence belongs to intuitionist logic ([40], [34, p. 24], [58, pp. 56ff]).[5]

At the beginning of this book Cusanus claims to have achieved a complete rational research method since he writes:

> I shall speak and converse with you, Ferdinand, [but only] on the following condition: viz., that unless you are compelled by reason, you will reject as unimportant everything you will hear from me. [22, 1108, no. 2]

An analysis of the logical features of this complex book would be too long. However, the task is facilitated by a subsequent book, _De Venatione Sapientiae_, written one year later. There Cusanus illustrates all the kinds of investigation he employed in order to approach God; in Chapter XIV he summarizes in two pages the investigation illustrated by the above book [23, Ch. 14, pp. 1303–4].[6] These pages include three sections, composed of 47 composite propositions.[7]

In the following I consider the five logical features which characterize the structure of the summary of _De non Aliud_.

---

application to reality. In this way classical logic is assured the continuation of the traditional monopoly in governing the real World, whereas intuitionist logic is left with the role of an interesting formal exercise of logical studies and is even excluded from linguistic studies.

[4]In order to clarify a double negation to the reader, I will often underline each of its negative words. In the following I will disregard an analysis of the various linguistic figures of the doubly negated propositions, because I will assume that the ancient scholars used them intuitively, i.e. by reference to rules that are tacitly semantic rather than formal.

[5]An analysis of the _De Non Aliud_ in the light of non-classical logic was attempted in 1982. The author wanted to characterize the new logical law applied by Cusanus; but he failed to formalize it correctly [63, p 120]. An interpretation of Cusanus's coincidence of opposites through paraconsistent logic was given by [61] but without obtaining significant results. I leave aside the several philosophical attempts to equate Cusanus' logic to Hegel's dialectical logic given that a paper [37] eventually refuted them.

[6]One more summary is usually edited at the end of the book; yet this summary develops the same subject in a more abstract way. The point of departure of both illustrations, i.e. the relationships between God, not-other and other, is well-developed also in ch. II of the book.

[7]I consider a "composite" proposition a sequence of words interrupted by a full stop, a colon, a semi-colon, a question mark. Each composite proposition may include several simple propositions.

2.1 The problem-based organization of the theory

Even a cursory reading of this short text suggests that it does not illustrate a dogmatic or an axiomatic theory. What kind of theory, then? In a previous paper I showed through a comparative analysis of several scientific theories that there exists an alternative organization of a theory to the apodictic one. (Drago 2012) Moreover, I extracted the main features of its ideal model; it is based on a general problem, whose resolution is not given by ordinary means. The author solves it by producing a new theoretical method, illustrated through doubly negated propositions of intuitionist logic (DNPs).[8] They are usually joined together in order to compose *ad absurdum* arguments (AAA).[9] The DPN concluding the last AAA is then changed through a general principle into an affirmative proposition, which works as a hypothesis to be checked against reality. I call this kind of organization a *problem-based organization* (PO).

In the following I will investigate to what extent Cusanus' text adheres to the features of the PO model of a theory.

2.2 The basic problem

It is easy to recognize that the text introduces a problem, i.e. how to find the best name for God. The following are the problems explicitly stated by Cusanus:

> ... what we are seeking is seen - in the way in which it can be known — in his [*God's*][10] definition [as <u>not</u>-other]. (p. 1303, n. 39)

> What is <u>Not</u>-Other? (p. 1303, n. 40)

> What, then, is <u>other</u>? (p. 1303, n. 40)

---

[8]For clarity's sake, let us consider one more instance of such a proposition. A Court judges a defendant as "acquitted owing to *insufficient* evidence of *guilt*"; i.e. the Court did not collect sufficient evidence for deciding either to send the man to prison or to grant him his freedom. Given that the above proposition is not equivalent to the corresponding affirmative proposition (his behaviour was lawful), in this case the law of double negation fails and only the doubly negated proposition is true.

[9]Here we meet one more prejudice, now concerning the AAA. It is currently maintained that such a proof can be converted into a direct proof, provided that one exchanges the thesis for the conclusion ([55, p. 15], [38]). But this exchange presupposes that the DNP concluding an AAA is previously translated according to the classical double negation law into the corresponding affirmative proposition. Without this application of classical logic the AAA is not convertible into a direct argument.

[10]In a quotation, an insertion of mine in square brackets is distinguished from Jasper's by writing it in Italics.

The last two problems are the consequences of having defined God as not-other; they are meaningfully and sequentially linked to first one.

Notice that this name is correctly distinguished by him from "other". The difference between the two expressions cannot be overemphasized; the word "other" denies any bridge between people and God. The words "not-other" allow, however, such a bridge, although it has to be discovered through an untiring search.

2.3 The doubly negated propositions

The third logical feature of this summary is an essential use of DNPs as all texts presenting a PO theory do.[11] Cusanus recognizes this specific logical form in *De Venatione Sapientiae*; here he calls double negations "negations that not are privative assertions" ; i.e. "assertions" which are not merely negative (i.e. "privative") but negative in a unusual sense, i.e. double negations. By following Plato, Cusanus adds that they have more affirmative content than the corresponding affirmations, which in this case are considered by him to be only partially true.

> Dionysius, who imitates Plato, made a similar pursuit within the field of oneness; and he says that negations that are not privative assertions but are excellent and abundant *affirmations* are truer than are affirmations,[23, ch. 22, p. 1318-19, no. 64].[12]

Moreover, he is aware that by making use of the DNPs he is exploring a new logical field.

> Pursuers who are philosophers do not enter in this field [of not-other] in which negation is not opposed to affirmation. [23, ch. 14, p. 1304, beginnings of no. 41]

---

[11]The recognition of DNPs in a text has to obey some rules; 1) the negative words which explain previous negative words have to be disregarded; 1) the word "absolute" is a DNP, because it means *ab-solutus*, i.e. *solutus ab* (= *without*) omnibus *vinculis* 2) also the word "only" summarizes a DNP because it is equivalent to "It is not other than..."; 3) a negative, interrogative proposition, whose implicit answer is manifestly "No" is counted as a DNP; 4) a modal word — such as it is "possible" or "likely", etc. — may be translated via the S4 model of modal logic into a DNPs [14, pp. 76ff], hence it is equivalent to a DNP; a word of this kind will be underlined with a dotted line. Notice that some cases usually remain dubious, because the negative meaning of either a word or a proposition may also depend on its context. For this reason the count of DNPs includes a percentage of error which, however, is small with respect to the large numbers resulting from the following measurements.

[12]Notice that Hopkins, by ignoring the logical role of double negations, maintains (see footnote 187) that in the text *affirmations* has to be read as "negative assertions".

The logical feature which Cusanus refers to is a consequence of exactly what occurs in intuitionist logic, which gives a truth value to a DPN rather than to the corresponding affirmation; hence, the affirmation is merely partially true, often being a notion with idealized content; whereas the negation, being weaker than classical negation, is not in opposition to the affirmation. Thus, Cusanus grasped one main feature of the new logic.

Let us investigate the DNPs occurring in the text. I identified 37 DNPs, which I do not list for brevity's sake. The density of DNPs is high; there are more than 10 per page. Moreover, with respect to the number of composite propositions (47) there are on average more than 3 DNPs out of 4 composite propositions. To my knowledge, no other text presents such a great density of DNPs. Moreover, these DNPs are concentrated in the last sections. All of which is evidence of Cusanus' indispensable use of DNPs.

2.4   The *ad absurdum* arguments

The question arises whether Cusanus' reasoning using these DNPs is effective.[13]

Although a short summary, the text under examination presents the subject through arguments on its crucial points. Remarkably, the classical process of reasoning, the syllogism, is lacking. Actually, this kind of deductive reasoning is convenient for an apodictic theory, while, in a text presenting a PO theory, the reasoning in intuitionist logic proceeds inductively through AAAs, each one concluding with the absurdity of the negated thesis, i.e. a DNP; in its intuitionist version this conclusion is not translated into the corresponding affirmative proposition, as only classical logic would allow. This concluding DNP may work as premise to a following AAA and thus start a chain of AAAs.

I have identified in the text at issue five AAAs, which in the following I will quote by adding some words and symbols in order to make it easy to follow the thread of their logic. First, since an AAA may be presented discursively, I will make clear this way of reasoning by putting between quotation marks the symbols characterizing an AAA (Ts, the thesis; $\neg Ts$, the negation of the thesis; and $\perp$, the

---

[13] As a first approximate answer to the above question, let us consider each proposition that is a candidate for being an effective argument since it includes a specific word for representing a logical inference belonging to either classical or intuitionist logic. Hence, I count as a possible argument each proposition including inferential words (in Latin: *ergo, propter, quia, enim, ob, unde, hinc, cum, aliter, alias, nisi*, etc.; but not the words *ante, praecedere*, since their meaning is looser than that of a logical inference).The total number of propositions of this kind is 31; it is less than the number of the composite propositions, i.e. 47, but it is close to the number of the DNPs (37). This high density of inferential words shows that Cusanus wants to present his illustration as rigorous logical reasoning.

absurd). Moreover, in order to further facilitate the reader I precede (by putting it in brackets) the conclusion of an AAA; instead of the doubly negated predicate I insert its affirmative version, since our minds grasp it more quickly than its doubly negated version.

I warn the reader that unfortunately the first AAAs are the most difficult. The first AAA is the least lucid one because, in my opinion, the edited Latin text is deficient, since the last proposition seems to be an iteration of the preceding idea; in order to improve the meaning of text I have inserted some words which avoid this defect. I will make use of the word "God" as a shortening of the long expression which Cusanus makes use of for designating the object of the mind's "hunting".

1) [*God precedes the other:*] ... the intellect, which pursues that which precedes[14] even the possibility-of-being-made[= *God*], must consider how it [= *God*] precedes [*read: have precedence*]. [*Ts*] [*An*] Other such that precedes the possibility-of-being-made [= *allusion to God*] cannot be [= *it is absurd that it is directly*] made, for [⊥] the other is [*impossible that is not*] subsequent to it. (p. 1303, no. 39)

2) [*God defines all things:*]...[*Ts*] all things have to be defined through it [= *God*], since [⊥] cannot exist [*better: they are nullified*] [¬*Ts*] unless they [*in the case they do not*] exist and are defined through it. (p. 1303, no. 39)

3) [*Self-definition of God as Tri-Unity expressed through only three "not-other":*] You can see that the Eternal, that Most Ancient, can be sought in this field by a very delectable pursuit. For inasmuch as it is the Definition of itself and other things, it is not found more clearly in any other [field] than in Not-other. For in this field you come upon [*better: perceive*] the trine and one Most Ancient, who is the Definition ~~even~~ of Himself. For [*better: Indeed,*] Not-other is not-other than Not-other. The intellect marvels over this mystery when it notices attentively that trinity, [¬*Ts*] without which [⊥] God does not define Himself, [*Ts*] is oneness, because the Definition is the defined ...(p. 1303, n. 40; *to be continued*)

4) ["*Not-other" defines "other"* :] ...Therefore, the trine and one God is the Definition defining itself and all other things. Hence, the intellect finds that God [*Not-other*] is not other than other, because He defines

---

[14]Within this AAA, from this point I depart from Hopkins' translation; in particular, the Latin word "*quomodo*" is not in my opinion "the fact that", but "how".

[rather: *it is not other from*] other. For if [$\neg Ts$] Not-other is removed, [$\perp$] other does not remain ... (p. 1304, n. 40; to be continued)

5) [*"Not-other" is the principle of the "other"* :] ... For if other is to exist, [Ts] it will have to be none other than other. [$\neg Ts$] Otherwise, it would be something other than other and hence [$\perp$] would not exist. (p. 1304, n. 40)

These 5 AAAs are aimed at answering the three above problems. The first AAA is a qualification of the notion of "other" with respect to God, called temporarily "that which precedes the possibility-of-being-made". This AAA states that God precedes "other". (The affirmative nature of this conclusion of an AAA, instead of its doubly negated corresponding proposition, will be explained in the following). The second AAA concludes that God defines not only "other", but everything. Regarding the third AAA, notice that God, by definition, has to define Himself; to this end God has to be a Tri-Unity (definition, defined, the relation between them). Cusanus suggests that through a triple reiteration of "not-other" one can obtain a proposition that defines itself and hence means the Tri-Unity. Hence, this AAA leads to defining God through the triple reiteration of "not-other".

From the result of this AAA Cusanus derives through the last two AAAs two important conclusions. They show that the words "not-other" play the same role as God: they define the notion of "other" and are the principle of "other". In total, the 5 AAAs constitute a chain of reasoning without interruption, except for the interruption constituted by the introduction of the proposition constituted by the triple "not-other", which actually is an invention.

Their general conclusion occurs exactly at the end of the last of the 5 AAAs; notice that this conclusion is correctly a DNP, which is how an intuitionist AAA should conclude

Therefore, since not-other is prior to other, it cannot be made other... (p. 1304, n. 41; to be continued)

This conclusion, concerning the name "not-other", is the same as the conclusion of the first AAA concerning God; hence, it terminates the arguments aimed at proving the similitude between God and "not-other" in His higher function of defining himself.

2.5 The application of the principle of sufficient reason

Let us now consider what constitutes the final logical step of the model of a PO theory, i.e. the application of the principle of sufficient reason (PSR).

$$\neg\exists\neg f(x) \Rightarrow \exists x f(x)$$

considered as a general principle translating a doubly negated, existential predicate into its corresponding affirmative predicate. Unfortunately, in the past it was disqualified by indiscriminate use. Only in recent times was its correct application to a final predicate of a PO scientific theory recognized together with its two constraints on the predicate; it has to be: 1) the conclusion of an AAA; 2) decidable. ([29, sec. 6], [32]) In our theological context the second constraint is to be interpreted as decidable by means of theological arguments.

From an inspection of the table of the implication relations between two intuitionist predicates [34, p. 27] it can easily be proved that the PSR translation of the main intuitionist predicate $\neg\exists x\neg f(x)$ into the corresponding classical one implies a translation of intuitionist predicate logic in its entirety into classical predicate logic. That means that PSR is capable of performing that logical step — i.e. a translation between two kinds of logic — which, like the principle of non-contradiction, belongs to a level of logic that is higher than that of any particular kind of logic.

At the end of the second of the three sections of the summary, Cusanus implicitly applies the PSR to the universal predicate which is the DNP concluding the 5 AAAs. So Cusanus concludes his PO theory with the following words:[15]

> ...and it [not-other] is actually everything which is at all possible to be [as God is]. (p. 1304, n. 40)[16]

Cusanus thus solved the basic problem of how to approach the name of God also as a Tri-unity, by qualifying through logical arguments both the name "not-other" and its triple reiteration.

---

[15]Unfortunately, past authors of a PO theory unwarily made use of PSR in order merely to enable the reader to quickly grasp the result of an AAA; therefore to the classically minded reader the undue conclusion appears to be a certain proposition, notwithstanding its lack of evidence, as it is the corresponding affirmative proposition of a DNP. E.g. Lobachevsky [50, theorems 17–21 and 23] applies the PSR to the conclusion of each AAA, so that the last proposition is an affirmative proposition. Cusanus also improperly applies the PSR to the conclusion of each AAA, except for the second one, where the thesis is expressed by means of the modal words: "must be".

[16]Notice that here not-other is identified with God; whereas he ought to insert "in" before "everything" (i.e., "God is in everything"); this move is necessary in order to avoid a charge of pantheism, which had already been directed at him and which obliged him to defend himself publicly [20].

The above analysis of the text, performed according to the features of the model of a PO, is summarized by the following Table 1. Notice that the last sec. is devoted to a commentary; there the specific features of an intuitionist reasoning, i.e. Problems, AAAs and PRS are correctly lacking. Hence, the distribution of the results in each column seems appropriate for a PO theory.

Section	Composite Propositions	Problems	DNPs	Possible Arguments	AAAs	PSR	Intuitionistic Logical Issues
39	12	1	6	9	1	1	
40	*22*	*2*	15	*13*	*4*	*2*	Double negation translation
41	13		*16*	9	–	–	Incommensurability of the two kinds of theologies (and kinds of logic). Failure of the double negation law. Negation does not oppose affirmation or double negation.
Total	**47**	**3**	**37**	**31**	**5**	**3**	
Legenda: In italics the highest score in each column							

Table 1: The main logical features of Cusanus' summary of *De Non Aliud*

2.6 An appraisal on Cusanus' way of reasoning

Cusanus' way of reasoning fits the alternative model of organization, because his text correctly presents all the features of a PO theory. Indeed, he clearly states a basic problem; he then pursues the resolution of it by means of an investigation making use of a large number (31) of DNPs and correctly builds a chain of (5)

AAAs. Moreover, he applies the PSR to the conclusion of the AAAs to obtain the conclusive hypothesis of the PO theory.

However, the first AAA is defective not only in the expression of the reasoning. The third AAA twice gives no explanations, i.e. i) when it appeals to the ability of the Trinity to give a self-definition; and ii) when it includes the triple reiteration of "not-other". Furthermore, in the end Cusanus does not clearly enunciate the demonstrated similitude, i.e. that "not-other" enjoys the same properties as God. Moreover, the continuity of the logical thread between any two AAAs requires the addition of some explanations, such as those added by myself in the above. These defects in the illustration of the arguments show that Cusanus did not clearly conceive this kind of logical reasoning (never called by its name); however, they do not lessen the importance of this chain of AAAs and the substantial correctness of their logical thread.

In conclusion, notwithstanding the above-mentioned defects, his reasoning as a whole is formally valid and substantially productive.

2.7 Cusanus' anticipation of the formal features of intuitionist logic

In addition, it is remarkable that Cusanus had such a command of reasoning with the new logic that he was able implicitly to point out some of its properties. In order to present them I will refer also to the book (edited one year before the text examined above).

When Cusanus is dealing with the main expression of his search, not-other, he remarks that these words are not the same as *idem*. Also in the summary of the book he lucidly reiterates this inequivalence:

> But notice that "Not-other" does not signify as much as does "same." Rather, since same is not other than same, Not-other precedes it and all nameable things. And so, although God is named "Not-other" because He is not other than any other, He is not on this account the same as any other. For example, it is not the case that just as He is not other than sky, so He is the same as sky. [23, p. 1304, n41]

Hence, he remarks that the following implication: $\neg\neg A \to A$ fails. This is only one instance of failure of the double negation law, as it occurs within intuitionist logic; yet, this failure surely plays a crucial role in Cusanus' thinking, because he defines "everything" X as "not-other than everything" X (being X any object; [22, ch. 1ff]; that means that the propositions with the addition of "not-other than" are inequivalent to the corresponding affirmative propositions; i.e. he conceives the above logical intuitionist law in its generality. The second logical issue suggested by

Cusanus' text is another intuitionist law, which he recognized by distinguishing "not-other" from "other" in a universal sense. He states that "negation is not opposed to affirmation". This proposition is precisely a law of intuitionist logic; when a double negation is true, both the corresponding negation and the affirmation, being true only partially, do not mutually oppose each other. The following quotation of the summary of the book shows how lucidly Cusanus reasons about this point.

> Pursuers who are philosophers did not enter this field [of not-other] in which, alone, negation is not opposed to affirmation. For Not-other is not opposed to other, since it defines and precedes other. Outside this [intuitionist logical] field negation is opposed to affirmation [...] Therefore, seeking for God in other fields, where [for cause] He is not found, is an empty pursuit. For God is not someone who is opposed to anything, since He is prior to all difference from opposites. Therefore, God is named *animal*, to which *not-animal* is opposed [...] in a more imperfect way than He is named *Not-other*, to which neither other nor nothing is opposed. For Not-other also precedes and defines nothing, since nothing is not other than nothing. The divine Dionysius said, most subtly, that God is *all in all and nothing in nothing* [23, ch. 14, p. 1403 no. 41].[17]

I have amended this quotation by leaving out some examples: "*immortal*, to which mortal is opposed" and "immortal to mortal, incorruptible to corruptible, and so on for all other things except Not-other alone." Here he erroneously makes use of the words "im-mortal" and "in-corruptible" as instances of negative words, whereas they are doubly negated words. In sum, although he cleverly establishes the general law, he sometimes chooses erroneous instances of his reasoning.

The third logical issue suggested by Cusanus' text concerns the translation from classical to intuitionist logic, i.e. the inverse operation of that performed by PSR. The textbooks of Mathematical logic teach that in order to translate a proposition or predicate of classical logic into intuitionist logic one has to place two symbols of negation before the classical proposition (or predicate; this translation is based on double negations, but it is inappropriately defined as "negative translation"). As a matter of fact, Cusanus emphasizes that in his theology everything is defined as "not other than" everything; i.e. he places two negative words before a proposition. Given that his words are specific negations, they are not enough to obtain the exact modern translation of predicate calculus; however, in a previous paper I showed that

---

[17]These remarks of Cusanus make clear his distance from pantheism, with which he was previously charged.

this difference is not significant for Cusanus' arguments [30]. Remarkably, the last section of the summary underlines this point by attributing "not other" to the very nature of everything:

> Therefore, all things have, from the fact that God defines them, their being not other than they are; and from Not-other they have the fact that they beget no other in species but produce what is similar to themselves. Therefore, goodness is good-making, and whiteness is white-making; and similarly for all other things. [23, p. 1304, n. 41]

In this way he translates the common vision of the world as composed of solid things, whose logic is classical, into the vision of the world as composed of things whose essence is expressed by "not-other, whose logic is intuitionist.

I conclude that, despite the defects of his AAAs and his imprecision in choosing the instances of the second intuitionist law, he was highly ingenious in introducing an intuitionist way of reasoning so early.[18]

3   A logical analysis of *De Deo Abscondito* (1440-1445)

In order to measure the extent to which Cusanus improved his way of reasoning over time, I consider a previous, short writing on the same subject — how man can or cannot in some way know God — but now illustrated through a dialogue: *On the hidden God*. A dialogue between two discussants - one a Pagan and the other a Christian. (Cusanus 1440-1445) It was written around 20 years before *De non Aliud*. It is 5 pages long in Hopkins' English translation,[19] composed of four parts divided into 15 sections.

A specific subject characterizing each of the four parts is easily recognized. Part I: Opposition between the Pagan and the Christian about the knowledge of God. Part II: Truth is absolute. Part III: Contradictions implied by naming God. Part IV: Analogies on the relationship between a believer and God. We understand from a cursory reading of the text that Cusanus illustrates a dialogue between a praying Christian and a Pagan who asks him why he is worshipping what he does not know. Cusanus' thesis, illustrated by the Christian's answers to the Pagan, is that God is

---

[18]It seems not by chance that the founder of intuitionist mathematics and logic, L.E.W. Brouwer, was inspired by mysticism, being familiar with Meister Eckart and maybe Cusanus also ([57, sec. 1.3, in particular p. 21]; [60, p. 114]. It is noteworthy that Brouwer's interpretation of original sin [10, pp. 3–10] agrees with both Cusanus' and Lanza del Vasto's.

[19]See http://jasper-hopkins.info/http://jasper-hopkins.info/DeDeoAbscon12-2000.pdf. It is also translated into many other languages.

not at all cognizable and communicable to others; remaining always hidden, He is only surmised by means of mere analogies.

To my knowledge two scholars only ([51, pp. 1–11], [52, pp. 99–106]) have analyzed this exceptional text in detail. Both remarked that the dialogue between the two believers in different ways in God presents an opposition between the two discussants, which has to be traced back to the Platonic difference between *dianoia* and *noesis*, by which Cusanus meant the difference between the two faculties of human mind, i.e. the discursive *ratio*, subject to the principle of non-contradiction, and the conjectural *intellectus*. In a previous paper I showed that these faculties work according to respectively classical logic and intuitionist logic [26, 27]. Hence, in the following, I will interpret the contraposition of the two discussants as based on a difference in the two different kinds of logic governing their arguments, i.e. classical logic for the Pagan and intuitionist logic for the Christian. My new method of analysis, relying on a distinction of a logical rather than a philosophical nature, improves the understanding of the text and provides a new accurate view of the subjects of the dialogue as well as their developments.

The crucial point of our investigation is again whether Cusanus' way of reasoning is effective or not; when one reads what the Christian affirms in sec. 1: "Because I am without knowledge [of Him], I worship [Him].", a doubt is legitimate.

Of course, a dialogue does not represent an apodictic theory, AO. Does the text represent a PO theory? In order to answer this question, I performed a quantitative analysis of the DNPs in the text in a similar way to the previous analysis of the summary of *De Non Aliud*. Appendix 1 shows this analysis. However, the above question is ambiguous since one has to ask for whom the theory may be a PO. For the Pagan, surely not, because with respect to the total of 94 DNPs he uses only 11 DNPs (of which 6 are modal words, which may represent a mere habit of common speech. Moreover, he does not use AAAs. The direct reading of the text shows that he always tries to reduce the Christian's answers to a contradiction, apart from the final sec. where he agrees with the Christian and also suggests an analogy which is equivalent to the Christian's; there he also makes use of (3) non-modal DNPs. I conclude that the Pagan does not develop a PO theory, but rather essentially makes use of classical logic in questioning the Christian.

The analysis of the Christian's propositions in order to decide whether the text represents a PO theory provides contradictory evidence (See Appendix 1). Only a direct and more detailed analysis of the text offers an explanation of this contradictory evidence. The result I obtain is that the complex arguments presented by Christian do not constitute a way of reasoning of a PO theory for the following reasons: 1) the main and concluding argument of the entire dialogue is a mere analogy (in sec. 14: just as a blind person cannot see colors, so a person who is not blind cannot see sight; like all analogies it can be interpreted as a DNP ("It is not false that it is ...), but not as an AAA, the logical argument which allows the theory to proceed; 2) in the intermediate part of the text the above separation between God and man is stated through metaphysical arguments which are applied without any precaution, although the metaphysical realm includes what in the real world is an absurdity. 3) All in all, this separation corresponds to the classical attitude of traditional negative theology which never achieved a specific way of reasoning.

In conclusion, the only discussant who reasons, is, oddly enough, the Pagan, who through *dianoia* alone, i.e. classical logic, tries to lead the Christian's arguments into inconsistency. The Christian does not reason, he manifests his belief in a God that is separate from him and in a conception of the truth that is only metaphysical in nature.

Cusanus' reasoning in this text manifests a considerable distance from his subsequent way of reasoning. In *De Deo Abscondito* he makes use of a large number of DNPs and AAAs, but few of the first ones are connected together and the latter ones are isolated.

By contrast in *De non Aliud* he correctly claims — as we saw in previous sec. — to be presenting only rational arguments about God and these arguments belong to intuitionist logic in a substantially precise way, even in his use of AAAs and PSR. In other words, whereas in *De Deo Abscondito* Cusanus stops before the wall of contradiction, by merely recognizing that this wall is composed of contradictions, in *De Non Aliud* the *intellectus* achieves the greatest improvement possible of human knowledge, i.e. not-other as the best name of God. This exalting result gives to the *intellectus* the highest possible dignity in exploring a kind of rational thinking based on a new logic. In other words, he overcomes the wall of contradictions. Hence, in the intermediate period of twenty years, Cusanus improved his new way of reasoning to the point where he was able to make a correct use of some laws of intuitionist logic and achieved a new kind of theology governed by intuitionist logic.

In the following we will see how far he proceeded in his adventure of exploiting new logical tools.

4 The Christian Trinity as a source of apparently insurmountable problems

Let us apply the previous results to Cusanus' capacity for reason on the subject of the Trinity, truly the most important subject of his theological research, after God's name.

Let us first consider the traditional way of approaching the Trinity. Augustine (354-430) brought together the Christian tenets on the Trinity into a system. (Augustine around 417) His thinking on the Trinity relied on analogies with triads existing in real-life. Among these triads, a celebrated one is the lover, the beloved and the love connecting the two.

The subsequent great work of scholars on this subject produced in particular a celebrated diagram summarizing the main tenets of the Christian faith regarding the Trinity, i.e. the "*scutum fidei*" (shield of the faith; [1]).

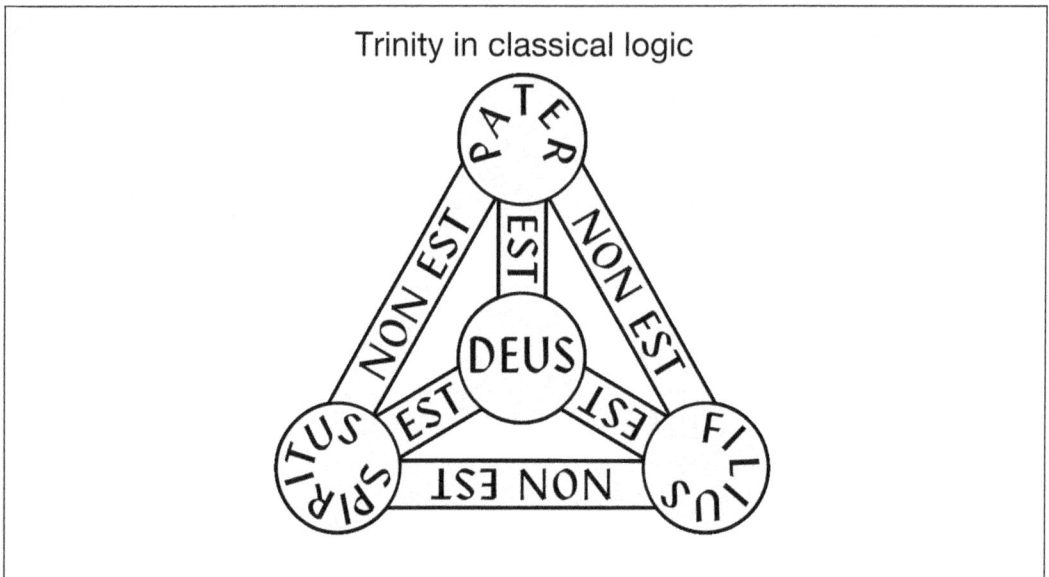

Figure 1

At a first sight the diagram suggests that we have before us four Beings, which, oddly, means four Gods. The words usually characterizing their relationships are aimed at correcting this first sight; they reduce the number of Gods to three (located at the vertices) and finally to one God only (located in the center but understood as subsuming all in Himself). Yet, this goal implies logical puzzles. Can 1 (God at the center of Diagram) be equal to 3 (Beings, located at the vertices of the triangle)? Are the 3 different from one another and yet merge into 1?[20] A clarification of all the relations among these Beings is necessary.

The inner relationships between each vertex and the center are usually characterized by means of the word "is". Yet, a copula implies that each of the 3 Persons[21]

---

[20]These two questions are assumed as the basic ones by the recent accounts of the paradoxes implied by the Christian notion of the Trinity ([12], [62], [56, sec. 1.4], [8, sec. 3]).

[21]For simplicity's sake I attribute the anthropomorphic name "person" to each Component of

is equal to one God. Yet, as an unfortunate consequence of the transitivity property of the copula, the 4 Beings represented by the diagram collapse into only 1 Being; this conclusion contradicts the initial hypothesis that the 3 Beings are different. In other words, if these Beings are different, in plain arithmetic the sum of 3 Beings cannot be posited as equal to 1; i.e. they cannot be added to obtain God.[22] Hence, the previous equality constitutes an absurdity. In logical terms, the simultaneous attributions of both unity and threefold existence to God constitute an oxymoron in classical logic where the principle of non-contradiction holds true; we cannot have at the same time 1 and not 1, i.e. 3.

However, the common justification for this strange situation emphasizes that God is not exactly equal to each of the three Persons, who only participate in the same divine substance of God; where the word "substance" (*sub-stare* (=stand under), *ousìa*) is in opposition to a *hypostasis* (person). The price of this intellectual operation is a surprising and quite inappropriate inner dualism within God as well as within any common person.

Given these insurmountable obstacles, the attention of scholars focused on other relationships, those between two of the three Persons. Given that they are surely different one from another, the diagram represents these differences through a "not". Yet, in classical logic a "not" means a mirror opposition, which implies a total difference, an exclusion, a full separation, without any degree of freedom in understanding the meaning of the negation. Hence, the meaning of classical negation is surely inappropriate to the relationships between two divine Persons.

At the present time no solutions to these puzzles exist, although a legion of theologians — and also philosophers — have pondered them for a long time.

It is easy to recognize that it is an anthropomorphic intuition rather than classical logic that allows our minds to conceive of a difference which nevertheless maintains a relationship. This appeal to the anthropomorphic images of the Persons is supported by several of Christ's propositions, suggesting e.g. a plain relationship of Father-Son generation. Yet, this gives rise to a disturbing question: since generation implies

---

the Trinity. The Bible seems to suggest analogies to persons rather than analogies with things (e.g. a temple) or ideas (e.g. love) which seems to give more insight into the idea of God; also because one may hope that an idealization — in the ancient Greek style — of the notion of "person" brings us to a closer conception of God.

[22]It was suggested, however, that, since each Being is in cooperation with the others, the operation of multiplication has to be applied. Thus, $1 \times 1 \times 1 = 1$, which is mathematically correct. Yet, the meaning of the verbal expression "multiplying together two persons" remains to be discovered. Hence, the idea is no more than a pleasant metaphor. Almost two centuries ago the great scientist Hamilton tried to invent a mathematical operation on three (imaginary) numbers such that the result is 1. He discovered instead the new numbers called "quaternions" (owing to their quadruple basis; [41])

a priority and a primacy, is there within the Trinity a hierarchy of one God over the other Gods? However, the fact that a relation was at least to some extent characterized was an encouragement for scholars to try to characterize the other two relations-differences. This clarification proved, however, to be difficult. The ancient specific notion, i.e. "procession" seems to solve the problem *grosso modo*. Yet, this word at the present time constitutes an artificial tool. Moreover, a crucial debate occurred about the procession relationship between the Son and The Holy Spirit as to whether the Holy Spirit "proceeds" from the Father only or also from the Son. The debate was acrimonious and caused one of the main divisions occurring between Eastern and Western Christendom. Almost a millennium has passed without an agreement on this point. Thus, even the anthropomorphic analogy leads to serious, unresolved problems.

In conclusion, the central tenet of faith of Christendom is a notion of Trinity whose inner relations between each Person and God are apparently plain ("is"), yet they lead to a manifest inconsistency. This faith adds a plainly anthropomorphic relation between Father and Son ("generation"), yet at the cost of abandoning a rigorous logical path; moreover, since this anthropomorphism produces mere analogies, one cannot hope to obtain anything more than informal ideas and as a result have generated a radical and unresolved disagreement within Christendom over the relations enjoyed by the Holy Spirit.

No improvements are obtained by merging the Trinity into mankind's history (Social Trinitarism), which Joachim a Flore (around 1130-1202) was the first to do. Actually, this introduced a new perspective on the "economic Trinity" (i.e. Trinity for us), but not new insights into the "immanent Trinity" (i.e. God's inner relationships).

Apparently, one has to conclude that the Trinity mystery manifests apparent absurdities implying a sharp separation between faith and reason, as several philosophers have stated.[23]

5 The logical features of Cusanus' Tri-unity

Did Cusanus apply intuitionist logic to the Trinity? Did Cusanus offer logical arguments also regarding the Trinity?

In the modern era Christian theology has been bound by one of St. Thomas' tenets, the logical principle: "that is and that is not are true propositions at same

---

[23]For instance, Rudolf Carnap wrote: "This [my scientific] examination has clearly shown that traditional theology is a remnant of earlier times, entirely out of line with the systematic way of thinking in the present century." [11, p. 8]

time." cannot apply to God [4, V, 2, 3]. Yet, according to Cusanus in this way Thomas and, before him, Aristotle, missed the possibility of establishing the basic connection within Trinity, that of One with itself ([22, chs. 18–29]; [23, ch. 14, p. 1303, no. 39]) In order to do this, Cusanus bravely suggests that the above principle limits not our knowledge of God, but our minds, or rather only one faculty of our minds, i.e. *ratio*. Hence, provided that one appeals to the other mind's faculty, *intellectus*, one may attain God by thinking beyond the law of non-contradiction.[24]

Cusanus believes that he was successful in proving the two tenets of Christian dogma, i.e. God is Oneness and God is Trinity [30]. In the following I will explain why these conclusions of Cusanus do not lead to the previously mentioned oxymora.

It is scarcely recalled that Western philosophy developed mostly ontological metaphysics, while in Greek philosophy metaphysics was of two kinds, i.e. henology (search for Oneness) and ontology; Aristotle merely preferred the latter, without declaring its supremacy over the former — as Western philosophy then did [54]. In modern times a few isolated philosophers have espoused henological metaphysics. Cusanus was prominent among them, but unfortunately his books seemed incomprehensible and no important theologians followed him.

On the issues discussed so far, while an ontological metaphysician has to establish truths by obeying the non-contradiction principle, a henological metaphysician reasons inductively. It is not surprising if the henological Cusanus claimed to be opening the human mind to new "great fields of hunting" [23], as he called his inductive search for divine beings; in fact, he explored fields which were disregarded by others (and which produced many new results).

Cusanus' effort to discover new names for God introduced a novelty of great logical importance. It was little noticed that within intuitionist logic, among the three truth values of a proposition, only the DNP is true, while both its corresponding affirmative proposition and negative proposition, by participating in the truth only partially, cannot be mutually opposed (see also [27]. As a matter of fact, in *De Non Aliud* Cusanus often stresses this logical law. Hence, the feared contradiction no longer constitutes an insurmountable barrier; the opposition between the affirmative and the negative proposition is only a partial one.

In the year 1462 Cusanus suggested that "Not-Other" was the best representation of the name of God with respect to human beings; there he stressed that it does not mean "*idem*", and even less "is". At the present time we know that the failure of the double negation law implies the use of intuitionist logic. Hence, through the notion of "not-other" Cusanus essentially overcame the law of non-contradiction

---

[24]Actually, in 1453 Cusanus wrote the book *De Visione Dei* whose chap.s 16 and 17 are devoted to the subject of the Trinity, yet still conceived through Augustine's classical analogy based on love.

and introduced intuitionist logic into the conception of God.[25] Thus, Cusanus could explore theological subjects using a different logic from the classical logic of Aristotle.

The above innovation is very important since it provides a different point of departure to his analysis of the notion of the Tri-unity. Indeed, by means of the above two words Cusanus successfully suggested a new way to describe Tri-Unity: "The not-other is not-other than not-other". In fact, this triple repetition of the words "Not-Other" is the best verbal expression for designating the Tri-Unity. This proposition is essentially a henological proposition, because it leads to understanding the entirety of God as Oneness from the multiplicity of three names "not-other" applied to the three Persons [28].

However, this expression is no more than an allusion to the divine reality, because it represents the Tri-Unity only allusively; formally, "not-other than" is different from the name "not-other" ; moreover, although the first and the last "not-other" are intended to represent two different Persons, they actually attribute the same name to both. This shows that even the highest expression of the divine reality is not exempt from criticism, owing to the imperfection of the results of all human thought.

6   Two improvements of Cusanus' insights through modern intuitionist logic

In the above-mentioned paper [30] I showed that Cusanus was well aware that he was introducing a new kind of logic; he did not, however, achieve a full comprehension of it — as the previous sec. 2.7 has also illustrated; hence, he did not derive all its consequences.

As a consequence of Cusanus' introduction of intuitionist logic I suggest that there are three innovations within the traditional diagram illustrating Tri-Unity; first, the relation between two of the three Persons should be understood to be no longer subject to classical logic; e.g. within the formula "Father is not Son", the negation should be understood not as a complete separation between the two Persons but in the vague sense suggested by weak intuitionist negation. Indeed, the

---

[25] According to Knuuttila [48, p. 1335], Abelardo (1079-1142) was the first to introduce a modality in order to solve the oxymora generated by an application of classical logic to the subject of Trinity; he made a distinction between "separate" and "separable" entities; he cleverly called it the "real distinction" or the "real difference". Unfortunately, this idea was not considered as a way out of classical logic, as the modal word separable (= it may be separated) suggests. Also Tuggy [56, p. 181] concludes that the relationship between Son and God is a qualitative sameness, i.e. the Son is *homoousios* with God; yet this appeal to a particular modality of "sameness" does not lead Tuggy to conceive this relation outside classical logic.

intuitionist negation of an identity may well represent the relationships of generation and procession, whatever the meanings of these words may be. This would clarify what Cusanus tried to express through the following words "they are not the same as one another" at the end of the following quotation:

> Now, it is evident that those who do not attain unto the fact that not-other is not **same** and that not-same is not other cannot grasp the fact that Oneness, Equality, and Union are the same in essence but are not the same as one another. (Cusanus [21], *incipit* of book II, VIII; I wrote in boldface the words which I understand as belonging to classical logic)[26]

Notice that, unlike the anthropomorphic relationships between Persons, the intuitionist relationships within couples of Persons do not present any logical disparity, i.e. they put all Persons on a par.[27]

I suggest a second innovation. By exploiting Cusanus'previous suggestion of a name for God, I attribute the words "Not-Other" not only — as Cusanus does — to God in His entirety, but also to the relationships of each Person with Oneness. As a consequence, a quaternary interpretation of God is no longer possible, because the

---

[26]This is the only point in the book where Cusanus refers to the Trinity by making use of a double negation ("not-other"). This fact may represent Cusanus' effort to adjust his language to the exclusively affirmative language of Muslims, to whom the book is addressed. As a matter of fact, the above quotation constitutes a very short anticipation of the contents of *De non Aliud* [22], written one year later.

[27]Let us quickly review how other scholars have approached what I have put forward in the above. Geach [39] and [46] remarked that without the transitivity property the word "is" does not give rise to the first oxymoron. For this logical reason these scholars suggested a "relative identity" ; it clearly constitutes a compromise with classical logic. Branson [9] performed an extensive logical analysis of the logical problems of the Trinity in formal terms. He admits his "prejudice" towards PLI = [classical Predicate Logic with Identity]" [9, p. 39]. However, he considered also the intuitionist relationships I introduced in the above; in his terms it pertains to the "Intuitionist-Identity-Counting-Family (NCICF)" (ivi, pp. 46-47). Yet, he adds that: "The rejection of PLI is in itself controversial... And it is hard to imagine what such an answer might look like, and what motivates such a view." (ivi, p. 49). Branson adds that Gregorius of Nyssa suggested a solution (ivi, ch.s 3 and 4). However, in my opinion this ancient author merely equivocated on the concept of God. Rather, Cusanus' suggestions appear to answer Branson's questions exactly, but the latter does not mention the former. The closest approximation to my above suggestion is the following: "Of course, if the [common] diagram [shield of faith] is interpreted according to ordinary logic, then it contains a number of contradictions... However, if the three links connecting the three outer nodes of the diagram [of the shield of Faith] to the center node are interpreted as representing a non-transitive quasi-equivalence relation (where the statement "A is equivalent to C" does **not** follow from the two statements "A is equivalent to B" and "B is equivalent to C"), then the diagram is fully logically coherent and non-self-contradictory. So the medieval Shield of the Trinity diagram could be considered to contain some implicit kernel of the idea of alternative logical systems." [2].

words "not-other" do not allow us to consider a Person as separate and independent from Oneness, since they do constitute connections and participations, although they are to be discovered. Hence, the mathematical addition of the three Persons together no longer leads to the paradoxical result of Oneness, because, since the addends are not separate from one another, this mathematical operation cannot be performed.

The previous logical oxymoron concerning the collapsing of all Persons into Oneness disappears, because one can no longer exactly equate each Person to Oneness. Furthermore, the distinction between the substance of each Person and His participation in God is dismissed.

Rather, the problematic nature of a double negation suggests that, given that our knowledge of the divine realm is always essentially limited, the precise kinds of relations that actually exist will remain, although hinted and imperfect, still to be discovered. This would seem to be quite appropriate to the relationship between man and God.

I introduce a third innovation concerning the name to be attributed to the third Person. According to most authoritative theologians He is not a person at all.[28] For this reason He is named using a verbal expression. However, the two words "Holy Spirit" manifestly constitute a very distant approximation to His name. Indeed, the adjective "holy" tries to redress the considerable ambiguity of the word "spirit", which in the human world applies to a variety of extraneous objects, wine and phantoms included. I suggest that these two words, "Holy Spirit", owing to their lack of correspondence with reality and hence owing to their idealistic nature, represent the result of an incorrect translation into affirmative words of a correct double negation; which by opposition to "spirit" is easily discovered, Im-material.

Indeed, the third Person is surely characterized by negating i) any reference to matter and its deterministic laws; ii) the material constitution of human beings; iii) the entire concrete World, whereas the other two Persons do have relationships with it (the Father has created (and/or creates) the World; the Son shared (or shares) human nature). One more reason for this name is that only through this doubly negated name can the entire Trinity be essentially called "Not-Other", otherwise the other two Persons can be mistaken for their materializations: God the Father with His Creation (pantheism) and the Son with every statue or painting of Jesus (fetishism). The previous suggestions change the traditional diagram representing the Tri-Unity into the following diagram essentially based on intuitionist logic. It

---

[28]"Both the personality and the role of the Holy Spirit can be expressed by no words in a perfect way. And they can be caught only in His effects [on the World]; instead in His essence, He is according to classical logic "only apophatic". His personality is absolutely transcending a whatsoever personality." ([35]; see also [53].)

may be called *Stella fidei* (Faith's star, or Star of the Faith).

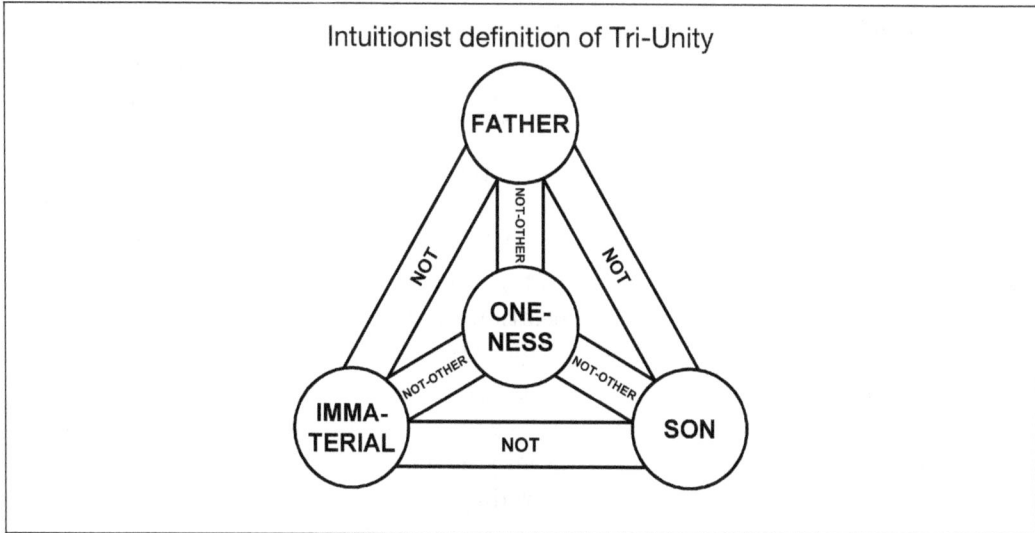

Figure 2

Notice that both the inner relationships of the Tri-Unity and the relationship between man and God are characterized by the same formula, "not-other", and this formula represents a symmetrical relationship, because also for God man is different but not other; indeed, he is "similar" to Him (Gn 1, 26). Hence, whereas theologians sharply distinguish between the two kinds of Trinity, my conclusion is that the immanent Trinity is governed by the same words "not-other" of the economic Trinity.

7 A consequence supported also by Cusanus' *Possest*: God's inner dynamics

The new diagram is pregnant with many important consequences whose theological validity proves the correctness of my logical viewpoint.

The first very important consequence concerns the immanent Trinity.

Notice that both the classical diagram and the idealistic (ontological) conception of the Trinity suggest a static nature of God. However, let us consider the two following points. First, God, being Oneness, as a single God performs actions in the World for which we have evidence; hence, the logic of His visible actions is classical.[29]

---

[29]This corresponds to Aristotle's conception of God as "*actus sine potentia*" (act without power)

This vision of His acts governed by classical logic suggests God as only Oneness, as He was conceived in the past; this vision is comfortable for a man living in the real World where the dominant logic is classical. Yet, we know from the previous sections that after the development of an entire PO theory the application of PSR changes a universal, doubly negated predicate into the corresponding affirmative predicate. In the case of Tri-Unity, as a consequence of the henological tension of all the three Persons towards Oneness, the intuitionist relations between each Person and Oneness, represented by the words "not-other", have to be translated into the classical logic of God as Oneness; Who indeed, according to the henological perspective, exists inasmuch as He fuses together the three Persons. This operation of fusion corresponds to a logical translation of the words "not-other", i.e. to an application of the PSR. Through this logical translation the human mind grasps a significant logical operation regarding the dynamics of inner relationships between the three Persons and Oneness, i.e. it reasons about the inner dynamics of God.

Hence, it is true that Tri-Unity essentially includes an operation; but not that operation which was naïvely suggested by tradition, i.e. an operation of mathematical addition of the three Persons; or even the operation of Hegel's three dialectical steps; rather, a logical translation from intuitionist to classical logic as it is performed by the PSR.[30]

Cusanus' search for better names of God had already suggested one more important one, to which he devoted an entire book [21]: *Posse = est*, shortened by him as *Possest*. This name summarizes Trinity through the relations among potentiality (*Posse*), act (*est*) and a relationship of equality between the two. This constitutes an Augustinian triad for representing Trinity; yet, since the modal word Posse is equivalent to a double negation, this name of God represents the equating of a doubly negated predicate (*Posse*) to its corresponding affirmative predicate (*est*);[31] this is exactly the result of an application of the PSR; hence, it implies the translation of the entire predicate calculus of intuitionist logic into that of classical logic (and also the change from a PO theory — based on the problem of the search for God — to an AO theory — the contemplation of God's intervention in the World) [29]. Thus, this name of God may be understood as the highest metaphysical representation

---

[5, 1071 b 20].

[30]Notice that these insights do not imply that God is subject to human reason (as Immanuel Kant said about the proofs of God existence) since a distance of God from man is preserved. Moreover, in our case reason is not only one of the two faculties of human mind, i.e. ratio, as Kant considered it, but is, as Cusanus maintains, the *intellectus*, i.e. the best link of similitude between the human mind and the divinity [18].

[31]Actually, the application of PSR translates *Posse* into *est*. Since of course *est* in all cases implies *Posse*, within God the implication between the two terms holds true in both directions; hence these terms are equal, as the symbol = means.

of the Trinity through a PSR application, because this principle can represent the inner dynamics of God. Notice that the ancients called God "Omnipotent" exactly in this sense; this word expresses, rather than the naive idea of a Being always doing everything (*Sempiter Omnifaciens*), a Being that more appropriately does what is impossible for a human being, owing to his finiteness; i.e. to change a mere possibility into either a being or a fact; or rather, to change the entire logic of possibilities into the logic of hard facts.

Cusanus knew PSR very well; he often enunciated either it or its equivalent versions, (e.g. [22, p. 1123, sec. 9, no. 32]), although he never called it by name nor focused his attention on it. Within *Possest* he emphasizes what he conceived as an operation of *Possest*, which actually represents the application of PSR to the "no-other" relationships of three Persons to Oneness in order to obtain Him:

> Oneness is the beginning of all multitude, as Proclus says. And, as Aristotle claims, what is maximally such [as it is] is the cause of all things such [as that] [*they are the images of the Father*]; and what is such [as it is] *per se* is the cause of all things that are such [as that] by participation [*they are the images of the Son*]; and what is simple per se is the cause of all things that are such [as they are] *per se* [*they are the images of the Im-material*], as the Platonists maintain; and what is *per se* without a [restricting] addition is the cause of whatever is *per se* with a [restricting] addition. And this thing that is unrestrictedly per se is the Cause of each and every cause, just as earlier-on [I showed that] the Beginning of all things is given various names on account of the various differences among its participants, even though the Beginning itself precedes everything nameable ...

> Accordingly, this name ["*possest*"] leads the one-who-is-speculating beyond all the senses, all reason, and all intellect unto a mystical vision, where there is an end to the ascent of all cognitive power and where there is the beginning of the revelation of the unknown God [23, p. 1352, n, 120]; insertions in Italic are mine).

The first period qualifies the relationship of each Person with the World through a modal expression, "such as", i.e. a similar DNP to "not-other". Then in order to obtain Oneness Cusanus dismisses the "[restriction] addition, i.e. "such as"; that amounts to translating the modality into a copula.[32]

---

[32] Also Cusanus wanted characterize a dynamics inside God. He presented this dynamics within the relationships of the Persons of God through his verbal formula for the Tri-Unity, yet according

Admirably, the second period stresses that: i) this name of God represents a high principle of reasoning — as does the principle of the PSR translation - because it surpasses both the reason (ratio) i.e. the classical logic, and the intellect (intellectus) i.e. the intuitionist logic; ii) this name is the highest point of the human mind's understanding of God — as is the translation between two kinds of logic. It differs from PSR in that Cusanus does not apply the PSR to the single relation of each Person with Onenenss, but to the relation of one only word, Posse, by which Cusano means all the potentiality of the three Persons.

8 One more consequence of my intuitionist viewpoint: A new interpretation of Christian revelation

A second consequence is astonishing. It is exactly what at the end of a previous quotation Cusanus claims, that is, his conception of Trinity implies that:

> Accordingly, this name ["*possest*"] leads ... *where there is the beginning of the revelation* of the [*in the past times*] unknown God [21, p. 921 no. 15]; Italic mine.

I take these words as a full explanation of the Christian revelation for the following reasons.

i) Christians believe that among the many manifestations of God narrated by the Bible, the one that has manifested the real God to human beings was that of the incarnation of the divine Person of the Son in a human being. Yet, classical logic unavoidably characterizes this double nature as an absurd oxymoron: at the same time God = man and God $\neq$ man. Instead, intuitionist logic can correctly represent the double nature of Christ through a plain DNP: "It is not true that Christ is not at same time true man and true God" (of course, the corresponding affirmative proposition equating the two natures, is theologically false). This DPN representing the double nature of Christ introduced men to an understanding of an intuitionist thinking. As a matter

---

to its Western Catholic church, i.e. "Not-other" Father generates "Not-other" Son, etc. [22, ch. 5, pp. 1116-7, n. 10]. This conception of Tri-Unity is not symmetric, as the star of Faith is, since it give a privileged role to the Father. Notice also that in *De Apice Theoriae* (1464) Cusanus defined the Trinity through three terms, posse, *aequalitas* and *unio*; both structure and logic of them are equal to the *Posse=est*; yet, the term *unio* represents the Oneness; hence, also this triad has a full logical meaning, because it accurately represents an application of PSR; its constitutes a verbal representation of the immanent Trinity, whereas *Possest* a verbal representation of the economic Trinity.

of fact, the Calcedonian Council (451 a.C.) which defined the dual nature of Christ, made use of four adverbs, which are all double negations: "without mutation and without confusion", "without separation and without division". This introduction into the history of mankind of intuitionist logic through an essential use of double negations for defining who the Christ was, is confirmed also by both Christ's mission and his teachings, whose meanings are apparent in intuitionist logic, as is shown in the following.

ii) In Saint John's Gospel, the hymn to the *Logos* (John, 1, 1-3 and 14) represents a hymn to the first step of the Son's incarnation in the World. Notice that Cusanus meant by *Logos* "the rational word of the principle", where the meaning of the adjective "rational" is very close to the meaning of the adjective "logical". In logical terms the incarnation of the Son represents the introduction of intuitionist logic, already subsisting within the inner relationships of God, into the human World, in order to overcome two separations; both the intrinsic separation of the dualistic truth of classical logic governing mankind's acting through the division of the world for selfish ends, in order to introduce love for those who present themselves as enemies, but actually are not enemies; and the traditional separation between men and God, in order to introduce a reconciliation between mankind and the divine realm, i.e. the reconciliation of recognizing themselves in a relationship represented by the two negated words "not-other".

Owing to the two natures of Christ and hence the two kinds of logic that He represents in Himself, the *Logos* represents the simultaneous actualization of the possibility of these two kinds of logic. Thus, this hymn is addressed to the possibility of introducing the coexistence of both kinds of logic and hence of a language enjoying a full faculty of expression (which means first the addition of the modal to the indicative conjugation of verbs, which occurred in Western culture in the period just before the birth of Jesus: van Der Auwera, Zamorano Aguilar 2016); it may be considered a hymn to logical pluralism, which in itself represents an epochal event in the history of mankind.

iii) In order to characterize the economic Trinity, a human being has, according to Cusanus, to perform the opposite logical translation to PSR, i.e. the opposite translation to that occurring within the Trinity; he has to perform the translation from classical logic governing the facts of daily life of human beings to intuitionist logic essentially included in the Trinity; i.e. he has to translate from the classical logic that dominates his sphere of existence into the intuitionist logic characterizing the inner relationships of God of Tri-Unity; hence, he has to succeed in naming Him through an essentially double negation, e.g. "Not-Other". This logical step corresponds to the historical way of introducing mankind to the knowledge of the Trinity; it began from the knowledge of the DNP expressing the double nature of the Son, as revealed by Jesus' birth; then it was enlarged by the preaching of the Son-Christ, who suggested to the human mind some ways of discovering God as a Tri-Unity, i.e. a God that essentially includes intuitionist relations represented by "not-other" (two words unfortunately misunderstood for two millennia by almost all theologians maintaining that classical logic was the only logic). In this logical leap of mankind the Jesus-Son rightly plays the role of the Mediator, in support of his role of Mediator for salvation, as theologians call Him.[33]

iv According to Cusanus original sin is caused by the human intellect supporting the *spiritus divisionis*, from which a propensity to evil is born [21, book II, n. 17]. Lanza del Vasto [49, ch. 1] adds that the role played by reason is to assume as a principle of life what the name of the forbidden tree means, the "knowledge-of-Good-and-Evil" as two separate and opposed realities to be exploited according to one's own tendency to achieve selfish ends, i.e. to obtain one's own material good while doing evil to others. This is a clear dualism within ethics and hence also within logic, which is therefore classical. As a social consequence, all mutually interacting men cooperate, either consciously or unconsciously, to build, even against God, social institutions that hide their evil purposes; in such a way their evil tendencies lead them to create social structures, imposing on the people formal laws that actually hide their sins that have become institutional and structural: e.g. the sins of dictatorship, capitalism, colonization, genocide, etc...

The mission of Christ was to teach how overcome this structural sin and in particular its root, the *spiritus divisionis*. The elected people usually obeyed the first (affirmative) commandments, while the other (social) commandments seemed impossible in all circumstances (mainly "Do not kill" within a radical and dramatic context of a war dividing two populations). The Jewish people (and even more so other peoples) preferred to obey the laws made by their social institutions (army, state, courts, market, capital, etc.) which they themselves had built in order to organize their society even against God's Law. In the history of mankind Christ's task was to bring mankind to accept also the social commandments even when social

---

[33]He is also a mediator in a conflict. Indeed, the first step of an act of love is not simply a dialogue, which in fact can occur also between deaf, but a dialogue that overcomes logical distances, i.e. a translation. That explains why the disciple who was the most beloved by Jesus starts his Gospel with a hymn to intellectual activity, that is, *Logos*.

structures are being opposed, i.e. by fighting the structural sins of evil power, which was offered by Satan in the second temptation of Jesus (Mt 4, 8-10).[34] He rejected it because Christ came into the World to establish, notwithstanding the evil laws of social institutions, the full validity of the social propositions located in the second table; in other words, the absolute validity of the social commandments which as a matter of fact are all DNPs of intuitionist logic (e.g. "Do not kill").

However, he radically changed their meanings from authoritarian commandments, whose main part is "not", as a person who espouses classical logic understands them, to paternal (recall how Jesus' prayer invites us to call Him: "Our Father...") warnings, to be considered by each person as — exactly in agreement with the role played by a DNP — a methodological principle for managing one's own life in the best possible way;[35] e.g. in the case of "Do not kill", for finding out a positive solution to each conflict potentially leading to killing the adversary.[36] In this way Jesus introduced to mankind the use of DNPs even in the most dramatic moments of human life.

Jesus' main teachings also manifest the intuitionist logical nature of his revelation, because they are DNPs, which in the past have been mistakenly understood as propositions of affirmative logic: "Do not resist evil [by means of evil actions]"; "Love [whoever actually is not] an enemy"; "Love your neighbour as [= neither more nor less than] yourself".

In conclusion, Jesus introduced into mankind's life a kind of logic which is very different from the ancient logic of obedience to compulsory commands of an absolute, separate authority as well as the logic of fighting other men in a war as an animal

---

[34]Notice that Jesus' rejection of the three temptations are also expressed through DNPs two of them necessarily include the word "only" (= not otherwise), the third response says: "Do not tempt God."

[35]Truly, Jesus' summary of the Law and prophets is a command: "Love God..., love your neighbor..." (Mc 13, 28-31). "Moreover: [If you want to behave servilely towards God] I give you a new commandment [which however is quite different from the previous ones] My command is this: Love each other as I have loved you." (John 15, 12). Really, this is a strange commandment, because no one can love on command. Actually, love implies a change of methodology: from that of a servant's blind obedience, to that of paying the greatest attention to relationships among people in order to understand, mainly within a conflict, the motivation of an adversary.

[36]It is not by chance that Jesus was condemned and killed by the two highest social institutions of his time, well representing evil institutional power par excellence. Both were essentially negative; the Roman empire was founded on worldwide military domination; the Jewish religious institution, claiming to be directed by God Himself, survived through profound compromises with the Pagan empire. The religious institution condemned Jesus precisely according to the deep meaning of original sin, i.e. its priests (dishonestly justifying their decision with the interest of the people) wanted to preserve their social power (their good) imposing the cost of their decision on another, i.e. the death of the Christ: "It would be good if one man died for the people." (John 18, 14)

against animals of a different species; he overcame the *spiritus divisionis* governing both these situations not only by setting himself as a bridge in the relationship between mankind and God, but also in the relationship of a man with others by introducing the love that overcomes selfish interest; in other words, with respect to the two polarities of mutually opposed good and evil he introduced the logic of searching for a third possibility aimed at mutual understanding. Of course, to follow him requires a conversion, which implies also a translation of the kind of logic, the inverse translation of that of PSR's.

To summarize, God applies, on the one hand, classical logic through His action as Oneness outside Himself, and, on the other, intuitionist logic within Himself through both the name of the Im-material, the inner relationships with Oneness and the manifestation of the Son-man in the World. Man applies classical logic through daily life and, after revelation, he also applies intuitionist logic through Jesus Christ, whose nature is dual in accordance with this logic, and God through both His name as "not-other" and the social commandments, which are all DNPs.

In sum, by essentially adding one more kind of logic to religious thinking the Christian revelation constitutes also a revelation of a logical nature.[37]

In the light of this the separation between God and human beings is overcome by two different kinds of translation between the two main kinds of logic, i.e. a perfect translation by God, as is stressed by Cusanus' idea of *Possest*, which is the PSR translation governing the Son's incarnation; an imperfect one by the human mind according to the inverse translation of PSR, that is, from classical to intuitionist logic; a human translation whose imperfection is first of all the result of the misleading human belief in the uniqueness of classical logic, and second by the uncomfortable feeling that an acceptance of DNPs leads to a loss of contact with the concrete human world, also because the human mind, in order to achieve a concrete conclusion of reasoning through DNPs, has to use its ingenuity to discover in each particular case a specific chain of AAAs allowing a correct application of PSR.

9   Cusanus' inconclusive studies on logic

The first study of logic by Cusanus appears in the book [20, p. 845, n. 10]; there he discussed the typical tool for logical deduction, a syllogism and introduced a new, yet ineffective one. Then in *De non Aliud* he arrived at some laws of a new kind of

---

[37] Of course, I do not claim that the Christian Revelation is *only* a logical matter, but that it is *primarily* a logical matter; e.g. true love comes after logic since without logic love is a foolish dispersion. Cusanus states (by reiterating Augustine): "For love is subsequent to knowledge and to the thing known, for nothing unknown is loved." [20, p. 845 n. 9]

logic. Klibansky [47, p. 308] remarks that one year after the *De Non Aliud* Cusanus is so attentive to logic that even Plato's *Parmenides* is read by him from a logical rather than the metaphysical point of view.

In the same year, one year before his death, within *De Venatione* Cusanus for the first time exalts the intellectual power of logic, as the best tool with which reason can capture truth:

> our intellect is endowed by nature with logic, so that by this means it infers and makes its own pursuit. For logic is, as Aristotle said, a most exact instrument for pursuit both of the true and of the truthlike. Hence, when the intellect finds [what is true] it recognizes [it] and eagerly embraces [it]. [23, p. 1292, n. 4]

There he devotes the subsequent four chapters to logic; in particular chapter 4 illustrates the various kinds of syllogisms. Yet, although he correctly starts from a clear DNP (stated at the end of the ch. 2: "What is impossible to be done, is not done", a negative version of PSR), he merely reiterates the usual considerations on syllogisms. Eventually, he failed to discover a new tool of reasoning, as the inconclusiveness of his search in ch. 4 shows. As a matter of fact, when studying the syllogism he sees it as the common tool for all kinds of logic.

However, after 1462 Cusanus claimed that *Posse ipsum* represents God. Moreover, he claimed also that only the word *Posse* represents God. In my opinion, he fell into two traps; in both cases he abandoned his previous speculations about *De Possest* because he expresses a possibility only, not an actuality.

In retrospect, we see that he ought at least i) to have guessed that a modality is equivalent to a DNP; ii) to have recognized the principle of the PSR; iii) to have recognized it as the logical operation concluding a PO theory. Surely too much, considering the stage his research had reached and the progress achieved in logic at that time.

Maybe he felt he was unable to proceed further.[38] One may suspect that for this reason, rather than out of modesty, he ends the above book by declaring his results "rough and unrefined":

> By means of the foregoing [reflections] I think that I have explicated as best I could a rough and unrefined conceptualization of my pursuits [of wisdom]. And I submit all [these explications] for one's better speculating on these lofty matters. [23, p. 154, n. 123]

---

[38]In fact, in the years 1462–1464 (the last years of his life) he illustrated through several books all that he had previously accumulated regarding both the different names of God and the different ways of "hunting the divine prey".

10 Conclusions

It has been shown that Cusanus' faith was supported by philosophical (and scientific) ideas, which were conceived through a rational activity that was so far advanced - as previous analyses proved — that they can be rightly called prophetical with respect to subsequent scientific progress; e.g. the possible failure of the double negation law was advanced only five centuries and half later by Brouwer, the founder of intuitionist mathematics and logic. One can no longer say with Dionisius [25, ch. vii] that "mystical theology [*as Cusanus' theology was commonly considered*] is irrational and insane, and a foolish wisdom...", full of contradictions and absurdities. Moreover, contrary to Hopkins' opinion, Cusanus' faith was not merely a "Christian cloak" in which metaphysical ideas were draped [43, p. 262].

Cusanus did reason in a correct logical way. His advances are mainly manifested in his thinking about the Trinity. His new representation of Tri-Unity can no longer interpreted as a linguistic joke, as many scholars (e.g. [33, p. 263]) understood Cusanus' combining together of three "not-others" to represent the Trinity. On the contrary, at present time in the light of intuitionist logic we know that Cusanus was right in claiming, when dealing with such an elevated subject as God, to be reasoning.

In the light of this, one ought rather to recognize the limitations of classical logic, which cannot avoid seeing intrinsic contradictions in the notion of Trinity (as well as in the psychic realm). Owing to this difficulty, in the past scholars (after Augustine) intuitively appealed to analogies, without realizing that, being essentially DNPs, they belong to non-classical logic. In fact, the introduction of intuitionist logic to govern thinking about Tri-Unity makes this theological notion a fully rational idea, in the sense that the intuitionist idea of Tri-Unity complies perfectly with logical thinking,[39] but according to a kind of logic that diverges from Aristotelian logic. Thus we can say, using Cusanus' figurative thinking, that the human mind, as it moves towards knowledge of Paradise (= house of God), no longer comes to halt before the "wall of the absurdity" erected by classical logic. Through conjectures, which is typical of the activity of the *intellectus*, or, in modern terms, through intuitionist logic, the human mind is capable of going beyond this wall and gaining some not inconsistent insights into the nature of Paradise, and even of the structure

---

[39]It is a "reasoned Trinity", as Hegel put it. Hegel tried to explore a new kind of logic, unfortunately, without precisely qualifying its basic laws. The application of his law of "the negation of the negation" starts from a concrete proposition (thesis) (while in intuitionist logic the affirmative proposition is only partially true), proceeds by an operation of negation of it, resulting in a new proposition (anti-thesis, considered as a new truth) (while, in intuitionist logic it is only partially true) and concludes through a further negation into a final new proposition (synthesis) (while in intuitionist logic this doubly negated proposition only is the true one).

of God; in particular, His relationship with the World and His inner relationships, all expressed through DNPs.

Finally, Cusanus' logical approach to Trinity is *vindicatus* by the discovery that his new logic is now recognized as being intuitionist.

In addition, his thinking belongs to a long tradition classified as "negative theology" including all theologies outside affirmative theology. Instead, there existed a long tradition of applying double negations to the crucial tenets of faith. First of all, let us recall the four doubly negated adverbs of the Calcedonian Council's definition of the dual nature of Christ "without mutation and without confusion", "without separation and without division". Moreover, App. 2 will show that the Athanasian creed also closely approached intuitionist logical thinking. With respect to this theological tradition, Cusanus plays the historical role of having improved it and achieved a close approximation not only to intuitionist thinking, but also to intuitionist reasoning; indeed, he correctly introduced some substantial laws governing the new logic.

In the light of the above, we have to conclude that Cusanus was not only the first modern philosopher [13, ch. I, sec. I]; he was also the first theologian to see and begin to express the primary logical nature of both the internal structure of the Tri-Unity and the Christian revelation; or, in other words, he was the first Christian theologian to begin to understand rationally the core of Christian faith; i.e. to join faith to modern reason in a perfectly consistent way.

Going beyond Cusanus' striking innovations, I have introduced some improvements in his introduction of some laws of the new kind of logic; they complete his logical advances in a new, deeper and more systematic knowledge not only of the Trinity but also of the Christian revelation.

First, the basic contradictions infesting traditional analyses of the notion of the Christian Tri-Unity have been eliminated. Second, the entire Christian revelation receives a new logical foundation, that joins faith and reason with such precision that no problem remained. Third, a subordinate result. An application of a new method of logical analysis of the literary text made possible a more precise interpretations of two of Cusanus'texts whose reading is difficult, as is proved by centuries of unsuccessful investigation into their essential meanings. The new interpretations in the two texts contributed to improving both the chronology of Cusanus' books and the historical development of his thought.

Appendix 1: Analysis of the *De Deo Abscondito* through the DNPs

Let us start with a short summary of this work. After a verbal confrontation between the Pagan and the Christian (Part 1), in sec. 3, the first section of Part II, a goodwill dialogue resumes by dealing with a metaphysical question put by the Christian, i.e. whether the truth is achievable outside itself or not. In sec. 5 the Christian answers the question with two AAAs. The first one states that any knowledge and any stage of the process of knowing leaves an insurmountable separation from truth. "Hence, he is irrational [= *absurd*] who thinks he knows something in truth but who is without a knowledge of truth." The second AAA suggests an analogy: as a blind person cannot perceive colors, so a man cannot perceive truth.

The next substantial part of the dialogue (sec.s 6-13) is devoted to Christian's rebuttals of the provocative arguments advanced by the unpersuaded Pagan. The Christian puts forward two strong propositions in a surprisingly incidental way; i.e. all that is conceived is not similar to God (sec. 8) and God is not truth, but precedes it (sec. 12). Both establish the Christian's opinion of a total separation between man's mind and God. This separation is reiterated in the next-to-last section (the no. 14), where the Christian explains why "God" is the common name of the divinity; this name is justified by a mere analogy: "...as God is to all things, as sight is to things visible" [19, 1305, n. 14]. As a matter of fact, in the last section the Pagan agrees with the Christian on a total separation between man and God; he indeed adds a similar analogy to the Christian's; it refers to the separation between composites and incomposites. In sum, the aim of the intermediate part of the dialogue (secs. 3–13) is to exclude the possibility that any name represents a possible knowledge of God; indeed, this part constitutes a systematic denial by the Christian of any suggestion of a possible relationship advanced by the Pagan; only an analogy regarding the above-mentioned relationship of separation is allowed. Hence, the intermediate part excludes any relation between man and God.

Now I perform an analysis of the logical features of this five-page long text. It is divided into four parts: it was divided by the author into 15 *short sections* which include 124 composite propositions. My only innovation with respect to the previous method is to distinguish among the AAAs those expressed as provocative questions, i.e. those expecting answers denying absurdities (e.g. "Is God nothing?", as the Pagan seems to implicitly ask in sec. 9); apart from one of sec. 2, these AAAs are all the Pagan's, whereas the other AAAs are advanced by the Christian only. Table 2 summarizes the results.

Let us remark that in the entire text the number of problems is very high (27;

	Section	Problems	DNPs	Possible reasonings	Provocative arguments	Christian's AAA	PSR
Part I: *Christian and Pagan in Opposition about the knowledge of God*	1	*2*	3	1	1	-	-
	2	*4*	5	2	*2*	2	-
Part II: *Truth is absolute*	3	2	6	3	-	*2*	1
	4	2	4	1	-	*2*	-
	5	1	*18*	8	1	*2*	-
	6	2	5	1	-	-	-
	7	1	6	1	-	-	-
Part III: *Contradictions implied by naming God*	8	1	2	-	-	-	-
	9	2	8	8	8	1	-
	10	4	11	4	1	1	-
	11	3	5	4	-	-	- -
	12	2	3	1	-	-	- -
Part IV: *Analogies about the relationship between the believer and God*	13	3	5	4	-	-	- -
	14	-	7	*10*	-	-	-
	15	-	4	2	-	-	- -
Total		**27**	**94**	**51**	**7**	**11**	**1**
Legenda: as in Table 1							

Table 2: Main characteristic logical features of Cusanus' *De Deo Abscondito*

more than 5 per page); it is the highest mean I know. Also the numbers of problems, DNPs and AAAs are exceptional. Also the number of DNPs is high (94; almost 20 for page).[40] The number of provocative questions (7; a mean of 1,4 for page; which means an intense debate) is remarkable, as well as the number of AAAs (12; i.e. 2 per page, which means a strong appeal to intuitionist logic),

The distributions of the issues (problems, DNPs, Possible arguments, Provocative arguments, Cristian's AAAs, PSR) constitute evidence for a well-reasoned discussion. Additional evidence is i) the absence of problems in the last two sections; ii) the greater number of DNPs in the second part of the dialogue, i.e. the part following the introductory one; and iii) the distribution of an even greater number of possible arguments. All this is evidence of the extent to which the Christian approaches a PO theory and its mode of reasoning.

Yet, there is also evidence for the contrary; it is given by *i)* the third and fourth parts contain a large number of problems to be solved, while these parts should be the conclusions to the dialogue; ii) the lack of AAAs in the last four sections that ought to conclude the entire dialogue; iii) the only application of PSR in a section (no. 3) which comes too early with respect to PSR's function of translating the conclusion of a chain of AAAs into classical logic.

The Christian also makes use of *noesis*, i.e. intuitionist logic, through some AAAs.

To decide whether the Christian's reasoning is effective, let us analyze his numerous AAAs. It is difficult to consider them as AAAs because the absurd is rarely declared explicitly. Moreover, they are strangely located as two disconnected groups. The aim of the first group, in sects. 2-5, is to prove that truth is unattainable. The last AAA reiterates that of the second of sec. 2 which had led there to the interruption of the dialogue. It appears as a complete chain of arguments (leaving aside the persuasiveness of the arguments advanced by the Christian, which are all of metaphysical nature).

In the second group of AAAs, those in secs. 9–11, the Christian wants to prove that God, although He has given all things a name, has no name. Being the second group, it ought to conclude all the substantial arguments. Let us examine these AAAs attentively.

1. $[\neg Ts]$ It is not the case that He is nothing, for $[\neg Ts]$ this nothing has the name "nothing" [*understood: and hence $[\bot]$ it is absurd that God is nothing*] (p. 302, no. 9).

---

[40] As well as the number of possible formal arguments whose argumentative words represent Cusanus' will to present formal arguments, 10 per page.

2. [¬*Ts*] He is not ineffable, though He is beyond all things effable; for He is the Cause of all nameable things. How is it [*understood: it is not absurd* ⊥], then, that He Himself, who gives to others a name, [¬*Ts*] is without a name?" (p. 393, no. 10).

3. When I said it, I spoke the truth; and I am speaking the truth now, when I deny it. For if there are any beginnings of being and of not-being, God precedes them. However, not-being does not have a beginning of its not being but has only a beginning of its being. For not-being needs a beginning in order to be. In this way, then, He is the Beginning of not-being, because [¬*Ts*] withhout Him [⊥] there would not be not-being (pp. 303-304, no. 11).

Let us remark that they do not constitute a chain, because they are not connected one to the other. The first two concern two distinct properties of God. The third one concludes that God precedes nothing. No concluding DNP summarizes the result of the chain of reasoning. Rather the beginning of the last quotation manifests the final point of the discussion: the Christian manifests his strange way of thinking to the Pagan; he is stating at the same time a proposition and its negation (sec. no.s 10 and 11). This is the apex of the Christian's way of thinking. This corresponds to modern paraconsistent logic, which it would have been temerarious to consider an easily understandable way of reasoning at his time. Indeed, sections 14-16 close the debate through an agreement of both to recur to analogies, i.e. no reasoning.

As a matter of fact, within the culminating sections (9-11) the Christian characterizes God by simultaneously affirming and negating an attribution to Him (without any name expressed by means of double negations). Not surprisingly, analogies remain the only means of guessing an unbridgeable reality.[41] He mixes classical and intuitionist logic paraconsistently;

Hence, the Christian's logical tools are not adequate for this purpose and are used mainly to oppose the Pagan's provocations rather than to show how to approach God, whose separation from man is declared to be insurmountable. In fact, the Christian does not reason, except when he is opposing the Pagan's arguments.

We conclude that in this short writing Cusanus considers reasoning, whether in classical or intuitionist logic (which the first group of AAAs may be considered to belong to) as merely instrumental to discussing local points of theology. Notwithstanding the exceptional numbers of both DNPs and AAAs, intuitionist logic can in no way be considered as supporting the dialogue as a whole, but rather, at most

---

[41]Notice that this method is not that of the *coincidentia oppositorum* that he applies in *De Docta Ignorantia*, because the latter essentially includes a limit process, i.e. the idea of infinity (or of being beyond any quantitative measurement) as essential to the name of God. This is strong evidence for the date of *De Deo Abscondito* being no later than that of the edition of the above book, i.e. 1440.

partially. All this seems to represent an obscure search by Cusano for the correct logic.

Appendix 2: The Athanasian Creed in intuitionist logic

I quote the Athanasian Creed — an invention traditionally attributed to Athanasius — by underlining some words with continuous and dotted lines in order to stress the astonishing number of double negations and modal words occurring in the original text. I moreover add a small number of "*n.o.t.*" (= "not-other than") to change the remaining affirmative propositions into DNPs and thus complete it as an intuitionist creed.

Whosoever will be saved, before all things it is necessary that he hold the catholic faith. Which faith except every one do keep whole and undefiled; without doubt he shall perish everlastingly. And the catholic faith is *n.o.t.* this:

That we worship one God in Trinity, and Trinity in Unity; Neither confounding the Persons; nor dividing the Essence. For there is one Person of the Father; another of the Son; and another of the Holy Ghost. But the Godhead of the Father, of the Son, and of the Holy Ghost, is all *n.o.t.* one; the Glory *n.o.t.* equal, the Majesty *n.o.t.* coeternal.

Such as the Father is; such is the Son; and such is the Holy Ghost. The Father un-created; the Son un-created; and the Holy Ghost un-created. The Father un-limited; the Son un-limited; and the Holy Ghost un-limited. The Father non-mortal;[42] the Son non-mortal; and the Holy Ghost non-mortal. And yet they are not three non-mortals; but one non-mortal. As also there are not three un-created; nor three in-finites, but one un-created; and one in-finite. So likewise the Father is Almighty; the Son Almighty; and the Holy Ghost Almighty. And yet they are not three Almighties; but one Almighty. So the Father is *n.o.t.* God; the Son is *n.o.t.* God; and the Holy Ghost is *n.o.t.* God. And yet they are not three Gods; but *n.o.t.* one God. So likewise the Father is *n.o.t.* Lord; the Son *n.o.t.*, Lord; and the Holy Ghost *n.o.t.* Lord. And yet not three Lords; but *n.o.t.* one Lord. For like as we are compelled by the Christian verity; to acknowledge every Person by himself to be *n.o.t.*

---

[42]Here and in the following I force the text by substituting "non-mortal" for "eternal". It seems to me that it is consistent with the previous "non-created" and "non-limited" and the next "in-finite". Surely, the word "eternal" was preferred by the original text because it is more common.

God and Lord, so are we forbidden by the catholic religion; to say, There are three Gods, or three Lords.

The Father is made of none; neither created, nor begotten. The Son is of the Father alone; not made, nor created; but *n.o.t.* begotten. The Holy Ghost *n.o.t.* of the Father and of the Son; neither made, nor created, nor begotten; but proceeding.

So there is *n.o.t.* one Father, not three Fathers; n.o.t. one Son, n.o.t. not three Sons; one Holy Ghost, not three Holy Ghosts. And in this Trinity none is before, or after another; none is greater, or less than another. But the whole three Persons are co-non-mortal, and *n.o.t.* coequal. So that in all things, as aforesaid; the Unity in Trinity, and the Trinity in Unity, is to be worshipped.

He therefore that will be saved, let him thus think of the Trinity. [3]

Given that there are 53 composite propositions in the original text, 29 original DNPs, 17 modal words and 19 added *n.o.t.*, we see that the additions are less than half the intuitionist expressions $(29 + 17 = 46)$ by the author. In other words, the Athanasius' creed was almost entirely conceived in intuitionist logic. This proves that intuitionist logic, far from being a cumbersome way of thinking, has implicitly been credited with being the best way of thinking about the divine realm for fifteen hundred years.

References

[1] Anonymous a (2015), "Shield of Trinity",
    Wikipedia, https://en.wikipedia.org/wiki/Shield_of_the_Trinity

[2] Anonymous b (2017), "Trinity",
    RationalWiki,   online   https://rationalwiki.org/wiki/Trinity   https://rationalwiki.org/wiki/Trinity

[3] Anonymous c (2017) "Athanasian Creed",
    Wikipedia, https://en.wikipedia.org/wiki/Athanasian_Creed

[4] Aquinas Thomas (1259), *Quaestiones quodlibetales* (Quodlibetal Questions, English translation by. Sandra Edwards, Quodlibetal Questions 1 and 2. Mediaeval Sources in Translation, 27. Toronto: Pontifical Institute of Mediaeval Studies, 1983).

[5] Aristotle (350 B.C.E.) *Metaphysics*.

[6] Augustine (around 417), *De Trinitate*, English translation online http://www.newadvent.org/fathers/1301.htm

[7] Agustinus., *De Deo loquimur, quid mirum si non comprehendis? Si enim comprehendis, non est Deus* (Sermo 117, 3, 5); [PL 38, 663]; *Si quasi comprehendere potuisti, cogitatione tua te decepisti* (Sermo 52, 6, 16); [PL 38, 360].

[8] Baber H.E. (2017) "The Trinity", in Fieser J and Dowden B, (eds.), *Internet Encyclopedia of Philosophy*, `http://www.iep.utm.edu/trinity/`.

[9] Branson B. (2014), "The Logical Problem of Trinity", PhD Diss. Univ. Notre Dame IN, online
`https://www.beaubranson.com/wp-content/uploads/2017/03/Branson`
`Dissertation-TheLogicalProblemOfTheTrinity.pdf`, pp. 46-47.

[10] Brouwer L.E.J (1976), *Collected Works*, Elsevier, New York.

[11] Carnap. R. (1927), "Intellectual Autobiography", in P.A. Schilpp (ed.): *The Philosophy of Rudolf Carnap*, La Salle Ill., Open Court, 1963, pp. 1-84.

[12] Cartwright R. (1990), "On the logical problem of Trinity", in *Philosophical Essays*, MIT, Cambridge MA, pp. 187-200.

[13] Cassirer E. (1927), *Individuum und Cosmos in der Philosophie der Reinaissance*, Damistadt: Wissenschaftliche Buchgesellscliaft, 1963.

[14] Chellas B.F. (1980), *Modal Logic*, Cambridge U.P, Cambridge.

[15] Cusano N. (1995), *Il Dio Nascosto*, L. Mannarini (ed.), Milano: Laterza.

[16] Cusano N. (2010), *Il Dio Nascosto*, L. Parinetto (ed.), Milano: Mimesis.

[17] Cusano N. (2002), *Il Dio Nascosto*, F. Buzzi (ed.), Milano: BUR.

[18] Cusanus N. (I440), *De Docta Ingornatia*. English translation online, `http://jasper-hopkins.info/`.

[19] Cusanus N. (1440-1450), *De Deo Abscondito*, in Opera omnia. Academia Literaria Heidelbergensis, Hamburg: Meiner, 1932ff., vol. IV edited by P. Wilpert, 1959.

[20] Cusanus N. (I449), *Apologiae Doctae lgnorantiae*. English translation online, `http://jasper-hopkins.info/`.

[21] Cusanus N. (1461), *Cribratio, Alkorani*, English translation online, `http://jasper-hopkins.info/`.

[22] Cusanus N. (1462). *De Non Aliud*, English translation online, `http://jasper-hopkins.info/`.

[23] Cusanus N. (1463a), *De Venatione Sapientiae*, English translation online, `http://jasper-hopkins.info/`http://jasper-hopkins.info/.

[24] Cusanus N. (1463b), *Compnedium*, English translation online, `http://jasper-hopkins.info/` http://jasper-hopkins.info/.

[25] Dionisius Areopagyte (450?) *De Divinis Nomibus*, English translation online `http://www.tertullian.org/fathers/areopagite_03_divine_names.htm`.

[26] Drago A, (2009), "Nicholas o! Cusa's logical way o! arguing interpreted and reconstructed according to modem logic", *Metalogicon*, 22, pp. 51-86.

[27] Drago A. (2010), "Dialectics in Cusanus (1401-1464), Lanza del Vasto (1901-1981) and beyond," *Epistetnologia*, 33, pp. 305-328.

[28] Drago A. (2011), "La migliore definizione della Trinità secondo la teologia «negativa» di Nicola Cusano", online https://mondodomani.org/teologia/drago2011.htm.

[29] Drago A. (2012). "Pluralism in Logic: The Square of Opposition. Lcibniz's Principle of Sufficient Reason and Markov's Principle", in *Around and Beyond the Square of Opposition*, J.-Y. Beziau and D. Jacquette (eds.), Basel: Birckhaueser, pp. 175-189.

[30] Drago A. (2017a), "From Aristotle's Square of Opposition to the "Tri-unity's Concordance" : Cusanus' Intuitionist Reasoning, in J.-Y. Beziau and G. Basti (eds.), *The Square of Opposition: A Cornerstone of Thought*, Berlin: Springer, pp. 53-78.

[31] Drago A. (2017b). "La pluralité des noms de Dieu selon Nicolas de Cues :leur progressive précision logique" in H. Pasqua (ed.), *Infini et altérité dans l'OEuvre de Nicolas de Cues (1401-1464)*, pp. 133-162.

[32] Drago A. (2017c). "A Scientific Re-assessment of Leibniz's prinicple of Sufficient Reason", in R. Pisano et al. (eds.) *The Dialogue between Sciences, Philosophy and Engineering. New Historical and Epistemological Insights. Homage to Gottfried W. Leibniz 1646-1716*, London: College Publications, (2017), pp. 121-140.

[33] Duhem P. (1913), *Le Système du Monde*, Paris: Hermann, pp. 262-286.

[34] Dummett M. (1977), *Elements of Intuitionism*, Oxford: Clarendon, p. 24.

[35] Dupuy B.-D. (1966), "Esprit Saint et anthropolgie chrétienne", in *L'Esprit Saint et l'Eglise*, Fayard, Paris.

[36] Flasch K. (2001), *Nikolas von Kues und Seine Zeit. Geschichte einer Entwnklung in seine Philosophie*, Klostermann, Frankfurt am Main.

[37] L. Gabriel. (1970): "Il pensiero dialettico in Cusano e in Hegel", *Filosofia*, 21, 537-547.

[38] Gardiè J.-L. (1991): *Le raisonnement par l'absurde*, PUF, Paris.

[39] Geach P.T. (1967), "Identity", *The Review of Metaphysics*, 21, pp. 3-12.

[40] Grize J.B. (1970), "Logique", in J. Piaget (ed.): *Logique et la connaissance scientifique, dans Encyclopédie de la Pléyade*, Paris, Gallimard, 135-288, pp. 206-210.

[41] Hankins T.L. (1977) "Triplets and triads: Sir Williams Rowan Hamilton Metaphysics of Mathematics", *ISIS*, 68, pp. 176-173.

[42] Hopkins J. (1988) *Nicholas of Cusa's Dialectical Mysticism: Text, Translation, and Interpretive Study of De Visione Dei*. Minneapolis: Banning Press.

[43] Hopkins J. (1994), *Philosophical Criticism: Essays and Reviews*, Minneapolis: Banning Press.

[44] Horn L.R. (2001), "The Logic of Logical Double Negation", in Yasuhiko K. (ed.), *Proceedings of the Sophia Symposium on Negation*, Tokyo: Sophia University P., pp. 79ff.

[45] Horn L.R. (2010), "Multiple negations in English and other languages", *The Expression of Negation*, Mouton, de Gruyter, pp. 111-148.

[46] Kelly C.J. (1994); "Classical Theism and the Doctrine of Trinity", *Rel. Studies*, 30, 67-88.

[47] Klibansky R. (1941-1942), "Plato's *Parmenides* in the middle ages and Renaissance", *Mediaeval and Renaissance Studies*, 19, p. 281.

[48] Knuuttila S. (2010), "Trinitarian Logic", H. Lagerlund (ed.), *Encyclopedia of Medieval Philosophy*, Springer, Berlin,, pp. 1335-1337.

[49] Lanza del Vasto (1959), *Les Quatre Fléaux*, Paris: Denoel.

[50] Lobachevsky N.I. (1840), *Geometrische Untersuchungen zur Theorie der Parallellinien*, Berlin: Finkl (English translation as an appendix to Bonola R. (1950), *Non-Euclidean Geometry*, New York Dover).

[51] Miller C.M. (2003), *Reading Cusanus*, Washington: Catholic University of America Press.

[52] Monaco D. (2010), *Deus Trinitas*, Roma: Città Nuova.

[53] Rahner K. (1979), *Foudations of Christian Faith. An Introduction to the Idea of Christianity*, New York: Sealbury P.

[54] Reale G. (2009) «Henologia» e «Ontologia»: i due tipi di metafisica creati dai Greci ", in Drago A., Trianni P, (eds.), *La Filosofia di Lanza Del Vasto. Un ponte tra Occidente e Oriente*, Milano: Il grande vetro / Jaca book, pp. 153-164.

[55] Russell B. (1903), *The Principles of Mathematics*, Cambridge U.P., Cambridge.

[56] Tuggy D. (2016), "Trinity", in N. Zalta (ed.) *Standford Encyclopedia of Phylosophy*, https://plato.stanford.edu/entries/trinity/

[57] van Dalen D. (1999), *Mystic, Geometer, and Intuitionist: The Life of L. E. J. Brouwer*. Oxford Univ. Press., Volume 1.

[58] van Dalen D. and Troelstra A.S. (1988), *Constructivism in Mathematics*, Amsterdam: North-Holland.

[59] van Der Auwera J., Zamorano Aguilar A. (2016), "The History of Modality ad Mood", in Nuyts J., van Der Auwera J. (eds.), *The Oxford Handbook of Modality and Mood*, online http://www.oxfordhandbooks.com/view/10.1093/oxfordhb/ 9780199591435.001. 0001/oxfordhb-9780199591435-e-4

[60] van Stig.W.P. (1990), *Brouwer's Intuitionism*, Amsterdam: North Holland.

[61] Ursic M. (1998), "Paraconsistency and dialectics as *coincidentia oppositorum* in the philosophy of Nicholas of Cusa", *Logique & Analyse*, 48, no. 161–163, pp. 203–217.

[62] Yandell K.E. (1994), "The most brutal and inexcusable error in counting?", *Rel. Studies*, 30, 201-217.

[63] Wyller E.A. (1982), "Indentitaet und Kontradiktion. Ein Weg zu Cusanus' Unendlichkeitsidee", *MFCG*, 15, 104-120.

 Received 27 May 2019

www.ingramcontent.com/pod-product-compliance
Lightning Source LLC
Chambersburg PA
CBHW080700110426
42739CB00034B/3351